"There are few theologians whom I regard more highly than the distinguished professor of Westminster Theological Seminary from years past, John Murray. For many years, his *Collected Writings* and Romans commentary have been a doctrinal landmark for me, as well as his great work, *Redemption Accomplished and Applied*. To now have his collection of expository sermons in print is indeed a treasure house of riches. Though this brilliant man is mainly known as a towering theologian and astute author, Professor Murray was, nevertheless, a distinguished preacher of the Word of God. Far from a dry lecturer in the pulpit, this Scottish-born expositor was a powerhouse whenever he stood before an open Bible and expounded its truths. He repeatedly instructed his students, 'To the text, men. To the text.' This is precisely what we see in the pages of these collected sermons. We observe a man relentlessly taking us to the text of Scripture, explaining it carefully, applying it wisely, and challenging us to live out the reality of its message. This book will be a profound aid to your Christian life as you read the pages of these masterful expositions."

—**Steven J. Lawson**, President, OnePassion Ministries

"If preaching is, as Dr. Martyn Lloyd-Jones described it, 'logic on fire,' then this collection of sermons by Dr. John Murray is a furnace ablaze with iron-tempering wisdom. And it is a conflagration that consumes human folly while imparting truth with white-hot clarity and disarming simplicity. I found myself involuntarily and yet audibly responding to these sermons with little outbursts: 'Yes! That's it! Ouch! That hurts so good!' The true mark of wisdom is to ably say much with few carefully selected

words. This collection is then true wisdom in preaching. The weight and wonder of each sermon almost forbids that one read them one after the other. You must push back from the table and rest the soul before you partake of more than one at a time. One is seated here before a feast of biblical delight! Savor it! Slowly taste it and deeply digest! There are sentences and even whole paragraphs that seem to me impossible to perfect. They are as poetically beautiful as they are theologically precise. If one thinks my words are hyperbolic or dramatic, that merely proves you have not yet read this outstanding collection."
—**Joseph Novenson,** Senior Teaching Pastor, Lookout Mountain Presbyterian Church, Lookout Mountain, TN

"Here is a collection of sermons without additives—no unnecessary words, no superfluous illustrations. How unlike so many of our current efforts. Professor Murray opens up the text and leaves us in no doubt about what it means and why it matters. Ever since reading his commentary on Romans, I have turned regularly to his *Collected Writings*. I am thrilled to have this new volume, which I commend with a measure of pride in the work of this Highland Scot!"
—**Alistair Begg,** Senior Pastor, Parkside Church, Cleveland, OH

"Those who appreciate John Murray's classic commentary on Romans for its clarity, profundity, and faithfulness to the text will also appreciate this collection of sermons for the same reasons. But those who know Murray only as a commentator and theologian will also enjoy encountering him in a different role, that

of preacher. These words weren't delivered in a classroom to train theological students in a seminary, but in a pulpit to edify the members of a local church. That's not to imply that Murray preached in a style that was light and breezy, and you won't find him padding his expositions with stories or lengthy illustrations. This is meaty preaching—exegetical, doctrinal, God-glorifying, Christ-centered, and welded to the text. Those who heard these sermons knew, and those who now read them will know, that Murray had no desire to preach himself, but only the Word of the living God."
—**DONALD S. WHITNEY**, Professor of Biblical Spirituality & Associate Dean, The Southern Baptist Theological Seminary

"Discovering hitherto unpublished sermons by John Murray is the equivalent of finding buried treasure. To those who know John Murray's writings, this book requires no recommendation. Borrowing a phrase from another context, this book is 'self-authenticating.' But to those who are not familiar with his name and reputation, these sermons represent the very finest sermonic material. Every word, carefully chosen; every argument, carefully analyzed. A book to read and re-read. Treasure indeed!"
—**DEREK THOMAS**, Senior Pastor, First Presbyterian Church, Columbia, SC

"Some of the best 'sermons' I ever heard were lectures by John Murray in systematic theology. The actual sermons in this collection have many of the same qualities. Although they are not as complex as the lectures, they are just as passionate and as precise in explaining the meanings of biblical texts. One must imagine the quiet intensity with which these were presented, urging the

hearers to appreciate the monumental importance of the doctrines involved and the grandeur of the realities to which these doctrines point."
—GEORGE MARSDEN, Francis A. McAnaney Professor of History, Emeritus, University of Notre Dame

"Our access to the edifying saints at rest is their writings, but until now we've only had John Murray's remarkable exegetical and theological insights. This volume rounds out his profile as a minister of the Word, which is, after all, the whole purpose of theology. These sermons are moving, faithful, and as relevant as ever. What a gift!"
—MICHAEL HORTON, J. Gresham Machen Professor of Systematic Theology and Apologetics, Westminster Seminary California

"The sermons that comprise this volume are so engaging that once we start reading them it is almost impossible to put them down. Their genius is that Professor Murray makes each one a journey of exploration in which he serves as an expert travel guide. We are first of all assured of making a complete exploration of the chosen text, and Murray's penchant for thoroughness is very winsome; a literary scholar would use the formula 'close reading' to name the process. We also journey through other parts of the Bible that bear upon the text and its doctrines. The ongoing momentum of each sermon is breathtaking, aided by numerical schemes, the pursuing of ideas to their logical conclusion, raising and answering questions that naturally arise, and moving toward application at the end. The form and craft of these sermons are as much a part of their excellence and appeal as is the edification that they impart. We expect edification in a sermon, but these sermons give us pleasure as well."

—**Leland Ryken,** Professor of English, Emeritus, Wheaton College

"These sermons have been held back for far too long. Doctrinally rich, heart-warming, and sometimes profoundly solemn, they deserve a wide circulation. Seldom has justification by faith been preached with greater clarity or the Father's love found a more passionate expositor. A feast for the hungry soul!"

—**Donald Macleod,** Professor of Systematic Theology, Emeritus, Free Church of Scotland College

"Professor Murray's commentary on Romans demonstrated the cogency of his exegetical attention to the biblical text. *Redemption Accomplished and Applied, The Imputation of Adam's Sin,* and the essays in his *Collected Writings* exhibited his reverent and discerning theological insight. Now in this sermon collection we hear careful biblical interpretation and incisive theological analysis in combination with a warm pastor's heart. Professor Murray preaches passionately, forthrightly, tenderly, and practically to the struggling, hurting, sometimes wandering hearts of God's people. He adores Christ the Redeemer and rejoices in the good news of his grace. His awestruck delight in the triune God is contagious. I was humbled and lifted up to worship as I heard Jesus proclaimed through these sermons."

—**Dennis E. Johnson,** Professor of Practical Theology, Westminster Seminary California

"The generations, now, who have been enriched by the teaching and writings of Westminster Theological Seminary's storied theologian, John Murray, and treasure his *Collected Writings* and commentary on Romans, will find this beautiful volume of sermons a particularly sweet treasure because of the great man's extraordinary simplicity and gospel-infused passion."
—R. Kent Hughes, John Boyer Professor of Evangelism and Culture, Westminster Theological Seminary

"Reading John Murray as a seminary student was a revelation. The Scottish theologian's careful attention to the biblical text, precise manner of theological expression, and unwavering focus on the saving work of Jesus Christ on every page of his books and essays enlivened my faith. In this beautiful volume, one of my favorite theologians takes his piety into the pulpit, expounding the gospel of Jesus Christ in some of the Bible's most well-known and influential texts."
—Philip Ryken, President, Wheaton College

"What a gift these collected sermons of John Murray are to preachers and Bible students! Here, the great Westminster professor's lucid voice is heard in stirring tones, both unfolding doctrine and stimulating doxology. And it is no surprise that Murray's consistent focus is Christ in the glory of his person and work and the blessing of union with Christ in faith. Reformed Christians should read everything Murray has written, and this small corpus of sermons demands our attention and thanksgiving."
—Rick Phillips, Senior Minister, Second Presbyterian Church, Greenville, SC

"John Murray was a tremendous biblical theologian, but he was not always the most accessible author. Thankfully, readers may now taste the fruits of some of his labors in a more welcoming medium. Through this collection of his sermons Murray speaks plainly and pastorally, allowing his insights to come through more clearly and personally. He speaks to the head and the heart, and we would do well to listen to his voice."
—**Kelly M. Kapic,** Professor of Theological Studies,
Covenant College

"What joy! To have Professor Murray leading us again so carefully, so thoughtfully, in our study of the Scriptures! Yes, there is a lot of the theologian in Murray the preacher. But then, there was a lot of the preacher in Murray the theologian. And anyone who fears there may not be enough of what moderns call 'application' in these sermons did not know my professor personally, the most loving saint I have ever known. His favorite theme is the boundless love of God and the lives God's love impels us to. Typical are his sermons on the Father's love from Romans 8:32 and his sermon on the compassionate love of the Son of God, our ascended High Priest, from Hebrews 4:14–16. Professor Murray had one goal as a preacher: to proclaim the Word of God—and in these sermons that Word speaks directly to our hearts in the power of the Holy Spirit."
—**Robert B. Strimple,** President & Professor of Systematic
Theology, Emeritus, Westminster Seminary California

"John Murray was a great man. Everything he wrote was done with great care, precision, and thoughtfulness. These sermons are hidden gems, now in view for us—especially pastors and theology students—to appreciate. Honestly, if John Murray wrote a grocery list I'd read it; so when he writes on such magnificent topics there isn't any good reason not to read him."

—**Mark Jones**, Minister, Faith Vancouver Presbyterian Church

"The sermons in this volume are, with a couple exceptions, not found in the four volumes of Murray's *Collected Writings*. Many of them are from Romans, a book on which Murray wrote an important commentary. As we would expect, the sermons are deeply theological, and they engage many of the themes stressed in Murray's systematic writings: definitive and progressive sanctification; the Father's love as the ultimate source of the atonement; Jesus's ontological and economic lordship; the believer's union with Christ in his death and resurrection; and many others. But these are actual sermons, and Murray here is concerned not just to validate doctrinal formulations. Again and again he addresses his hearers, exhorting them to attend to the very practical consequences of the teachings. We often see how a frequently overlooked doctrinal distinction brings the believer to a new dimension of heart-commitment and consistent discipleship. Let me exhort you now to take advantage of this feast. Learn from the depths of Scripture from one of its best students."

—**John Frame**, J. D. Trimble Professor of Systematic Theology and Philosophy, Reformed Theological Seminary, Orlando

"The apostle Paul's spiritual nutrition plan offers two basic food groups: meat and milk. Readers of these sermons will be in no doubt as to which Professor Murray served for his Sunday dinners. A bite-sized sample from any paragraph would prove the point. 'The marvel is that everything that belongs to Christ becomes the possession of the person who is united to him.' Christ's 'righteousness is not simply something that *grounds* the justifying act of God, but it's something that *demands* the justifying action of God.' There will never be a John Murray for the masses, and yet the gospel preached in these pages is just the food that seasoned saints, hungry sinners, and thoughtful reading groups most clearly need."

—**Chad Van Dixhoorn**, Chancellor's Professor of Historical Theology, Reformed Theological Seminary, Washington, DC

"This collection models to us the (increasingly) lost art of doctrinal preaching embedded in the expository sermon. Here we find fine distinctions and logical connections, we trace the arguments and flow of thoughts, and we are led along by turns of phrase which unlock the grandest of theological storehouses. These sermons are rich soul food for shepherds and their sheep. I will return to them again and again."

—**David Gibson**, Minister, Trinity Church, Aberdeen, Scotland

"John Murray is well known for his eagle-eyed theology and scholarly exposition of the Scriptures. However, in this book we hear the voice of John Murray the gospel preacher—a voice that tenderly and urgently calls us to Christ as our righteousness, our life, and our all. These messages are a feast for the soul. Highly recommended!"

—**Joel Beeke**, President & Professor of Systematic Theology and Homiletics, Puritan Reformed Theological Seminary

"John Murray enjoys a well-deserved reputation as a keen biblical and systematic theologian. With the publication for the first time of this collection of his sermons, the homiletical fruit of Murray's exegetical and theological insights will also be gratefully acknowledged. Just as Calvin's exegetical and theological work bore fruit in sermons that were faithful in the exposition and application of biblical texts, so we witness the same in Murray's sermons. Readers of these sermons will find them rich in gospel content, Christ-centered in focus, and urgent in their summons to faith in Christ. If the surest test and most important fruit of a careful reading of Scripture are its homiletical payoff, Murray's sermons are more than equal to the challenge."
—**Cornelis Venema**, President & Professor of Doctrinal Studies, Mid-America Reformed Seminary

"When one thinks of the legacy of Professor John Murray, it would be natural to remember him for the precision and clarity of his treatises in systematic theology. What may not readily come to mind is the power and passion of his preaching. Thankfully, this book helps remedy that by providing for readers a collection of his sermons that showcases a balance of biblical and theological precision with pastoral and compassionate devotion. Read it to be gripped by what gripped Professor Murray—the Christ of all the Scriptures."
—**Julius Kim**, Dean of Students & Professor of Practical Theology, Westminster Seminary California

"I still remember the first time I heard a recording of a John Murray sermon and its impact upon me. I was a young Christian with a growing sense of God's call to preach. This sermon was the clincher. Never before had I encountered such a unique combination of careful exegesis, profound theology, fresh insight, clear expression, and spiritual application. It inspired me with a vision of how glorious Reformed, experiential preaching could be. May this beautiful collection of Murray's sermons touch and motivate a new generation of preachers and revive those who have lost sight of their high calling."

—DAVID MURRAY, Professor of Old Testament and Practical Theology, Puritan Reformed Theological Seminary

"Professor Murray has long been celebrated as one of the clearest, most penetrating, helpful theologians the church has enjoyed. In this collection of sermons, we see that Preacher Murray was just as clear, penetrating, and helpful. In these pages a feast is laid before the hungry soul. Devour these sermons to your eternal benefit."

—JASON HELOPOULOS, Associate Pastor, University Reformed Church, East Lansing, MI

"Professor Murray helps the discerning heart to appreciate the biblical distinction between teaching and preaching. These sermons do not call us into the classroom to hear Westminster's legendary teacher—as profitable as that would be. Rather, they send us up into the heavenly sanctuary to learn at the feet of our exalted Savior, who alone is full of grace and truth."

—A. CRAIG TROXEL, Pastor, Bethel Orthodox Presbyterian Church, Wheaton, IL

"It would be impossible for me to overstate the influence of John Murray on me as a young man; his writings were crucial to my embrace of the Reformed faith. Now his sermons in print will surely stimulate the mind, warm the heart, and edify the spirit of a new generation and prompt us all to adore the majesty of God and glory in Christ Jesus."

—**Liam Goligher,** Senior Minister, Tenth Presbyterian Church, Philadelphia, PA

"Murray's sermons feel more modern than many good sermons I hear today. His insights are fresh, his posture is warm, his language is clear. Scripture comes alive!"

—**Paul Miller,** Author, *A Praying Life*

O DEATH,
WHERE IS THY STING?

COLLECTED SERMONS

JOHN MURRAY

With a foreword by SINCLAIR B. FERGUSON
And an introduction by K. SCOTT OLIPHINT

WESTMINSTER SEMINARY PRESS
Philadelphia, Pennsylvania

O Death, Where Is Thy Sting? Collected Sermons
Copyright © 2017 Westminster Theological Seminary and Logan Murray

Published by Westminster Seminary Press
P.O. Box 27009, Philadelphia, Pennsylvania 19118

All rights reserved. No part may be reproduced without the prior written permission of the publisher, except for brief quotations for the purpose of review or comment.

Email wsp@wts.edu to contact the publisher.

Cover design by Push10 Design Studios

Printed by Legatoria Editoriale Giovanni Olivotto
in Comune di Lavis, Trentino, Italy.

Most Scripture quotations and allusions are based on the author's memory of the King James Version (KJV). When a quotation substantially differs from the KJV, the deviation is the author's own rendering or an alternate Bible translation. Both are identified in the body of the text or in parentheses.

Print ISBN: 978-0-9980051-6-4

In Memory of A. Dickinson Dabney III (1936–2014)

*"So when this corruptible shall have put on incorruption,
and this mortal shall have put on immortality,
then shall be brought to pass the saying that is written,*

*Death is swallowed up in victory.
O death, where is thy sting?
O grave, where is thy victory?*

*The sting of death is sin; and the strength of sin is the law.
But thanks be to God, which giveth us the victory
through our Lord Jesus Christ."*

—1 Corinthians 15:54–57

Contents

Foreword xix
Sinclair B. Ferguson
Editor's Preface xxiii
David Feister
Acknowledgments xxvii
James Baird
Introduction xxxi
K. Scott Oliphint

One The Power of God unto Salvation 1
(*Romans 1:16–17*)

Two Reckoned to Us as Righteousness 19
(*Romans 4:9–11*)

Three Dead to Sin 35
(*Romans 6:5, 10, 14*)

Four Triumph over Sin 55
(*Romans 7:6*)

Five The Father's Love 73
(*Romans 8:32*)

Six Be Ye Transformed 89
(*Romans 12:1–3*)

Seven Put on the Lord Jesus Christ 117
(*Romans 13:11*)

Eight	Let This Mind Be in You 131
	(Philippians 2:5–9)
Nine	The Lordship of Christ 145
	(Acts 2:36)
Ten	The Priesthood of Christ 157
	(Hebrews 4:14–15)
Eleven	The Cost of Discipleship 171
	(Matthew 16:24)
Twelve	Lazarus and the Rich Man 187
	(Luke 16:31)
Thirteen	This I Call to Mind 203
	(Lamentations 3:21–22, 24)
Fourteen	Where Two or Three Are Gathered 219
	(Matthew 18:20)
Fifteen	Appointed Once to Die 239
	(Hebrews 9:27–28)
Appendix	Charge to Edmund Clowney 259
	John Murray

Scripture Index 267
Subject and Name Index................ 273

Foreword

Reading these sermons brings back a vivid memory from my teenage years. Shortly after my eighteenth birthday, I was sitting in a small committee meeting of the InterVarsity group at the University of Aberdeen, Scotland, when I heard the president say, "Professor John Murray is retiring from Westminster Theological Seminary, and we will be able to have him speak next session." I remember thinking, "Who, in all the world, is Professor John Murray? And where on earth is Westminster Theological Seminary?" Little did I realize then that the answers to these questions would loom so large in shaping my life.

In due course, Professor Murray joined us for a Friday night meeting, and we gathered to hear him speak in the splendid wood-paneled Graduation Hall. I had never heard such a combination of profound theological learning and gospel passion. The experience can best be described metaphorically. It felt as though John Murray came to my seat and said, "Son, come with me to the back wall of this room. You thought it was covered in wood panels. But look! One of them has a handle; it is a door. Trust me; come with me through the door and I will show you treasure you have never seen before." Now, more than fifty years later, I remain deeply grateful for that winter night. It is, therefore, a special joy and honor to commend this new volume of John Murray's sermons.

Soon after Professor Murray's death in 1975, his colleague Cornelius Van Til described him well:

> John Murray I held in high esteem as a Christian. . . . As to his character there was, first, his deep *humility* before God. . . . There was, second, his *boldness.* He feared God and therefore feared no man. His reputation as a scholar was never of primary concern to him, so long as by his work, the triune God of Scripture was magnified. In both of these respects he resembled Dr. Machen and Dr. Vos. . . . There was, third, his *faithfulness,* faithfulness toward God and then toward men. . . . John was of inestimable value to Westminster Theological Seminary, equally to its students and to its Faculty. He was the "conscience" of all of us. Blessed be his memory.[1]

The spoken word of some preachers transfers to print almost seamlessly; not so with Professor Murray. The printed page cannot convey his unique mannerisms—the slapping of the thigh when he was excited; the occasional examination of his fingernails as though somehow his notes were microfiched onto them; the measured and quiet-voiced opening of the sermon, and the rising vocal power that followed; and the way his whole person exuded what can only be described as a fierce devotion to Christ and a passion to glorify God.

He was, of course, unique in several ways. No one before him (and none in quite the same way since) had his personal faith and preaching style shaped on the one hand by the highland ethos of the Free Presbyterian Church in which he was reared, and on the other hand the theology of Old Princeton,

---

1. Iain H. Murray, "The Life of John Murray," in *Collected Writings of John Murray,* ed. Iain H. Murray (Edinburgh: Banner of Truth, 1976–82), 3:157–58.

permeated especially by the biblical theology of Geerhardus Vos. Professor Murray's preaching combined light and heat, the "theology on fire . . . logic on fire" which Dr. D. Martyn Lloyd-Jones would later describe to Westminster students as the marks of true preaching.[2]

But while not everything transfers to the printed page, words do. Some of these sermons have already appeared in print, notably in volume 3 of the *Collected Writings of John Murray*. What we have here is not Professor Murray's *manuscripts* but the *transcripts* of the messages themselves, and this adds interest and vitality to the words written. So, our thanks are due to Westminster Seminary Press for tracking down and transcribing these sermons that are now brought together in this little volume.

Like many others, I owe Professor Murray more than words can express. May these pages introduce a new generation to the ministry of a man to whom God providentially gave great gifts but who never appeared to think of himself more highly than he ought.

—Sinclair B. Ferguson
Senior Minister
St. Peter's Free Church of Scotland

---

2. D. Martyn Lloyd-Jones, *Preaching and Preachers* (London: Hodder & Stoughton, 1971), 97. The book contains lectures given at Westminster Theological Seminary in the spring of 1969.

Editor's Preface

This coming May (2018) will mark the forty-third anniversary of the death of Professor John Murray. This Scottish Presbyterian is best known for his thirty-seven years of service as professor of systematic theology at Westminster Theological Seminary and for his numerous written works. But what is less well-known about this eminent scholar and Reformed theologian is his pastor's heart. Though a dedicated professor and writer during the school year, Murray spent many summers in Ontario, Canada, or in the Scottish Highlands, preaching to congregations of two to four dozen people. One of Murray's friends described his preaching and pastoral labor in these small, rural churches as his "first love." This collection finally provides us with a window into this underappreciated facet of John Murray's ministry.

The sermons and prayers in this book were transcribed from fifteen audio recordings preserved in the media archives of Westminster Theological Seminary. It was not simple or easy to bring these sermons from their auditory format into written form. Our process consisted of three painstaking steps. First, every sermon went through an initial transcription, in which we captured each and every word. Second, the transcriptions were compared carefully with the audio to correct vocabulary errors, identify punctuation, insert paragraph divisions, add italicizations to words that Murray emphasized, and include Scripture references for biblical quotations or allusions. Considerable care was spent identifying words when the quality of the recording was poor or Murray's voice was obscured. At points where the recording was inaudible, words were omitted or replaced with contextually appropriate alternatives. In the following lines of this book, words have been omitted due to unclear audio: page 12, line 12; page 41, line 2; page 152, line 16; page 163, line 13; page 164, lines 13 and 16; page 166, line 7; page 168, line 18; and page 169, lines 3–5. On page 153, line 8, the word "splendors" was substituted for unclear audio with contextual accuracy. On page 155, line 19, the word "sovereignty" was substituted for unclear audio with contextual accuracy. The final step focused on editing the clarity, style, grammar, punctuation, et cetera. While these sermons do not represent merely a word-for-word transcription, the goal has always been to preserve the content as well as the voice and preaching style of Murray. Unfortunately, no transcription can perfectly capture the power of Murray's preaching style. Readers cannot hear when Murray raises his voice to a climax or lowers it to nearly a whisper, nor can they tell when he pounds the pulpit with zeal or prays with fervor. I have attempted to preserve some of Murray's vocal emphases by italicizing words and phrases, but I encourage interested persons to listen to the sermons themselves at students.wts.edu/resources/media.html.

Though this is primarily a book of *sermons*, these sermons were not originally intended to stand alone in isolation from the rest of the congregation's worship. In about half of the recordings, we have the privilege of hearing Murray's opening prayers. Scripture permeates his prayers just like it filled his sermons—so much so that it seems as though his prayers are merely verses sewn together. These are prayers and sermons by a man who knew God's Word, who prayed God's Word, and who interpreted his particular passage by the whole of God's Word.

You will find in these sermons not only robust theology but also accessible and practical application. Murray focused on bringing the text to bear on his hearer's lives with concrete practicality. One of his favored methods of applying the passage was to verbalize a practical objection that his audience might have or to describe a real-life scenario in which the passage was particularly relevant. In his sermons, he addressed women as well as men, and occasionally drew out an application for the "young people." Almost all of his sermons end with a call or an exhortation. Because of the historical and cultural distance between us and Murray's audience, there may be words and phrases that are not clear to us, but this is not due to a lack of concern to preach in a clear and accessible way.

—David Feister

Acknowledgments

The team at Westminster Seminary Press has many to thank for their help in bringing this volume through to publication. First, we would like to thank the churches that had the foresight to record Professor Murray's sermons and prayers. Special thanks are due to David Feister, who tirelessly oversaw the transcription process, and to Ashley Feister, for her indispensable support. Thanks are also due to Charles Williams, Jane Hunt, Pierce Hibbs, Mary Ruth Murdoch, Noelle Wells, Mary Davis, Jessica Doerfel, and Rachel Stout for their editorial help. We are grateful to Jeremy Eshelman, Matt Moutoux, and Spencer Ewing for providing necessary IT support. Thanks also to John Meuther for his dedicated work in creating the indices for this volume. Sandy Finlayson and Larry Sibley also must be acknowledged for their tremendous encouragement throughout the project.

We would also like to express our gratitude to President Peter Lillback, our fearless leader at Westminster. He provided the vision for this project after being memorably moved to tears when listening to the opening prayer of the final sermon in this collection.

We are deeply appreciative to Dr. Logan Murray, the son of John Murray, who has shown deep support for this project and has granted us permission to publish the transcribed sermons in this volume. We would like to thank John Rawlinson for his permission to publish sermons 5, 8, and 15 in this volume, which were preached from the manuscripts included on pages 194–98,

215–21, and 236–41 of volume 3 of the *Collected Writings of John Murray* (Edinburgh: Banner of Truth, 1982). We are also thankful for permission to republish, in the appendix, the charge Professor John Murray delivered on October 22, 1963, at the installment of Dr. Edmund Clowney as professor of practical theology. This charge was previously published on pages 107–109 of volume 1 of the *Collected Writings of John Murray* (Edinburgh: Banner of Truth, 1982).

We are additionally grateful to Tom DeVries for his permission to publish Murray's sermons on Romans, which clearly depend on (and often paraphrase) his commentary on Romans (2 vols; Grand Rapids: Eerdmans, 1959 & 1965). The following citations note where in the present volume Murray paraphrases his Romans commentary. On page 3 of the present book, Murray paraphrases volume 1, page 27, lines 1–10 and 14–16 of his commentary on Romans. On page 5 of the present book, lines 10–12, Murray paraphrases volume 1, page 28, lines 38–40 of his commentary on Romans. On page 8, lines 18–19, Murray paraphrases volume 1, page 30, lines 10–16. On page 9, line 27, Murray paraphrases volume 1, page 31, lines 1–2. On page 13, Murray paraphrases volume 1, page 32, lines 27–31. On pages 19–20, Murray paraphrases volume 1, pages 135–36. On page 39, lines 15–18, Murray paraphrases volume 1, page 211. On pages 41–42, Murray paraphrases volume 1, page 213, lines 11–13 and 211–32. On page 44, Murray paraphrases volume 1, pages 219–20. On page 46, Murray paraphrases volume 1, page 220, lines 15–20 and page 221, lines 4–20. On page 47, lines 3–4, Murray paraphrases volume 1, page 222, line 21. On page 51, lines 6–8, Murray paraphrases volume 1, page 225, lines

14–20. On page 52, Murray paraphrases volume 1, page 26, lines 1–4. On page 58, Murray paraphrases volume 1, page 241, lines 20–28. On page 62, Murray paraphrases volume 1, pages 250–51. On page 63, lines 12–15, Murray paraphrases volume 1, page 257, lines 9–12. On page 64, Murray paraphrases volume 1, page 259, lines 3–5. On page 71, lines 8–10, Murray paraphrases volume 1, page 270, lines 9–18. On page 74, Murray paraphrases volume 1, page 323, lines 15–22. On page 75, lines 5–7, Murray paraphrases volume 1, pages 323–24. On page 76, Murray paraphrases volume 1, page 323, lines 24–34, and page 324. On page 81, Murray paraphrases volume 1, page 325, lines 6–28. On page 82, lines 21–22, Murray paraphrases volume 1, page 325, lines 30–32. On page 84, lines 19–24, Murray paraphrases volume 1, page 326, lines 8–10. On page 93, Murray paraphrases volume 2, page 111, lines 8–11. On page 95, lines 13–16, Murray paraphrases volume 2, page 111, lines 2–4. On page 96, Murray paraphrases volume 2, pages 111–12. On pages 99–100, Murray paraphrases volume 2, page 112. On page 101, lines 20–22, Murray paraphrases volume 2, page 113, lines 32–34. On page 103, lines 1–3 and 23–27, Murray paraphrases volume 2, page 114, lines 8–12 and 15–22. On pages 104–105, Murray paraphrases volume 2, pages 114–15. On page 108, Murray paraphrases volume 2, page 116, lines 30–39. On page 109, lines 9–16, Murray paraphrases volume 2, page 117, lines 6–17. On page 119, lines 12–18, Murray paraphrases volume 2, page 165, lines 26–29.

Last, but not least, we have dedicated this book to our former chief operations officer, Dick Dabney, who went to be with the Lord suddenly in 2014. Without his passion and administrative oversight in the early stages of the project, the book would have never seen the light of day. We could not be more thankful for his many years of faithful service to the seminary.

—James Baird
Publishing Director
Westminster Seminary Press

Introduction

The sermons of John Murray contained in this volume show a man who was deeply committed to the Reformed faith and to its faithful exposition. Such could be said of a multitude of men. What must be highlighted here, however, is that Murray was, throughout his adult life and by virtue of his calling, bathed in the system of theology that finds its home in the Reformation. The glorious and majestic content of that theology, unlike much that went before it and unlike much that passes for it today, is intrinsically and inextricably related to its *proclamation*. It would not put it too strongly to say that the *reason* for the content of Reformed theology is its proclamation and communication to the church, to the glory of God.

Murray recognized the importance of this inextricable connection, which is sidelined by many today who would want to maintain the label "Reformed." Abstract systems of theology that purport to be Reformed are ill-suited, even antithetical, to Reformed, gospel proclamation.[1] Murray knew such abstractions

---

1. One example of a theology that cannot preach should suffice here. Let's take as an example the question of how the wrath of God relates to his eternal love toward his own. How might we articulate that relationship? Specifically, how can those whom the Father loves from before the foundation of the world (Eph 1:3–4) be objects of his wrath (Eph 2:4) and then of his grace (Eph 2:8) in history? Does God's disposition toward us change in history? Paul Helm says no. With respect to a transition from wrath to grace in history, he says, "there is no change in God; he loves us from eternity. There is, however, a change in us, a change that occurs as by faith Christ's work is appropriated. *The change is not from wrath to grace, but from our belief that we are under wrath to our belief that we are under grace*" (*John Calvin's Ideas* [Oxford: Oxford University Press, 2004], 395, my emphasis). It should be noted here that Helm's view is not John

to be theological aberrations. We see this in Murray's deeply rich and biblical understanding of God's wrath, contained in this collection. In his sermon on Romans 1:16–17, Murray notes,

> When God created the heavens and the earth, there was no wrath of God. There was no need for it. There was nothing that was a contradiction of himself, and so God wasn't pouring out his wrath upon anybody. The creation in its primitive perfection didn't call forth the wrath of God.[2]

Murray recognizes that God's wrath is a response to sin; when there was no sin, there was no wrath. He goes on to proclaim that, given sin, God's wrath is "an exigency . . . a demand." The only thing that can "meet the contradiction that sin offers" is God's righteousness in Jesus Christ. This is no mere change of subjective belief. It is a change from God pouring out his wrath on sinners to pouring out his grace on his people. God *must* pour out his wrath against sin, says Murray. But as we are made alive, he pours out his grace upon us. Surely this is a change of God's ac-

---

Calvin's view. Quoting Augustine, Calvin says, "Thus in a marvelous and divine way *he loved us even when he hated us*," and later on he says, "For, in some ineffable way, *God loved us and yet was angry toward us at the same time*, until he became reconciled to us in Christ" (*Institutes of the Christian Religion*, ed. John T. McNeill, trans. Ford Lewis Battles [Louisville, KY: Westminster John Knox Press, 2011], 1: 507, 530, my emphasis). An abstract understanding of God's immutability applied to the historical reality of the Christian's transition from wrath to grace relegates that transition, for Helm, to a mere change of our own subjective beliefs. This, Helm thinks, protects God's immutability. It would be interesting to see how someone might preach such a thing. This is "theology" that is light years away from any orthodox pulpit.

2. Page 7 of this present volume.

tions toward us and not simply a change of our subjective belief. Murray proclaims such a change because Scripture demands it.

In another sermon, Murray moves us more deeply into a discussion of God's wrath. We could focus it with this question: if the transition from wrath to grace in the redeemed is a transition *only* of our beliefs, then what might we say about the wrath of God *in history* that the Father visited on his *eternally* beloved Son? Would the wrath of the Father on the Son be simply a *belief* that the Son had on the cross, since he, too, was loved "before the foundation of the world" (1 Pet 1:20)?

Here again, Murray's Reformed and biblical roots dig much deeper and spring up into a healthy flower of full-orbed, "whole-counsel-of-God" proclamation. In his sermon on "The Father's Love" (Rom 8:32), Murray takes us to the heavenly throne room of God's majesty. This one paragraph is worth a lifetime of Christian meditation. Addressing the Father's love of the Son *together with* his wrath on the Son, Murray proclaims,

> Here again we have this unheard-of conjunction: infinite love and divine wrath. The Son bore the stroke of the Father's wrath, and there was no amelioration. Don't be deceived by the widespread current of thought that denies the real doctrine of propitiation. The essence of sin's curse and judgment is the wrath of God. So, if Jesus bore sin and if he bore our curse and if he was made sin, then the vicarious bearing of the wrath of God belongs to the very essence of his atoning accomplishment. *How cramped the understanding and how narrow the perspective of those who think that the infliction of wrath is inconsistent*

with the exercise of infinite love. Oh, my friends, the truth is that it was just because the Son was the object of this immutable, infinite, and unique love that he could at the same time be the subject of the wrath of God.[3]

These two examples from Murray's sermons should whet the appetite of every Christian who longs for the spiritual meat of the Word. It is Reformed theology—with its deeply biblical and exegetical roots—that alone can produce the richest and most glorious sermons. It is this deep theology that naturally blossoms forth into the pulpit. Whether it's the difficult doctrine of predestination, or Reformed pneumatology, or any other Reformed *locus*, all of it must be suitable for preaching, or else it cannot be biblical and thus not Reformed. This is one reason why Murray's courses in systematic theology included significant exegetical content. For Murray, doctrines were not based on abstract deductions of logic but rather found their home in the God-breathed texts of Holy Scripture.

What this means is that orthodox theology, by definition, is *practical* because it is meant to be *preached*: "Oh, what folly when people speak of doctrine as being impractical. Of course, we may make what we conceive to be doctrine very impractical, but it isn't because *doctrine* is impractical."[4]

Murray emphasized the practicality of doctrine in his charge to Edmund Clowney. There he made two points about the relationship of systematic theology to preaching that help frame the context of the sermons in the present volume. First, Murray said to Clowney,

---
3. Page 78 of this present volume, my emphasis.
4. Page 141 of this present volume.

> Your department is that of practical theology. The bane of much that goes under this title is the divorce of practics from theology. You are well aware of this evil and you have determined to counteract it. But it may not be out of place to put you in remembrance. Practical theology is *principally systematic theology* brought to practical expression and application. And this means the whole counsel of God brought to bear upon every sphere of life, and particularly upon every phase of the life and witness of the church. He would be a poor theologian indeed who would be unaware of, or indifferent to, the practical application of God's revealed counsel.[5]

Murray recognized that our preaching is constituted by our systematic theology. Because Murray saw systematic theology as being *exegetical,* and not philosophical, at root, he recognized that any minister ascending the pulpit must be grounded in the exegetical theology of Holy Scripture. Poor theology, said Murray, is measured by its distance from the *application* of biblical truth.

Second, Murray said,

> But likewise, and perhaps more tragically, he would be a poor exponent of practical theology who did not know the theology of which practics is the application. I charge you to make it your concern to be the instrument of inflaming men with zeal for the proclamation of the whole counsel of God and of doing so with that

---

5. Page 262 of this present volume, my emphasis.

passion and power without which preaching fails to do honour to the magnitude of its task and the glory of its message.[6]

Murray's second point is implied by his first. How might one go about preaching if he is unaware of the rich and deep theology that Scripture alone can provide? Preaching a *text* without a view to the majesty and glory of Scripture's systematic coherence with respect to that text is to bleed the life and power from the passage preached. To preach the *part* without the background of the *whole* is to truncate the task of preaching. It is the *whole* counsel of God that is the minister's duty and privilege to preach.

The whole counsel of God is exactly what Murray preached. In the pages that follow, you will be fed a rich and nutritious diet of biblical truth that is inextricably tied to the systematic unity of Scripture. You will be treated to Murray's assessment of the "very *meaning* of salvation." He will proclaim the death of the "old man" in every Christian. He will declare to you what is "at the very basis of sanctification." He will convince you that the most distinguishing characteristic of a believer is union with Christ.

In the following sermons, Murray shows how difficult passages provide for true Christian holiness in life and thought. He will show you why Romans 7:15–25 describes the Christian at war with sin. He will ask and answer the question of the Father's disposition toward you when Christ hung on the cross. In his exposition of Philippians 2:4–7, Murray proclaims,

---

6. Pages 262–63 of this present volume.

> So when it is said of Christ Jesus that he was in the "form of God," that has richer meaning than to say simply that he was God. The accent falls, you see, upon the fullness of his Godhood, upon his being originally, natively, and essentially God in the full possession of all that is distinctive of God in his glory and majesty. That is the dignity of his divine identity, the dignity of unabridged deity.[7]

This is where difficult and deep theology penetrates the Christian soul and prompts Christian worship.

Murray knows that Christians need to understand their doctrine in order to understand right living. So, in his proclamation of Scripture, he will ensure that you know what the word "propitiation" means. And, as one who was keenly able to transfer his own passion to his listeners, in an exposition of the Father's love to his people, he will ask, "Do you stagger with amazement? Does your mind reel with amazement? Oh, let that not be the amazement of bewilderment, but may it be the amazement of believing and adoring wonder!"[8] This is no dry, dusty theology; this is the Word of God proclaimed, persuading us to bend the knee to his triune majesty!

There is a rich, spiritual meal awaiting you in the following pages of Murray's sermons. It comes from one who spent his life devouring the God-breathed Scriptures in order to feed the sheep of Christ. Every word preached by Murray has its foundation in the Word inspired by God's Spirit. A proper reading of these sermons will, if Murray's desire becomes yours, contribute

---

7. Page 132 of this present volume.
8. Page 77 of this present volume.

to a life of holiness that has its foundation in the Reformed theology of Scripture. Take, read, and meditate on these sermons. Reformed theology preached is unsurpassed as a catalyst to the worship of the one true and triune God.

—K. Scott Oliphint
  Dean of Faculty
  Westminster Theological Seminary

Sermons

1

The Power of God unto Salvation

For I am not ashamed of the gospel of Christ: for it is the power of God unto salvation to every one that believeth; to the Jew first, and also to the Greek. For therein is the righteousness of God revealed from faith to faith: as it is written, The just shall live by faith.
—Romans 1:16–17

Oh God, who dwellest in thy holy temple, who art high and lifted up but who also dwellest with the humble and the contrite, do thou grant unto us that we may have a profound sense of thy glory and of thy presence. May the knowledge of the Lord captivate our minds and our hearts, and may we have an all-pervasive sense that thou art the Lord God Almighty—Father, Son, and Holy Spirit. Grant us thy presence in thy sanctuary in accordance with thy promise that where two or three are gathered together in thy name, there thou art in their midst. May we, oh Lord, have the experience of this inestimable grace. And may the words of our mouth and the meditations of our heart be acceptable in thy sight, oh Lord, our strength and our Redeemer. Amen.

It might appear to us that the apostle would have drawn the curtain of concealment over the things that he described in the latter part of this chapter, because these sins, which he enumerates in the latter part of this chapter (Rom 1:24–32), are in that class of which it is written elsewhere that it is a shame even to speak (Eph 5:12). But instead of drawing over the curtain of concealment, the apostle Paul draws the curtain aside, and he opens to our view the abominations of moral and religious degeneracy into which the nations of the world had fallen. And we can very readily see the reason. Because it is only in the context of that degeneracy, which the apostle depicts in this chapter, that we can appreciate the word that is the keynote of this epistle: "I am not ashamed of the gospel of Christ because it is the power of God unto salvation to every one that believeth" (Rom 1:16).

Now you might think that this is a rather weak way of expressing his confidence because the apostle Paul in other places, where he abounds in confidence regarding the efficacy of the gospel, uses rather different language. In the companion epistle, the Epistle to the Galatians, he says, "God forbid that I should glory, save in the cross of the Lord Jesus Christ, by whom the world is crucified unto me, and I unto the world" (Gal 6:14). And in another epistle, he says, "Thanks be unto God, that always causeth us to triumph in Christ, and maketh manifest the savour of his knowledge by us in every place" (2 Cor 2:14). And so you might think that what he says in Romans 1:16 is a rather weak and negative way of expressing his confidence: "I am not ashamed of the gospel of Christ."

But if we remember the reproach with which the enemies of the gospel encountered its message, if we bear in mind the scorn that was oftentimes placed upon the gospel as it confronted the pomp of Roman political power and as it confronted the pretended wisdom of the Greeks, then we can discover, in Paul's particular way of expressing his confidence, the undertones of exultant assurance. "I am not ashamed of the gospel because it is the power of God unto salvation" (Rom 1:16). With reference to the worldly pomp that was manifest in the Roman political power, he said, "I am ready to preach the gospel to you that are at Rome also" (Rom 1:15). With reference to all the degeneracy that the apostle Paul portrays in verses 24 to 32 of this chapter, he says that the gospel is "the power of God unto salvation," reaching down to the lowest depths of degradation and lifting men and women from the dunghill, placing their feet upon a rock, establishing their goings, and putting a new song in their mouths (Ps 40:2–3; 113:7).

What is the gospel of which the apostle here is speaking? We must always remember that the gospel is a proclamation. It is a message, and it is of that message that the apostle Paul is speaking when he says, "I am not ashamed of the gospel." I am not ashamed of the gospel message. I am not ashamed to proclaim it. We must never forget that that Word of proclamation is the Word of power. It is the Word that transforms men, and it is that Word *alone* that transforms them, that translates them from darkness to light and from the power of Satan unto God.

It is true enough that this Word of the truth of the gospel is never efficacious unto salvation except as it is accompanied by the demonstration of the Spirit and of power. As Paul says in another epistle, "Our gospel came not unto you in word only, but also in power, and in the Holy Spirit, and in much assurance" (1 Thess 1:5). But we must likewise remember that it is the gospel that the Holy Spirit witnesses to. It is only through the gospel that the Holy Spirit is working unto salvation. And where that gospel is absent, then there is not the regenerating and sanctifying work of the Holy Spirit. It is the gospel, after all, that Paul says in this passage "is the power of God unto salvation." Therefore, he is drawing our attention to this great pronouncement that it is the gospel that is the Word of reconciliation and the Word of salvation unto a lost and perishing world.

Why is the gospel so powerful? Why is the gospel the omnipotent power of God operative unto salvation? Just for this reason: that it is the Word *of God*! And the Word of God is never void of power! "The Word of God is living and powerful, and sharper than any twoedged sword. It pierces to the dividing asunder of soul and spirit . . . and is a discernment of the thoughts and intents of the heart" (Heb 4:12). The Word of the gospel is the Word of God, and it isn't a dead word; it's a living voice! It's the living voice of God as surely as those who heard the Word of God the Father on his Holy Mount, witnessing to his own Son, "This is my beloved Son, in whom I am well pleased" (Matt 17:5; cf. 2 Pet 1:17).

So, let us never be deceived by the allegation that is so frequently made that the Word of the gospel itself is a dead word. If we do not hear it as the living voice of God, it's precisely because the god of this world has blinded our minds lest the light of the knowledge of the glory of God in the face of Jesus Christ should shine into our hearts (2 Cor 4:4). The Word of the gospel is the omnipotent power of God operative unto salvation—salvation from sin in its defilement, in its degradation, in its guilt, and in its power. It lifts men out of the degradation and squalor of iniquity and makes them the sons and daughters of the Lord God Almighty, clothing them with righteousness and establishing them in the ways of integrity.

Why does the apostle Paul say, "I am not ashamed of the gospel"? Because it is the power of God unto salvation. And *why* is the gospel this omnipotent power of God operative unto salvation? "For therein is the righteousness of God revealed from faith to faith." The gospel is the power of God unto salvation just *because* there is revealed in it the righteousness *of God* that is operative unto salvation. So, you have this combination of power and righteousness.

It is well for us to appreciate this combination in the gospel because the gospel is never simply bare omnipotence. Bare omnipotence, as exercised by God himself, could never save a single soul. If we emphasize the omnipotence of God to the prejudice of his righteousness, then we fail to appreciate what is at the very center of the provision of God's grace. Bare omnipotence could, indeed, create this mighty universe. God created the world simply by the command of his will. "He spake, and it was done; he commanded, and it stood fast" (Ps 33:9). "By the word of the Lord were the heavens made; and all the host of them by the breath of his mouth" (Ps 33:6). But not so with salvation. There are certain exigencies that are at stake in this matter of salvation so that salvation can never be wrought by the exercise of bare omnipotence.

Two considerations explicit in this very context draw attention to that fact. There is, first of all, the degradation, the squalor of iniquity that the apostle Paul describes in the latter part of this chapter. We must remember what that involves. What is, after all, the essence of sin? People will say sometimes that sin is selfishness. Well, that's a woefully inadequate definition of sin! All selfishness is sin, but sin is not simply selfishness. There's something far more serious about sin than the fact that we are absorbed in ourselves. Sin is the contradiction *of God*. When sin came into the world, something came into the world that was the very contradiction of God—the contradiction of his sovereignty, the contradiction of his authority, the contradiction of his holiness, and yes, the contradiction of his righteousness. And that contradiction of God is what exists in all the description that the apostle gives in Romans 1 of the degradation and degeneration of the world. When God created the heavens and the earth, when he created all creatures at the beginning, there was no contradiction at all; there was nothing that existed that was in contradiction to God because there was nothing that existed *but* God himself. When he spake and it was done, when he commanded and it stood fast, there was no contradiction at all. Therefore, God could create simply by the command of his will.

The second consideration in the context of this passage that points to the impossibility of salvation simply by the exercise of God's omnipotent power is the wrath of God. You see, the very next verse to our text is, "For the wrath of God is revealed from heaven against all ungodliness and unrighteousness of men, who hold the truth in unrighteousness" (Rom 1:18). The wrath of God, of course, is God's necessary reaction to that which is the contradiction of himself. There *must* be the wrath of God wherever there is sin because sin is the contradiction of God!

Again, when God created the heavens and the earth, there was no wrath of God. There was no need for it. There was nothing that was a contradiction of himself, and so God wasn't pouring out his wrath upon anybody. The creation in its primitive perfection didn't call forth the wrath of God. But now there is the reality of the wrath of God, and it is inseparable from the degradation and degeneracy that the apostle Paul depicts. Consequently, when we come to this matter of salvation, what is indispensable is *righteousness* and *nothing less than* the righteousness of God. The only thing that can meet human degeneracy is the righteousness of *God*! And the only thing that can meet God's *own* wrath is his *own* righteousness.

You see what a situation there is! It's a situation for God himself, you see. It's an exigency, it's a demand, that God *himself* cannot waive. If there is going to be salvation, then there must be righteousness—righteousness to meet the contradiction that sin offers and righteousness to meet even his own wrath. Oh, how magnificent is the apostle's explanation! "I'm not ashamed of the gospel." Why? "Because it is the power of God unto salvation." And why is it the power of God unto salvation? "Because therein the righteousness of God is revealed." Oh, my friends, do appreciate that sequence because we're getting to the heart of that which is the most precious thing for human beings in this whole universe! It is the supreme manifestation not only of the *grace* of God but of the *wisdom* of God, and it is something that will cause the eternal ages to ring with joy! Don't fail to get hold of the glory of this: "Therein is revealed the righteousness of God."

What is this righteousness of which Paul is speaking in this instance? You might say, "Oh, the righteousness of God is simply his attribute of justice: that God is just, 'that justice and judgment are the habitation of his throne' (Ps 97:2), 'that he is just in all his ways and holy in all his works' (Ps 145:17)." It is quite true that there could be no salvation except as the demands of divine righteousness were fully met. There cannot be any salvation but the salvation that completely comports with the righteousness of God. Perfectly true! And Paul draws our attention to that in this very epistle when he says,

> Whom God hath set forth to be a propitiation through faith in his blood, to declare his righteousness for the remission of sins that are past, through the forbearance of God; to declare, I say, at this time his righteousness: that he might be just, and the justifier of him who believeth in Jesus. (Rom 3:25–26)

It's a great truth that there could be no salvation except a salvation comported with the righteousness of God. But that is not the righteousness that the apostle is speaking of in this instance. It's not the *attribute* of righteousness that is here called "the righteousness of God." It's very closely related to the attribute of righteousness, but it's not the attribute of righteousness itself. Why isn't it the attribute of righteousness? It's very easy to discover the reasons in this epistle and elsewhere.

First of all, this is a righteousness that is made over to us (that is, to those who fall into this category). In Romans 3:21–22 we read, "But now the righteousness of God without the law is manifested, being witnessed by the law and the prophets; even the righteousness of God which is by faith of Jesus Christ unto all and upon all them that believe." Don't you see, there is a righteousness that is by faith of Jesus Christ *unto all* and *upon all* them that believe. It's a righteousness that is made over to men and women. Now men and women don't come to possess God's attribute of righteousness, just as they don't come to possess his attributes of omnipotence or eternity or immutability. They don't become divine. So, this righteousness that is made over to us must be something different from God's attribute of righteousness.

Secondly, Paul teaches us in another epistle that this is a righteousness that we have: "Not having mine own righteousness, which is of the law, but that which is through the faith of Christ, the righteousness which is of God by faith" (Phil 3:9). Then again, in another epistle, he tells us that it is a righteousness that we *become*, not simply a righteousness that belongs to us or that we have: "He gave him to be sin for us, who knew no sin; that we might become the righteousness of God in him" (2 Cor 5:21). We *become* the righteousness of God. And of course, then, another consideration is that it is the righteousness that is appropriated by faith: "righteousness . . . from faith to faith," as Paul says in Romans 1:17.

So what is this righteousness? It is something very different than the attribute of righteousness. It's a righteousness that belongs to men. It's a righteousness that they *have*, it's a righteousness that they *become*, and it's a righteousness that is *mediated to them* through Jesus Christ and that becomes theirs in actual possession by faith. And yet, my friends, we must not tone down that which the apostle here calls it: "the righteousness of God."

It's a God-righteousness, a divine righteousness, after all. It's not the attribute of righteousness in God, but it nevertheless is a righteousness with divine attributes, qualities, and properties.

And oh, my friends, don't fail to get that grand lesson, because it's the central theme of this epistle! If there is any book in the Bible that portrays to us the gospel, it's the Epistle to the Romans. And the great central theme of the epistle is just precisely this: the righteousness of God that becomes ours by faith, a righteousness that is not the divine attribute but that nevertheless has divine properties. It's a God-righteousness, and, oh, that's the magnificent thing about the gospel. Don't you see that *that* is something that will meet the awful exigency of our sin and even the exigency of the wrath of God—a righteousness that is divine?

Remember, also, that this righteousness of God is contrasted not simply with human unrighteousness but with human righteousness. Do you know that the greatest enemy of the gospel is not human unrighteousness? The greatest enemy of the gospel is not that degradation and degeneracy that the apostle Paul portrays in the first chapter of Romans. But the greatest enemy of the gospel is human *righteousness*! When Paul says in the Epistle to the Galatians, "God forbid that I should glory, save in the cross of our Lord Jesus Christ, by whom the world is crucified unto me, and I unto the world" (Gal 6:14), he wasn't there talking about outward, notorious iniquity. Paul was never given to that—never. Paul had never been a notorious person; he had always been a person who was outwardly above reproach: "Circumcised the eighth day, of the stock of Israel, of the tribe of Benjamin, a Hebrew of the Hebrews; as touching the law, a Pharisee; concerning zeal, persecuting the church; touching the righteousness which was in the law, blameless" (Phil 3:5–6). That's the character of the apostle Paul. So, when Paul says, "God forbid that I should glory, save in the cross of our Lord Jesus Christ, by whom the world is crucified unto me, and I unto the world," he means that he was crucified unto his own righteousness, crucified unto self-righteousness.

That's the greatest contradiction to the gospel: human righteousness offered to meet the contradiction of sin and the wrath of God. Oh, what a complete insult to God to offer human self-righteousness to the contradiction of sin and to the wrath of God. But in the gospel we have a righteousness that is divine, and that's the righteousness that can go down to the deepest depths of our degradation and can lift us up from the dunghill and place us among princes and princesses (1 Sam 2:8). That righteousness alone is equal to our situation.

So what exactly is this righteousness of God that is made over to us—that we have, that we become, and that is mediated to us through faith? The apostle tells us in this passage that it's nothing else but the righteousness of Christ. And Christ's righteousness is "the righteousness of God" because he *himself* was God. It's a righteousness that's made over to men, that they come to have, and that they become just because *Christ* becomes theirs. That's the gospel: "therein is revealed the righteousness of God," the righteousness of the Redeemer. Paul says in a later part of this epistle, "As by one man's disobedience many were made sinners, so by the obedience of one shall many be made righteous" (Rom 5:19). That's the grandeur of the gospel: we become the righteousness of God *in Christ*! "Him, who knew no sin, he made to be sin for us that we might become the righteousness of God in him" (2 Cor 5:21). The marvel is that everything that belongs to Christ becomes the possession of the person who is united to him. And he becomes even this righteousness.

Now this righteousness is not simply something that *grounds* the justifying act of God, but it's something that *demands* the justifying action of God. The righteousness of Christ cannot meet with anything else than God's approbation. Wherever there is a sinner, however degraded, who is united to Christ in *his* righteousness, that sinner possesses a righteousness that God must justify because it is a righteousness that is undefiled and undefilable. It is a righteousness that reaches down to the deepest depths of human degradation and rises to the highest heights of divine approbation, a righteousness that covers to the fullest extent the righteous wrath of God and the unrighteous contradiction of men! I ask you, my friends, to consider *this righteousness* because it stretches to the utmost confines of reality. That is why the gospel is the power of God unto salvation.

Now you will ask me, "Oh, well, if the gospel really is the power of God unto salvation, then why isn't it the power of God unto salvation *to everyone*?" It is a question that cannot be evaded. If the righteousness of God is all that I have said it is, why doesn't it take the whole of humanity into its grasp? The reason is in our text. First of all, it is the righteousness of God *revealed*. When Paul here uses that word *revealed*, he's not talking simply about that which is made known to us for information. He's using the word *revealed* in the sense that you find frequently in the Old Testament and particularly in the prophet Isaiah: the Word of God in saving action. "My salvation is near to come, and my righteousness to be revealed" (Isa 56:1). These two are the same thing; it is the righteousness of God revealed, or brought to bear upon us, in effective action! It isn't efficacious simply because it is made known to us for information, not simply because it is made known to us in the word of proclamation; it's the righteousness of God *revealed* in *saving*, effective action.

So then we must ask the question: in whom is this righteousness of God revealed in saving and effective action? The apostle Paul tells us in verses 16 and 17: the gospel is "the power of God unto salvation to *every one that believeth*," and this righteousness of God is "revealed *from faith to faith*." We must not allow our minds to escape that this righteousness of God is operative unto salvation *only for this faith*! Don't for your life disjoin that which God has placed together. It's a righteousness of God revealed *from faith to faith*. The gospel is the power of God unto salvation *to every one that believeth*. That's the line of discrimination defined in this text, and with that line of distinction all great issues—tremendous issues—are bound up. And don't let us escape the greatest.

Now, faith is a very simple thing. Oh, it's not simple to the person who is imbued with his own self-righteousness; it's the very contradiction of self-righteousness. But faith is a very simple thing after all. And faith in its essence is simply self-commitment; it's entrustment. When the apostle speaks of faith here, as elsewhere in this epistle, he is speaking of that faith by which we become joined to Christ in self-commitment and self-entrustment. When Christ becomes the only one who can stand between us and the degradation and contradiction of sin, when Christ becomes to us the only one who can stand between us and the holy wrath of God, *then* he has become all to us. We have committed ourselves to him, we have entrusted ourselves to him, we have become united to him. And being united to him, we become the righteousness of God in him. That is the gospel that is implicit here when Paul says it is "the righteousness of God revealed from faith to faith."

Now, that's very precious. Here is a sinner, and he knows that he's a sinner, and he's perhaps very deeply convicted of his sin. (You know a person who is not yet regenerated can be very deeply convicted of sin.) And his reply is, "Well, I could never hope or expect to be the recipient of salvation. I'm just too far gone and beyond repair. I'm so utterly bound to sin and so utterly degraded in my own iniquity that I can't entertain any hope." My friends, here there is a very great, important lesson conveyed to us, and it is contained in that very little expression "from faith to faith." This righteousness of God is operative unto salvation through *faith*, and it is operative unto salvation to *everyone* who has faith. It is necessary to emphasize both. It is by faith, and by faith alone, that we are justified in God's sight. And everyone who has faith, however weak that faith may be, is just as effectively united to Christ and to the righteousness of God as is the person who is strong in faith. That's the great truth expressed in "from faith to faith": this righteousness becomes ours by faith and it becomes the possession of anybody who is exercising faith.

Oh, my friend, however degraded you may feel yourself to be, however bound in the bondage of sin you may feel yourself to be, however great may be your consciousness of the contradiction that you are to the gospel and to that which God demands of you, remember that the greatest insult you could offer to God is to offer insult to the sufficiency and the perfection of his righteousness! People sometimes think that they're doing God great honor by pleading their own degradation, their own corruption, their own wickedness, and all that. They think they're doing God great honor by pleading *that* as a reason why they should not commit themselves, in the simplicity of faith, to the righteousness of God in Christ. That's the greatest insult because you are offering insult to that which is sufficient for the deepest depths of human degradation and meets the highest demands of God's glory. There is nothing in this universe that offers greater contradiction to God than to offer contradiction to the overture of his righteousness in Christ Jesus! "This is the condemnation, that light is come into the world, and men loved darkness rather than light, because their deeds were evil" (John 3:19). And, my friend, however deeply involved in the contradiction you may be, remember that the gospel is the power of God unto salvation and that the righteousness of God is operative unto salvation to *everyone* that believes.

On the other hand, I have every confidence that there are a lot of people in this congregation who are very well advanced in the knowledge of the Lord, who are a long way on the pilgrimage to "the city which hath the foundations, whose builder and maker is God" (Heb 11:10). For such people, the more they pilgrimage to the city which hath the foundations, the more they are being convinced of their own utter helplessness and their own utter vileness. You might think that's a contradiction, but it is always the case that wherever there is the true advance in holiness, in sainthood, that person becomes more and more deeply convinced of his own utter depravity. That was true with the apostle. When Paul penned later in this epistle these words, "O wretched man that I am! Who shall deliver me from the body of this death?" (Rom 7:24), and when he says, "I see another law in my members, warring against the law of my mind, and bringing me into captivity to the law of sin which is in my members" (Rom 7:23), he was far along on the way of advancement to the celestial city. And he was imbued then with a profound sense of his own depravity and his own utter helplessness.

What is it that the saint of God can continue to offer as he is confronted with the demands of God's holiness and righteousness upon him? What is it that he can present to God in order to offset the awful liabilities that are his because of his degradation and sin? It's simply the righteousness of Christ mediated through faith. This is the gospel for the person who has never known the power of God unto salvation, and it's also the gospel for the saint who is a long, long way in his pilgrimage and who is just about to enter into the celestial city. It's the gospel for saints as well as for sinners! I know nothing that I can present with greater confidence as I am confronted with the demands of God's holiness and with the liabilities of my own iniquity. What can I present to God as my plea? My friend, it's just this righteousness—this righteousness that is divine, this righteousness that meets not only my unrighteousness but my self-righteousness, and this righteousness that meets all the demands of God's holiness and justice and truth.

This is the grandeur of the gospel. I have the confidence that as I make this righteousness my plea, I have not simply something that God will justify, but I have something that God *cannot but* justify, because it is the righteousness of the Redeemer, a righteousness that is undefiled and undefilable. Remember, my friend, though your faith be at the lowest ebb of a possible exercise, though it be the weakest faith that exists, nevertheless, if it is a faith that looks to Christ as the only plea against human sin on the one hand and God's wrath on the other, then that is the righteousness that is the power of God unto salvation. It's yours just as fully with the weakest faith as it is yours with the strongest faith. It is a righteousness of God from faith to faith to everyone that believes.

Are your hearts drawn by the irresistible appeal of the gospel of God's provision? Oh, how can we be indifferent as we are confronted with the greatest thing that can occupy the minds of rational beings? How can we be indifferent as we are confronted with that which is the supreme manifestation of the wisdom, grace, and righteousness of God? What an awful commentary upon the depravity of human nature when we can be unmoved and indifferent in the presence of that grand thing that will be the preoccupation of the saints of God throughout eternal ages. Oh, may our hearts be drawn by that irresistible appeal of the glory of the gospel of God's power and of God's righteousness.

Oh Lord our God, do thou grant unto us that our hearts may be drawn irresistibly to the Redeemer in all his glory and perfection, and that we may each be united to him in the bonds of enduring and abiding faith, for Jesus's sake. Amen.

2

Reckoned to Us as Righteousness

Cometh this blessedness then upon the circumcision only, or upon the uncircumcision also? For we say that faith was reckoned to Abraham for righteousness. How was it then reckoned? When he was in circumcision, or in uncircumcision? Not in circumcision, but in uncircumcision. And he received the sign of circumcision, a seal of the righteousness of the faith which he had yet being uncircumcised: that he might be the father of all them that believe, though they be not circumcised; that righteousness might be imputed unto them also.

—ROMANS 4:9–11

The argument of the apostle in Romans 4:9–11 is based upon the fact that Abraham was justified before he was circumcised. That is such an obvious fact that it might not seem at all necessary for the apostle to conduct any extended argument concerning it. For the statement with reference to Abraham, which occurs in Genesis 15:6, "And Abraham believed in the Lord; and he reckoned it to him for righteousness," is a statement that applied to Abraham at least fourteen years before the rite of circumcision had been instituted. We don't find reference to circumcision until we come to Genesis 17, when Ishmael was thirteen years old—therefore, about fourteen years at least must have elapsed between the time that Abraham believed in the Lord and it was "reckoned to him for righteousness" and the time when circumcision had been administered to Abraham and to his seed when he was ninety-nine years old.

So, why labor the point? It's an obvious fact of history. And yet, you see that the apostle Paul, in this particular chapter, is taking great pains to point out that Abraham was justified long before he had been circumcised. Why? Because a great many of the Jews have completely misinterpreted the relation of circumcision to Abraham's justification (or to Abraham's righteousness). They have completely misunderstood the relationship of circumcision to faith. Consequently, it was necessary for Paul to base an argument on this very simple and obvious historical fact that Abraham believed in the Lord and it was counted to him for righteousness long before there was any institution of circumcision.

What was the misunderstanding on the part of the great many Jews with whom the apostle Paul was concerned in this particular epistle? It is that they had, in one way or another, regarded the circumcision of Abraham as that by which he attained to righteousness. Their thinking had been controlled by the principle that a man was justified in the sight of God by his works, by what he himself is and by what he himself does. They had regarded circumcision as definitely pointing to that conclusion because, after all, circumcision is a certain work that is performed. It is something that Abraham *did*—did in obedience to the divine command, but nevertheless something that he performed—and so in that respect it is in the category of a work. They had regarded circumcision, therefore, as an index to that kind of working on the basis of which Abraham was accepted with God and was justified. And they had applied that misunderstanding of the relation of circumcision to the justification of Abraham to the whole of their own thinking. The great fundamental error of their thinking was, of course, that a man was justified and accepted in the sight of God by reason of what he himself is or by reason of what he himself does.

The argument of the apostle in this chapter is directed very definitely to the correction of that fundamental error. There is no more basic or fundamental error in the whole realm of what we call religion than to think that a man is accepted in the sight of God, that he is justified by God, on the basis of what he himself is or on the basis of what he himself does. Therefore, it was not at all superfluous for Paul to appeal to that very simple fact of history, because it was a very cogent and effective way for exposing this fundamental error of Jewish thinking. You can see the relevance and the effectiveness of his appeal to certain simple historical facts: Abraham was justified before God and had been righteous in the sight of God long before he had been circumcised. Therefore, circumcision could have had absolutely nothing to do with his actual acceptance with God. It had its own place, but it was not anything on the basis of which he could have been accepted with God as righteous, since he had been accepted with God as righteous long before he had been circumcised.

Now, we might well ask the question, "Is this of any consequence to us? The simple historical facts to which the apostle Paul appeals are well known to us, and therefore, surely it isn't necessary for us nowadays to argue the point as the apostle Paul did." That is very, very far from being the case. It is just as relevant to us in our present situation, here in the year of our Lord 1958, to base an argument upon these simple historical facts, as it was when the apostle Paul himself did so at the beginning of the Christian era. According to the most reasonable evidence, the apostle Paul penned this epistle in A.D. 58. That's just exactly nineteen hundred years ago and a few months. And the lapse of nineteen hundred years does not make in the least degree irrelevant this particular argument of the apostle.

Why not? Why is it not irrelevant for us? Why is it just as necessary for us today to take account of simple historical facts as it was for the apostle nineteen hundred years ago? Just for this very reason: I said a moment ago that the fundamental error of all that we call religion is to think that we are accepted in the sight of God on the basis of what we ourselves are or on the basis of what we ourselves do. That's the fundamental religious error. There is nothing that is in more direct contradiction to the faith of God's people or to the revelation that God has given us or to the gospel of God's grace than the particular tenet that we are accepted in God's sight on the basis of what we are or what we do.

And yet, the native bent and tendency of our hearts and minds—and I mean for every one of us—is just that fundamental religious error. There's nothing that is more characteristic of us naturally than to think along that very pattern of thought. Let me give you just a few examples. I suppose you know, just as well as I do, that when a great many people are confronted with the question of their relationship to God and their hope for eternity, the spontaneous, natural response of their hearts and minds is after this pattern: "Well, I don't steal. I don't lie. I don't commit adultery. I don't murder. I live a very honest, upright life. I'm very decent in my behavior. I'm a good neighbor. I don't want to do harm to anybody." And they begin to talk to you about their own decency of behavior and conduct. Then they will say (and whether they say it or not, it's the implication of their thinking), "Well, since I'm such a decent person, I don't believe that the Lord will cast *me* off."

Now, it's a grand thing for people to be decent. It's a grand thing for people not to be notorious transgressors of God's law and to live outwardly an upright life in society. It's a splendid thing indeed. We're always very thankful for people who are decent, who are good neighbors, who are helpful members of society, and who do not transgress God's law outwardly. But don't you see that in that kind of response to the question, "How do I expect to be justified in the sight of God, how do I expect to be accepted with God as righteous?" there is a characteristic response of heart and mind just after the pattern of the basic, fundamental religious error: that we are to be accepted in the sight of God and justified by him on the basis of what we are and on the basis of what we do?

Let's take another person. He or she is confronted with the question, "What is your relationship to God? How do you expect to stand before God in the day of his reckoning and his judgment?" And perhaps you will get an answer after this type: "Well, I was baptized, I am a member of the church, I go to the

Lord's Table, and I do a great many things that are connected with the church of Christ."

Again, there is nothing necessarily objectionable about any of these things. Baptism is a divine ordinance. The Lord's Supper is a divine ordinance. Attendance upon the means of grace is an obligation resting upon us. Woe betide the person who casts any aspersion or scorn upon these institutions of God's appointment. But don't you see again the fact that this response is just after the pattern of the basic religious error of which we are speaking: that a person is going to be accepted in the sight of God on the basis of what he does and, particularly in this case, on the basis of what he does in connection with the church of God?

Take another instance. I suppose you find such people too, as I have, who, when you confront them with the great, basic question of their relationship to God, will answer, "Well, I had a very godly mother. I had a very godly father." And you get a long story about the godly forebears that the person had. Your only inference related to this fundamental religious question can be that they're really basing their expectation of acceptance with God on their godly ancestors. It almost amounts to ancestor worship—very close to it.

It's a grand thing to have a godly parent, and woe betide the person who despises the godliness of his parents or his ancestry. It's an inestimable privilege, and the grace of God normally flows along the lines of covenant godliness. "The mercy of the Lord is from everlasting to everlasting upon them that fear him, and his righteousness unto children's children; to such as keep his covenant, and to those who remember his commandments to do them" (Ps 103:17–18). I say again, woe betide the person who despises a godly ancestry, and woe betide still more the person who contradicts and runs counter to that great heritage that is his by reason of his godly parents. But again, don't you see that, in relation to the central question of relationship with God, you have the same fundamental religious error, because it all comes back to the idea that we are going to be accepted with God in one way or another on the basis of some particular *human* relationship?

It was just precisely that pattern of thought, coming to expression in various ways, that the apostle Paul was dealing with in this particular chapter. That is why he takes such pains to show the simple, obvious religiousness that is to be derived from the fact that Abraham was justified long before he was circumcised. That circumcision was not the ground of his justification but simply the theme, the final theme, of that justification that he had with God on an entirely different base.

Now, in Romans 4, the apostle Paul is giving us the gospel of the grace of God, and he's propounding for us that in which the blessedness of the righteous man consists. In other words, he's giving us the marks of that blessedness that consists in our acceptance with God as righteous. What are they? Well, I'm going to mention them for you briefly, in order to show how necessary it was for Paul to provide us with this argument in Romans 4:9–11 and how necessary it is for us to take account of the relevance of this argument on this great saving and fundamental question—namely, our acceptance with God and our justification by him.

The first criterion of the blessed man that I shall mention is this: the first thing that looms up on the horizon of the truly blessed man, the man who enjoys the favor of God, when he is confronted with this basic religious question of his relation to and his standing before God, is not at all his righteousness, not at all his decency, not at all his relationship to his fellow man in the sort of pressure of society, but the thing that looms up first of all on the horizon of the truly blessed man is his sins. In other words, he doesn't think first of all spontaneously and immediately of his goodness but of his wickedness and iniquity. That seems very strange indeed, doesn't it? But it's the only thing that is commensurate with the situation that belongs to us as sinners before God.

I tell you that there is no blessedness, no true and final blessedness, belonging to a person unless the first thing of which that person thinks when he is confronted with this question is his sin and his iniquity. A truly blessed man is the man who is overwhelmed, first of all, by his sins—by his own wickedness, his own iniquity—and by the fact that he has no standing with God at all on the basis of who he is or on the basis of what he has done, except the standing of condemnation. That's the first criterion of the blessed man, the person who recognizes that the only thing he deserves on the basis of who he is or what he has done is not acceptance with God or justification before God, but damnation.

It's easy for us to talk about this—-it's easy for you to listen, perhaps, and it's easy for me to speak—but it's another thing for us to search our hearts and see if that is really our spontaneous response and reaction when we are confronted with this basic religious question of our relationship to God and our acceptance with him.

The second criterion of the blessed man is that his sins have been forgiven. You see the emphasis that the apostle Paul places on that criterion in Romans 4 because he appeals to David, to what we find in the thirty-second Psalm:

> Even as David also describeth the blessedness of the man, unto whom God imputeth righteousness without works, saying, "Blessed are they whose iniquities are forgiven, and whose sins are covered. Blessed is the man to whom the Lord will not impute sin." (Rom 4:6–8, quoting Ps 32:1–2)

Remember, my friends, that the blessed man is not simply the man in whose consciousness looms the sense of his own iniquity, of his own wickedness, of his own guilt, and of his worthiness of damnation. But the blessed man is also the man into whose consciousness has come the efficacy of the forgiving grace of God. He is at least the person who is not content to have a sense of his own sinfulness, but who yearns before God and pleads before God that he may receive the full remission of his transgressions.

Oh, my friends, if we have a sense of our own unworthiness, our own sinfulness, our own ungodliness, and our own hell-deservedness, there is nothing that is more indispensable to our peace of mind and to our peace of conscience than to also have some sense of the forgiving grace of God. How marvelous it is that God can forgive! How marvelous that "if we confess our sins, he is faithful and just to forgive us our sins, and to cleanse us from all unrighteousness" (1 John 1:9), that he will "blot out, as a thick cloud, [our] transgressions and, as a cloud, [our] sins" (Isa 44:22), and that they will be cast forever into the sea of his forgetfulness (Mic 7:19). That is the blessed man! That is the man of whom the psalmist was singing in the fifty-first Psalm, the man whom David was as he penned the psalm—the psalm that breathes the atmosphere of divine forgiveness. "Blot out my transgressions. Wash me thoroughly from mine iniquity, and cleanse me from my sin" (Ps 51:1–2). Now that's the language of the blessed man!

I ask you very frankly to interrogate yourself. I don't suppose it's humanly possible, at least under all normal circumstances, for a person to remember all his sins at any one particular time. It might be at the judgment seat of Christ; I don't know what may be possible under very abnormal circumstances. But under normal circumstances it's just not humanly possible. But I tell you that if you are among the blessed of the Lord, there comes to your mind again and again particular situations, instances, and exigencies in connection with your whole life that cause you to have an overwhelming sense of your own iniquity. Perhaps you have completely forgotten something, you just didn't think that it would ever loom up in your consciousness at all, and perhaps sometime, when you least expect it, there comes across the threshold of your memory a particular situation thirty, forty, fifty, sixty, or seventy years ago, and you remember. Your sins are brought to remembrance in your own consciousness, and you are overwhelmed with the enormity and the iniquity of that particular expression of the depravity of your own heart. You never thought that it would ever invade your consciousness but there it is, vivid in your memory and stinging in your consciousness. Well, that must inevitably be the way with a blessed man. The psalmist gives expression to it in that very song we were singing earlier: "Let not the errors of my youth nor sins remembered be; in mercy for thy goodness's sake, O Lord, remember me" (Ps 25:7; author's translation).

In order to pass on from this point, may I ask one question, and may I ask it very pointedly? To what extent is the need of forgiveness and the blessing of forgiveness occupying your conscience? To what extent does it enter into your supplications before God as you prostrate yourself in humble contrition before him? To what extent does this matter of forgiveness and pardon enter into your consciousness? What kind of place does it occupy in your religion? My friends, if this isn't central in your interest, if it isn't central in your prayers, and if it isn't central in your faith, you're not a blessed man. "Blessed are they whose iniquities are forgiven, and whose sins are covered" (Rom 4:7).

Now the third criterion of the blessed man, according to the argument of the apostle in Romans 4, is that he is in the same category as Abraham. Abraham believed in the Lord, and it was reckoned to him for righteousness (Rom 4:3). Very simply stated, the blessed man is the man who is justified by faith. He is not only the person in whose consciousness looms up the reality of sin. He is not only the person in whose consciousness looms up the blessing of forgiveness. He is also the person in whose consciousness there looms up the grandeur of that article of justification by faith, justification by God's free grace on the basis of a righteousness that is not our own.

Now what is justification? It's a very great mistake to equate justification with the forgiveness of sin. Forgiveness of sin is a very important element in justification—an all-important element—and it's central in our justification because there cannot be any justification or acceptance with God unless our sins are "blotted out as a thick cloud" (Isa 44:22). But don't equate justification with the forgiveness of sin because justification is much more than the forgiveness of sin.

So what, then, is the central idea and meaning of justification? It is that we are accepted with God as righteous. The blessed man is the man who realizes that forgiveness of sin is not sufficient for him. Yes, forgiveness of sin will give you a clean slate, it will blot out your transgressions, but that's not sufficient for acceptance with God. If we have any sense of God's justice and of God's holiness, we shall not be satisfied simply with the forgiveness of sins. There must be something very much more positive. And that positive thing is that we must be accepted in his sight as righteous; there must be a positive righteousness to our account. God cannot be satisfied with a clean slate, if I may use that figure, with a slate from which all sin is blotted out. God can only be satisfied with a full slate—specifically, a slate full with the credit of righteousness. To put it in other terms, God cannot be satisfied simply with the blotting out of debt. In order to have acceptance with him, there must be full credit, and credit that is unto everlasting life.

What is that credit? What is that full slate? What is that full quota of righteousness that will satisfy God? Oh, here is the grandeur of the article of justification by faith of which the apostle is here speaking! It is expressed in this epistle in terms of the righteousness of God. In Romans 1:17 he says, "Therein is the righteousness of God revealed from faith to faith." In the third chapter of this epistle, he says, "Now the righteousness of God without the law is manifested, being witnessed by the law and the prophets; even the righteousness of God which is by faith of Jesus Christ" (Rom 3:21–22). In the tenth chapter of this epistle, he says, "They being ignorant of God's righteousness [referring to these Jews], and going about to establish their own righteousness, have not submitted themselves unto the righteousness of God" (Rom 10:3). And in the Second Epistle to the Corinthians, he says, "He who knew no sin was made to be sin for us, that we might be made the righteousness of God in him [that is, in Christ]" (2 Cor 5:21). Finally, in the Epistle to the Philippians, he says, "Not having mine own righteousness, which is of the law, but that which is through the faith of Christ, the righteousness which is of God by faith" (Phil 3:9). You see, that is what is central: the righteousness of God!

Now that doesn't mean the attribute of God's righteousness. The righteousness of God sometimes, of course, refers to the attribute of justice, of equity, in God. But that is not the righteousness that is spoken of in these instances because this is a righteousness that is available for us. It's a righteousness in which we come to have property. "Not having mine own righteousness . . . but that which is through the faith of Christ, the righteousness which is of God!" And we don't come to have property in the essential righteousness of God, in what we call God's attribute of justice. Of course not!

But what, then, is it? What, then, is this righteousness of God in which we come to have property? I'll come to that in a moment, but I want to emphasize, first of all, that the only righteousness that is adequate to our situation as sinners, that measures up to the gravity and desperateness of our need, is a righteousness that has a divine quality. That's the wickedness of a works-righteousness. You see, a works-righteousness, however good it may be, is human after all. If I'm justified on the basis of what I am or on the basis of what I do, then, after all, my righteousness is human, and it doesn't measure up to the gravity and to the desperateness of my need. But the grandeur of the great article of justification is that we are justified by a righteousness that is *not* our own, by a righteousness that is a God-righteousness, a divine righteousness. Therefore, it is a righteousness that measures up to *all* the exigencies of our situation and to all the demands of our need. That's the blessed, blessed man.

That righteousness, of course, as the apostle Paul clearly indicates in the sixth chapter of this epistle, is the righteousness of our Lord and Savior, Jesus Christ—the righteousness of his obedience. And because it is his righteousness, it is a divine righteousness. And it's a divine righteousness, therefore, that can be appropriated by us or imputed to us. It's a righteousness in which we come to have property, and therefore a righteousness that gives us a perfect standing before God. It is a righteousness that not only *warrants* divine justification, but a righteousness that, we can say with all reverence, *demands* divine justification. Wherever this righteousness is present, there *cannot but be* the divine justification, there *cannot but be* acceptance with God, for the simple reason that it is a righteousness that is of divine property and divine quality.

That is the righteousness of justification by faith, a righteousness not of the law. It is a righteousness that is undefiled and undefilable, that not only *merits* eternal life but that *must* accord, to every person who is the beneficiary of it, eternal life in the presence and in the fellowship of God. "Grace reigns through righteousness unto eternal life through Jesus Christ our Lord" (Rom 5:21).

Now, we have been dealing with the great fundamental question of religion. It's not the only question, remember, but it's the basic religious question of our acceptance with God. We cannot build for eternity, we cannot build acceptably for God or to God, except that we stand solidly upon this one foundation. As this particular question is answered, so will be our whole religion. And if it is answered according to that which Paul is controverting in the Epistle to the Romans, then there is nothing for us but "the blackness of darkness" (Jude 13). But if it is answered in terms of the argument of the apostle in Romans 4, then there is for us the hope of eternal life.

Stand upon that foundation against which the very gates of hell will not prevail (Matt 16:18). Here, my friends, is the blessed man. Here are answered by the apostle the great fundamental questions of our holy faith. Let us examine ourselves as to the foundation which we make (1 Cor 3:10). That is, examine ourselves as to the answer that *we* give for ourselves as individuals to the great fundamental question of religion—namely, our acceptance with God as righteous and our justification by him. Do we meet the criteria that the apostle enunciates in this chapter for the blessed man? These are questions that are pertinent to the basic religious question. They are questions that cannot be evaded. They are questions that we must answer, each one for himself as in the presence of God, at the tribunal of God's judgment and in the tribunal of our own conscience. Are we accepted in God's presence?

Oh Lord our God, we pray that thou wouldst bless to us our meditation upon thy Word. May it be mixed with faith in our hearts, may we receive it in faith and love, and may we lay it up in our hearts and practice it in our lives. May we be brought, each one of us, out of the thralldom of sin and iniquity into the liberty and glory of thy children, that we may walk in the light as thou art in the light, that the blood of Jesus Christ, thy Son, may cleanse us from all sin. May we be washed and cleansed, so that we may give evidence that we are not our own, but we have been bought with a price, and therefore may we glorify thee, our God and our Father, through Jesus Christ our Lord. In his name, amen.

3

Dead to Sin

For if we have been planted together in the likeness of his death, we shall be also in the likeness of his resurrection . . . For in that he died, he died unto sin once: but in that he liveth, he liveth unto God. . . . For sin shall not have dominion over you: for ye are not under the law, but under grace.
—Romans 6:5, 10, 14

Oh God, high and lifted up, holy, holy, holy, Lord God of Hosts, who art ever blessed in thyself, who dwellest in light that is unapproachable and full of glory, blessed forever be thy great and holy name. Thou art holy and inhabitest the praises of Israel. Do thou, therefore, oh Lord, grant unto us that as we come into thy holy presence, we may give thanks upon remembrance of thy holiness.

We confess unto thee, oh Lord, that the fear of thy great name, that reverence for thy majesty, is not native to us. We confess that we are ungodly in ourselves and that we are utterly alienated from thee because of our sin and our iniquity. We confess unto thee the hardness of our hearts and the darkness of our minds so that in thy light we might see clearly. We would come with a confession of our sin, remembering that if we confess our sins, thou art faithful and just to forgive us our sins and cleanse us from all unrighteousness.

Blessed be thy great name, that thou hast brought all the perfections of thy being, all the dictates of thy justice and of thy holiness, to bear upon that salvation that is in Christ Jesus, and that in the salvation wrought by thee thy glory is made great. Therefore, may we have confidence to draw nigh to thee in full assurance of faith, having our hearts sprinkled to cleanse us from a guilty conscience and our bodies washed with pure water.

As we come ostensibly and professedly to worship thy great and holy name, may we appreciate the unsearchable riches of grace that thou hast proffered to us in the gospel: that in Christ Jesus, our Savior, are all the treasures of wisdom and knowledge, that he is full of grace and truth, that in him dwells the fullness of the Godhead bodily, and that therefore we may have strong consolation—we who have fled to take refuge on the hope set before us—and that out of his fullness we all may receive grace for grace.

Deliver us, oh Lord, from that besetting sin of unbelief by which we do dishonor to thy truth and to thy faithfulness. Enable us to take hold of all the promises that are yea and amen in Christ Jesus. Therefore, may we have confidence that thou wilt meet every situation of ours, every circumstance in which we are placed, with the all-sufficiency of thy grace and with thy strength that is made perfect in weakness.

We pray, oh Lord, that we may realize the claims of the vocation wherewith we are called to the high calling of God in

Christ Jesus. Help us, therefore, to live not on the level of this present evil world, but to mount up on wings like eagles, that we may run and not be weary, and that we may walk and not faint. May we know what it is to have participation in the great power that thou didst work in Christ when thou didst raise him from the dead and set him at thy own right hand. Therefore, we pray that we may increasingly experience the might of Jesus's conquest when he destroyed him who had the power of death, the devil, and delivered them who, through fear of death, were all their lifetime subject to bondage. Oh grant that into this glorious liberty of thy saints, the sanctified ones, we may enter and be more than conquerors through him who loved us—that neither death nor life, nor angels nor principalities, nor powers, nor things present nor things to come, nor height nor depth, nor any other creature, will be able to separate us from the love of God that is in Christ Jesus our Lord. Make every situation of life demonstrate more and more to us the sufficiency of thy grace and that overcoming faith that overcomes the world. And do thou grant, we pray thee, that all thy people may be enriched with the fullness of grace and truth in Christ Jesus so that, in whatever situation thou dost place them in thy sovereign providence, they may bear aloft the testimony of the Lord and Savior, Jesus Christ.

We pray, oh Lord, that thou wouldst revive thy church in these days when there is such widespread apostasy from the faith of Jesus, such widespread indifference to the claims of his glory. Do thou, oh Lord, graciously arise and have mercy upon this world in all its confusion and staggering unbelief. We pray, oh Lord, that thou wouldst send forth the Holy Spirit with more manifest unction and demonstration of power, so that sinners may be converted, that thy people may be built up, and that there may be added unto the church daily such as are appointed to salvation.

We would not be unmindful of those who are in authority in the civil realm. Do thou grant unto them to be given wisdom that we may lead a quiet and peaceable life in all godliness and gravity. May those in authority know that thou art God, and may they bring the various affairs of their administration into conformity to the will of him who is King of kings and Lord of lords, who is given all authority in heaven and on earth. And now, oh Lord, while we wait upon thee, do thou grant that thy blessing might be vouchsafed unto us, that thy Word may go home to our hearts with its convicting, converting, sanctifying, and enriching power, all in Jesus's name. Amen.

It is not by my own choice but by request that I am speaking to you today on the teaching of chapter 6 of the Epistle to the Romans. And I am not focusing attention on any one particular verse but on the leading emphasis and teaching of the chapter. It should be noted that there is a transition at the beginning of this chapter to a new phase of doctrine. In the preceding part of this epistle, the first five chapters, the apostle is dealing with the great doctrine of justification by faith on the basis of the righteousness of Christ. This doctrine is very well defined in our Westminster Shorter Catechism when it says that justification is "an act of God's free grace, wherein he pardoneth all our sins, and accepteth us as righteous in his sight, only for the righteousness of Christ imputed to us, and received by faith alone" (Q. 33). Justification is, in a word, the acceptance of sinners as righteous with God, that God is just and "the justifier of him who believeth in Jesus" (Rom 3:26).

Justification is, of course, a once-for-all action—it is as complete and perfect once it is executed as it will be at the day of judgment and throughout eternity. There are no degrees of justification, and it is not a process. It is well emphasized in the catechism that justification is an act of God's free grace. It has reference to the relationship that we sustain to God or, more accurately, the relationship that God comes to sustain to sinners when they are received into his favor on the basis of the righteousness of Christ.

But you will notice, or at least you should notice, that at the beginning of chapter 6 the apostle proceeds to deal with an all-important aspect of the salvation that is in Christ Jesus, which we generally speak of as sanctification. There is an all-important distinction between justification and sanctification because sanctification is concerned with the sanctifying of our hearts, our minds, and our lives. It is the making of us more and more conformed in our hearts and in our persons to the image of God, more and more conformed to the norm of holiness, righteousness, and truth. It is that all-important aspect of the salvation that is in Christ Jesus with which the apostle begins to deal at the beginning of this chapter.

Now you notice that the chapter begins with a rather striking question: "What shall we say then? Shall we continue in sin, that grace may abound?" (Rom 6:1). And that question is posed by what the apostle Paul states earlier in the preceding chapter, particularly Romans 5:20: "Moreover the law entered, that the offence might abound. But where sin abounded, grace did much more abound." The entering of the law is the action of God, and the action of God is said to be to the end that the trespass might abound. Then, in the latter part of this verse, we have this statement that where sin abounded, grace did much more abound. Therefore, it might seem that the logic of the grace of God is that we should multiply transgression in order that the grace of God might be all the more illustrated and magnified. If sin is abounding and if grace abounds all the more where sin abounds, the logic might seem to be, "Well, let us sin all the more so that God's grace might be glorified and magnified."

Now that, from the standpoint of human reasoning, might be good logic, but it is perverse logic. It is not the logic of the order of heaven; it is the logic of the pit. And it is that objection, or that logic, that the apostle meets when he says, "Shall we continue in sin that grace may abound? God forbid." Paul is using the strongest kind of negation that would be at his disposal in the language that he used. In the idiom of the Old Testament, as well as in English, the only proper way of expressing it is, "God forbid!"

Then, of course, the apostle goes on to tell us the reason why: it would completely violate the logic of God's salvation. To continue in sin that grace may abound would be a complete contradiction of the very nature of salvation, of the very grace the apostle speaks of in Romans 5:20 when he says, "But where sin abounded, grace did much more abound." What is salvation?

Well, it's salvation *from* sin! It's salvation *to* righteousness and glory, but it is first of all salvation from *sin*.

But it isn't that *general* consideration that the apostle pleads in this particular case as the answer to the question, "Shall we continue in sin, that grace may abound?" He deals with something that is much more specific: "How shall we, who have died to sin, live any longer therein?" (Rom 6:2). That is to say, he interprets for us one particular aspect of this salvation that God has wrought and that God has imparted, and it is that we have *died to sin*. Now, if I may give a more literal translation, it would be this: "How shall we, who are such as have died to sin, live any longer therein?"

What the apostle Paul is dealing with in this chapter is that which has its starting point, its pivot, in the truth that we died to sin. That is to say, if we are the partakers of that justification that Paul is dealing with in the preceding chapter, if we are the possessors of salvation, if the grace of God has supervened upon us and has come to be operative in us, *then* we died to sin. We are in that category, and it is only because we are in that category that we have come to be partakers of the salvation of which Paul is speaking.

But what does that mean, that we died to sin? It is just a little misleading in our version to translate it, "How shall we who are dead to sin." It's not the most accurate expression because the thought in this verse is focused upon the momentary action, or at least the momentary event, of having died to sin. If this is the pivot of Paul's teaching in this passage, it is all-important that we should understand precisely what he means by saying, "We are such as have died to sin" (Rom 6:2; author's translation).

Paul is using language with which we are very familiar. We

are very familiar with the event of death in the ordinary realm of our human experience. When a person dies, that person has no longer any communication with us who are left behind. Has it not been a very painful experience for some of us, perhaps all of us, that a very loved one has died and you could just wish that you had one minute more in which to express to that person your love, your affection, and the great sorrow that will be yours when that person will depart this life. But you can't get it. The person has gone with no further communication. You can't tell that person anymore, "Oh, how I love you! How regretful I am that I have not been a more faithful son, or a more faithful daughter, or a more faithful husband, or a more faithful wife (as the case may be)." But you cannot communicate. The person is gone and has no further communication with this life.

That person, you see, is therefore no longer active in this sphere. The person, indeed, as respects the disembodied spirit, is active in *another* sphere (about which we know very little). We know enough for the comfort of the godly and the warning of the ungodly, but very little about that unseen realm to which the departing spirit goes. But that spirit is undoubtedly active in another realm, it is just not the realm of our life here. How eloquent the Scripture is in portraying that very fact with which we are all familiar. "The wind passeth over it, and it is gone; and the place thereof shall know it no more. . . . I have seen the wicked in great power, and spreading himself like a green bay tree. Yet he passed away and, lo, he was not: yea, I sought him, but he could not be found" (Pss 103:16; 37:35–36). That is the very thought the apostle Paul is expressing in Romans 6, when he says, "We are such as have died to sin" (Rom 6:2; author's translation).

What does this mean? It means that this person, who is in

possession of the salvation that is the theme of this epistle, died to sin and therefore died to the realm of sin. This person is no longer active in the kingdom of sin; he has been translated to another realm. That is often expressed in the Scripture as being translated from the kingdom of darkness to the kingdom of light, from the kingdom of Satan to the kingdom of God (Col 1:13). But it is a reality that we must never underestimate and that we must never tone down: that the very *meaning* of salvation, in its very inception and in its fundamental character, is that we died to sin. If we died to sin, we have been translated out of the realm of sin and are no longer active in that realm. That is the way the apostle Paul expresses it here: "How shall we, who have died to sin, live any longer therein?" (Rom 6:2; author's translation). It's not possible, if we have died to sin, to live any longer in the realm of sin.

You may be surprised at that thought because the believer, the possessor of salvation, is not yet perfect and hasn't been completely delivered from all sin. But, you see, the apostle Paul is making an all-important distinction between *living in sin* and what we might call *sin living in us*. There is a fundamental, radical distinction between living in sin and having sin still active in us. The apostle Paul makes perfectly plain in a later chapter in this epistle how active sin is in the believer and in himself (Rom 7). But nevertheless, although sin is active in the believer, he does not *live* in sin.

There are various ways in this chapter in which the apostle unfolds that basic truth of having died to sin. We find, for example, in Romans 6:6 another way of expressing this very same truth of having died to sin: "Our old man has been crucified with him" (Rom 6:6; author's translation). It is not correct to simply say "is crucified"; it's past tense and a very definite event. "Our old man has been crucified with him, that the body of sin might be destroyed, that henceforth we should no longer serve sin" (Rom 6:6; author's translation). It is one thing to be serving sin; it is another thing altogether for sin to be soliciting our service and to be constantly plaguing our hearts and minds by its solicitations. To express the same thought in a different way, the person who is in this category does not live in sin and he does not serve sin.

But there are other expressions in Romans 6:6 that need to be noted. The first is, "Our old man has been crucified" (Rom 6:6; author's translation). Now, I suppose that you have often heard it said that in the believer there is the old man and the new man. Indeed, that is the characteristic way of expressing the conflict that goes on in the believer. He refers his sins to the old man and that which is good and acceptable to God to the new man. But that is not the way to express the biblical teaching. When Paul says that our old man has been crucified, he means that the person who is in this category of which he is speaking is *no longer* the old man. He is a new man in Christ Jesus. It is an utterly unbiblical way of representing the life of conflict in the believer as being between the old man and the new man. Paul makes that very clear in other epistles as well as in this epistle. This man is a new man, and he's no longer the old man, for the old man is the unregenerate man, the unsaved man, the man who has not died to sin. Know this: our old man has been crucified. And remember this, beloved: if you are in the category of the person of whom Paul is speaking, you are no longer an old man; you are a new man in Christ Jesus, a new creation in him. You are not an old creation because the old man has been crucified, and he's been crucified once-for-all. Just like death itself, death to sin—the crucifixion of the old man—is a once-for-all, definitive event.

I fear, my friends, that there is far too much in the way of excusing sin and apologizing for sin in the life of a believer by saying, "Oh, that's just the old man in me," or, "That's just the old man in him." And there is the tendency to excuse ourselves in the sins that we commit. My beloved, the great truth that the apostle Paul is emphasizing is that the *old man has been crucified.* Therefore, we are not to indulge those sins that are characteristic of the old man. We are not to be harking back, as it were, to Egypt from which we have come. We are not to be harking back to the old man who has been crucified. But we are new men in Christ Jesus, and we should exemplify that. And we should bank all our interests and all our concerns on this fact: that we must live according to the new man in Christ Jesus, and therefore "put on the Lord Jesus Christ, and make no provision for the flesh, to fulfil the lusts thereof" (Rom 13:14).

Then there is another expression in verse 6: "That the body of sin might be destroyed." This is language just as strong as the language you have in the earlier part of the verse when Paul says, "Our old man has been crucified with Christ" (Rom 6:6; author's translation). "That the body of sin might be destroyed" means that it might be brought to naught, and it is the very term that Paul uses when he says, with reference to Christ at his second coming, that he will bring to naught death (1 Cor 15:26). Death will be swallowed up in victory, and we will be able to say, "O death, where is thy sting? O grave, where is thy victory?" (1 Cor 15:55). Christ will bring the last enemy, death, to naught. This is the same term that is used in Romans 6:6 when we read "that the body of sin might be destroyed."

I know it has been common for interpreters to speak of the *body of sin* as the *mass of sin*, but I do think that in this particular instance the apostle Paul is speaking about our physical body. When he says the body of sin has been destroyed, he's talking about the physical aspect of our being and is characterizing the physical body as a sinful body. Now, it is the body of the unregenerate person, of the unsaved person, of the person who has not died to sin, that is a sinful *body*, a body characterized by sin. The body is not the *source* of sin; the spirit is the source of sin or the heart is the source of sin. Nevertheless, the sin that has its seat in the heart or the spirit of the man permeates his whole being, so that his body is brought into captivity to sin and is therefore a sinful body.

What I believe the apostle Paul is emphasizing here when he says that the body of sin has been destroyed is that, as the old man has been crucified and he is now a new man, so also the sinful *body* has been destroyed. His body hasn't been annihilated (he still has a body), but just as the new man is complete, so is the very body that a believer possesses—it's no longer a sinful body. Oh, sin still inheres in it, but it's one thing to have sin attaching to us; it's another thing to have a body of sin. Paul is emphasizing this because the human body is an all-important aspect of the human person. There is no underestimation or depreciation of the significance of the human body in either sin or in sanctification. "The body of sin might be destroyed, that henceforth we should not serve sin" (Rom 6:6).

Then the apostle also uses another expression in verse 7: "For he that is dead has been freed from sin" (Rom 6:7). That is a rather apt rendering of what Paul says, literally, "He that died is justified from sin." What he really means is not so much the justification of which he speaks in the preceding chapters, but rather what is rendered in our version as "freed from sin." It means this: the person who has died to sin is quit of sin. Judgment has been executed upon sin. He is no longer sin's slave, no longer under its thralldom. Sin is no longer the ruling principle for him nor the sphere within which he lives and moves and has his being, because he has been translated into the kingdom of righteousness and holiness and truth.

There is one further characterization of what it means that we died to sin that the apostle uses in this chapter (at least one more on which I wish to reflect). "For sin shall not have dominion over you: for ye are not under the law, but under grace" (Rom 6:14). Notice how the apostle Paul has led up to this extraordinary statement that sin shall not have dominion. He has said that we died to sin, that the old man has been crucified, that the body of sin has been destroyed, that we no longer serve sin, and that we are quit of sin (that is to say, we have been effectively delivered from the thralldom of sin). And now he makes this astounding statement: "Sin shall not have dominion over you: for ye are not under the law, but under grace."

This statement has so frequently been interpreted as an exhortation to believers that they should not *let* sin have dominion over them. But that is not what Paul is saying in this instance. It is perfectly true that in a preceding verse he gives exhortation that is in very much the same terms: "Let not sin therefore reign in your mortal body, that ye should obey it in the lusts thereof" (Rom 6:12). But in verse 14 he makes a categorical statement to this effect: "Sin will not have dominion over you." And he gives the reason, of course, that we are not under law but under grace. That is an express statement that the person who is in this category is no longer under the dominion of sin.

That's awfully difficult to believe, isn't it? A believer himself, who is perhaps long on the pilgrimage to glory and who is far advanced in what we call saintliness, is coming perhaps more and more to experience the awful power of sin. And the longer he lives, the more intense becomes his conviction of the power of sin and of the iniquity that resides in his own bosom. It is very difficult to believe that he is not still, to a very considerable extent, under the dominion of sin. But, you see, the truth of God is not to be measured by our experience but by the teaching of God's own Word. This is the truth: sin will not have dominion and cannot have dominion over this person because he is not under law but under grace.

What does that mean? It means that, although sin still lives in the believer, although sin is still active in him, and although he still commits sin, the sin that inheres in him and the sins that he commits are no longer the master. Sin no longer has the dominion. It is this very truth that we must accept as the teaching of Scripture, however much it may seem to be contradicted by our own experience. The sin that we commit doesn't exercise dominion, and the sin that resides in us doesn't exercise dominion. And *why* not? It is just because *Christ* is our Lord, and Christ *never* abdicates the throne of the believer's heart. He never gives up his kingship, his hegemony, in the heart of the believer. And it is just because Christ exercises the lordship, not only in the whole domain of the universe but also in the heart of the believer, that it *must* be said, "Sin does not have dominion over you: for ye are not under the law, but under grace" (Rom 6:14).

This is something, my friends, to appropriate in faith when you are afflicted as a believer by the iniquity that resides in your own heart, and when you become more and more acutely conscious of the gravity of the sin that you commit and that inheres in your very being. Remember the great assurance that God gives: your sin, however grievous it is in God's sight and however grievous it is in your sight, does not exercise the dominion. "For sin shall not have dominion over you: for ye are not under the law but under grace."

These are the characterizations that the apostle gives of this person who has died to sin, and this, my friends, is at the very basis of sanctification. We often use the word *sanctification* as it is defined in the Shorter Catechism: "Sanctification is the work of God's free grace, whereby we . . . are enabled more and more to die unto sin, and live unto righteousness" (Q. 35). And we generally think of sanctification as a process (and it certainly *is* a process). Yes, sanctification is progressive as justification is not. But we must remember this: there is a once-for-all sanctification that lies at the very inception of the believer's life and that belongs to the salvation that is in Christ Jesus. It is with that *once-for-all* sanctification, by which a believer is made a sanctified one (a saint) in Christ Jesus, that the apostle Paul is dealing in Romans 6.

It is one of the great oversights of our theology and our teaching within orthodox churches that we have overlooked, to a very large extent, the emphasis that we find in this chapter and in this particular part of the epistle in connection with this basic sanctification. And too often, in certain circles where the teaching of the sixth chapter of Romans has been taken into account, it has been distorted and instead used to press home the necessity for sanctification as a second blessing or second gift. That has been a grave distortion—prejudicial to the truth of salvation—that has been propounded in perhaps the last seventy-five years or so in the application of this particular passage. What Paul is teaching in this passage is that everyone who is the possessor of salvation has died to sin, that his old man has been crucified, that the body of sin has been destroyed, that he no longer serves sin, and that sin does not exercise dominion over him. We'll find out in a moment why that is so.

If that is the description or the characterization of sanctification, we have now to turn very briefly to the basis. How is it that this person has died to sin? Paul unfolds the answer in this chapter. You notice the emphasis that falls in this chapter on the death and resurrection of Christ, and the reason is this: the person who is in *this* category has been united to Christ in the virtue of his death and the power of his resurrection.

Too frequently in evangelical circles, the doctrine of union with Christ has been overlooked and has not received the place that it occupies in biblical teaching. If you want to describe a Christian, a person who is a believer in Christ, there is no more characteristic way of describing that person than that he or she is united to Christ. It takes place at the very inception of salvation. Those who are the partakers of salvation are called into the fellowship of Jesus Christ, and it is in this fellowship or union with Jesus Christ that they come to possess all that is involved in salvation. Christ himself is the embodiment of salvation, and it is just because believers are united to Christ that they are partakers of salvation, because they are partakers of Christ.

It is the death and resurrection of Christ that receives the emphasis in Romans 6. "In that he died [that is, Christ], he died unto sin once" (Rom 6:10). He made an end of sin, he finished transgression, he made reconciliation for iniquity (Dan 9:24)—it was a once-for-all, definitive action on his part. It's not a process; it's *finished*! That is expressed in our passage by saying, "In that he died, he died unto sin *once-for-all*" (Rom 6:10). The person who is the possessor of this salvation died with Christ, and if he died with Christ, he died to sin once-for-all. That's the efficacy, that's the dynamic, that's the power effecting this momentous change from the sphere of sin to the sphere of life and holiness. It is by virtue of union with *Christ*, and the whole dynamic proceeds from that union. We likewise have union with him in his resurrection: "That like as Christ was raised from the dead by the glory of the Father, even so we also should walk in newness of life" (Rom 6:4).

Now, the next point would be: what are the corresponding exhortations that belong to the obligation of this person? You find them here in this passage as well. For example:

> Let not sin therefore reign in your mortal body, that ye should obey it in the lusts thereof. Neither yield ye your members as instruments of unrighteousness unto sin: but yield yourselves unto God, as those that are alive from the dead, and your members as instruments of righteousness unto God. (Rom 6:12–13)

The exhortation is summed up, my friends, in this expression in verse 11: "Reckon . . . yourselves to be dead indeed unto sin." It is not this reckoning that brings the reality to pass. This has been the mistake of a great many teachers who have appeared in this country in the last eighty to eighty-five years and who have taught that it is by reckoning ourselves dead unto sin that we become dead unto sin and attain to this victorious life. My friends, that is a complete distortion of Paul's teaching. This exhortation, "Reckon yourselves to be dead indeed unto sin," is not that which puts the death to sin into effect at all. It's an exhortation that belongs to those people who *have* died to sin, whose old man *has been* crucified, whose body of sin *has been* destroyed, and who are no longer under the dominion of sin. Reckon to be a fact what *is* a fact. Don't reckon it in order to put that fact into existence, but reckon it to be a fact because it is a fact. It is a fact by virtue of our union with Christ.

My friends, when we come to a realization of the implications of union with Christ in his death and resurrection, then there is nothing that is more important for sanctification than reckoning to be true that which is a fact by reason of our union with Christ. It is simply another way of saying, "We should take a full accounting of what our heritage is." If a person has become the possessor of an estate by virtue of the death of a relative, he has to reckon with it, he has to calculate henceforth on the basis of what he has come to inherit. That's the way here as well. We have to calculate on the basis of what Christ has done with reference to us in order that we may worthily exemplify that which has been accomplished once-for-all, by virtue of union with Christ, in the efficacy of his death and the power of his resurrection. "Just as Christ was raised from the dead through the glory of the Father, we also should walk in newness of life" (Rom 6:4).

What a contradiction it is, therefore, for us to take to ourselves the ways of this world in all of its sin and squalor and iniquity if we are new men in Christ Jesus! What a contradiction it is to take to ourselves those things that are characteristic of the old man and characteristic of the realm of sin and death, where sin reigns unto death and in which the devil is paramount. Oh, let us more and more appreciate what the grace of our Lord Jesus Christ is. Let us bask in what has its embodiment in him, that he is "full of grace and truth" (John 1:14).

Oh God, receive us more and more fully into the experience of the grace that is in Christ Jesus, and may we live not according to the course of this world but according to the power and the grace of the almighty, exalted Savior. In his name, amen.

4

Triumph over Sin

But now we are delivered from the law, that being dead wherein we were held; that we should serve in newness of spirit, and not in the oldness of the letter.
—ROMANS 7:6

Oh Lord our God, as we come into thy house and into thy holy presence, do thou sprinkle us with the blood of Christ Jesus the Savior, so that we may have true access unto thee and acceptance by thee. For we all have sinned and come short of the glory of God. If thou, Lord, shouldst mark iniquity, oh Lord, who shall stand? Do thou grant unto us that our sins may be real to us in all their gravity of defilement and guilt and curse, and do thou therefore imbue us with a broken spirit and a contrite heart, which are pleasing sacrifices unto thee. Do thou imbue us with a humble spirit, for thou, oh God, resisteth the proud and giveth grace unto the humble. We would remember, oh Lord, that he that falleth upon the stone that is set in Zion, the chief cornerstone, shall be broken, but on whomsoever it will fall, it will grind him to powder.

Do thou therefore grant that we may be thus imbued with a broken spirit, so that we may confess unto thee our sin with all sincerity and truth, and be delivered from that pride of self-righteousness, which we may entertain because of our uprightness in this world, in this social and political order. Oh grant that we may know that in thy sight there is no good in us except as thou dost implant by the efficacious operations of thy grace. Therefore, oh Lord, let us come to thy throne of grace with a purged conscience, with a renewed heart, and therefore present ourselves at thy throne of grace for the supply of all our needs—the needs of this life and the needs against all the issues of death and eternity. May our needs be so amply and fully supplied out of the riches that are in Christ Jesus that we may rejoice with a joy that is unspeakable and full of glory, because we receive the end of our faith, even the salvation of our souls.

We pray, oh Lord, that we may glorify the Redeemer by not taking to ourselves positions that do not belong to us, but that we may accord to the Redeemer all the glory and the honor that belong unto him. Therefore, may we rejoice in him who is the first begotten from the dead, who is the Prince of the kings of the earth, who is exalted in glory and given the name that is above every name. Therefore, may we exalt him in all our ways so that we may have that true dedication of heart and devotion of spirit by which we shall serve thee acceptably with reverence and godly fear.

We pray, oh Lord, that our hearts may be sanctified more and more. May we not only be set upon that one foundation, but may we build upon that foundation, and not build upon it with wood and hay and stubble but with gold and silver and precious stones, knowing that every man's works shall be tried and that thou will bring every work into judgment with every secret thing, whether it be good or whether it be evil.

And we pray, oh Lord, that thou wouldst bless this congregation. Oh may the presence of God be manifest here from Sabbath to Sabbath and from week to week. Do thou endue thy servant with richness of understanding and with completeness of consecration, and do thou grant that he may be an abundant blessing in this community as he ministers, unto these who are gathered in this place, the Word of life, the Word of the living God, which abides forever. May many be begotten anew unto everlasting life, begotten unto a living hope by the resurrection of Jesus Christ from the dead, and may they thus be heirs of the inheritance incorruptible and undefiled and that fadeth not away.

Do thou, oh Lord, grant that, to the ends of the earth, the testimony of the Lord Jesus Christ may be unfurled. Where thy church has been unfaithful, do thou give that reformation, that radical transformation, whereby thy church may again be arrayed in her garments of glory and beauty, bearing a pure testimony to the whole counsel of God and to the institutions of thy grace. Now, while we wait upon thee, grant us thy presence, the unction of thy Holy Spirit, so that the Word may be registered to our hearts with true conviction, that we may know that it is the Word of the living and abiding God, effectually working in our hearts and bringing forth corresponding fruit in our lives, for Jesus's sake. Amen.

We are looking at the Epistle of Paul to the Romans, chapter 7. May I say again, as I said this forenoon, that I am speaking on this subject by request and not simply by my own individual choice. In the forenoon we noted, in reference to chapter 6, that

Paul is laying great emphasis upon dying to sin by union with Christ and living again in newness of life by virtue of his resurrection. The pivot upon which his teaching turns in Romans 6 is that we died to sin, and that this death to sin is just as once-for-all as was the death of Christ when he died upon the accursed tree. It is because of union with Christ that believers died to sin and live again in the newness of life represented by Jesus's own resurrection. "Like as Christ was raised up from the dead by the glory of the Father, even so we also should walk in newness of life" (Rom 6:4).

That is the theme of chapter 6, and you should notice that in chapter 7 the same theme is being continued through the first six verses. Only, Paul changes the perspective in Romans 7:6 and views this momentous change that took place by union with Christ, in the virtue of his death, from the angle of its implication with reference to the law. That is inevitable because "the strength of sin is the law" (1 Cor 15:56), and where no law is, there is no transgression. If there were no law, sin would be void. Since the strength of sin is the law, if there is to be death to sin, there must be also death to the law.

That is exactly what Paul says in verse 4: "Wherefore, my brethren, ye also are become dead to the law by the body of Christ." In the first three verses he is using the parallel of what occurs in the marital relationship: the woman who is wed to the husband is bound by the law to that husband as long as he lives, but if the husband dies, she is free from that law and is ready to be married to another man so that she is no adulteress. Having used that analogy, the apostle proceeds, "We have been put to death to the law through the body of Christ, that we might be married to him who was raised again from the dead" (Rom 7:4). Then in verse 6, Paul says (as it should properly be read), "But now we are delivered from the law, having *died* to that wherein we were held" (Rom 7:6; author's translation). It isn't the law that is put to death at all—*we* died to that wherein we were held; *we* were put to death *to the law*. The law is not represented as having died at all, but we are represented as having died to the law.

Now, of course, as Paul points out in the latter part of this chapter, the law is not evil: "The law is holy, and the commandment holy, just, and good" (Rom 7:12). He says later on that "the law is spiritual" (Rom 7:14), and by that he means that it is of the Holy Spirit, that it is of divine origin, divine sanction, and divine authority. The law is spiritual, and it is holy, just, and good. But we must remember this: Although the law of God was ordained to life—and, in a state of innocence, in a state of integrity, it would have been the means of securing and attaining to life—nevertheless, in our sinful situation, the law as law is totally impotent. Once sin has entered, the function of the law is to condemn and to inflict curse. Consequently, law simply as law has absolutely no power to produce life in a sinful situation. That, of course, is the refrain of Romans 7:4–6:

> Wherefore, my brethren, ye also are become dead to the law [or, ye have been put to death to the law] by the body of Christ; that ye should be married to another, even to him who is raised from the dead, that we should bring forth fruit unto God. For when we were in the flesh, the motions [or the passions] of sins, which were by the

> law, did work in our members to bring forth fruit unto death. But now we are delivered from the law [we are discharged from the law as the way of attaining to life, as the way of righteousness, as the way of acceptance with God], having died to that wherein we were held; that we should serve in newness of the Holy Spirit, and not in the oldness of the letter [that is, in the oldness of the law principle, which, in a sinful situation, is utterly incompetent to impart to us any life or any righteousness].

As I said, in a sinless situation, the law of God would have been the minister of life. It was ordained to life even as Paul said in this chapter. But once sin has entered, the whole situation has been changed. In a sinful situation, the law of God is utterly incompetent and utterly impossible as a way of obtaining to acceptance with God, as a way of righteousness, as a way of justification, and as a way of life. Therefore, we have to be put to death to the law, we have to die to the law, in order that we may be united to him who has come into this sinful situation and who himself, by his obedience unto death, fulfilled the law on our behalf and is therefore able to deliver us from the condemning power of the law and from the law as the principle regulative of salvation.

In Romans 7:7–13, the apostle provides us with what could probably be called the *period of conviction* in his own experience and in the experience of many believers. It isn't that in these verses he is describing a believer, but he is describing a person who has come under the convicting power of the law of God. It might be called the transition experience from indifference and carelessness to the life of faith and new obedience, which is delineated later in this epistle. In fact, I think you can see very well that he is not in this passage (that is, in verses 7 to 13) describing a believer, but that he is describing a believer who is in, what you might call, the vestibule of faith. This is the person who is convicted now of sin and who is no longer self-satisfied, no longer prepared to remain in his own self-complacency and self-righteousness.

You can see this when he says, "For I was alive without the law once: but when the commandment came, sin revived, and I died" (Rom 7:9). There he is not talking about dying with Christ or dying to sin in virtue of the death of Christ; he is referring to the destruction of his self-righteousness, of his self-righteous hope and his self-complacent confidence. Then Paul says:

> And the commandment, which was ordained to life, I found to be unto death. For sin, taking occasion by the commandment, deceived me, and by it slew me. Wherefore the law is holy, and the commandment is holy, and just, and good.
>
> Was then that which is good made death unto me? God forbid. But sin, that it might appear sin, working death in me by that which is good; that sin by the commandment might become exceeding sinful. (Rom 7:10–13)

So you see in this passage a portrayal of what happened in reality in the apostle's experience but also what happens in the experience of numberless others. They are quite content with their own legal self-righteousness, they have a self-complacent confidence, but the commandment comes with conviction, and that self-complacent confidence is taken away. "I was alive without the law once: but when the commandment came, sin revived, and I died" (Rom 7:9). That old self-complacent, self-righteous confidence was destroyed, the ax was laid at the root of the tree, because the law of God came with convicting and condemning power into his consciousness, and he found that he had no ability to keep the law. The more knowledge he came to possess of the law of God, the more that sin was aroused to activity and to virulent opposition to what the law of God commanded.

I take it that the main interest of the person who asked me to speak on this subject is concerned with verses 14 to 25 in this chapter. I think you are bound to recognize that at verse 14, or at least at verse 15, there is a complete transition, for Paul is no longer speaking as a convicted sinner; he is speaking in the present tense. He begins verse 14 by saying, "For we know that the law is spiritual," that is, it is divine (of divine origin, of divine sanction, of divine authority); the law is holy, just, and good because it is divine. Then he goes on: "But I am carnal, sold under sin," and you notice the present tense.

There are a lot of people who have taken the position that in verses 14 to 25 the apostle is not describing the experience of a believer, but that he is describing the same situation as that which is delineated for us in verses 7 to 13. They think that he is still describing the person who is laboring under the conviction of sin, who is still, as it were, under the sentence of condemnation because of the condemning power of the law of God. But I consider this impossible. The person who is being described in verses 14 to 25, or at least in verses 15 to 25, cannot be a person who is still in his unregenerate state, who is simply convicted of sin and under the curse and condemnation of sin. But these verses are describing the person who has passed from death to life. I want to mention just a few considerations that point to the necessity of that conclusion.

The apostle Paul describes himself in this passage, that is verses 14 to 25, as the person who consents unto the law that it is good. And he has a preponderant will to that which is good— he wills that which is good. He's not able to carry it into effect, because, as we shall see, there is another principle, but he is the person who, nevertheless, consents unto the law that it is good.

But now more than that, he says, "I delight in the law of God after the inward man" (Rom 7:22). That statement cannot possibly be construed to describe a person who is still under the dominion of sin, who has not really died to sin by union with Christ! The person who is still under the dominion of sin, who is still in what we call the state of nature, does not delight in the law after the inward man. He is still controlled by the carnal mind (that is, the mind of the flesh), and "the carnal mind is enmity against God; it is not subject to the law of God, neither indeed can be" (Rom 8:7). That's the description of the unregenerate man, even the convicted and condemned and self-condemned unregenerate man. He cannot be said to delight in the law of God after the inward man.

And there is another consideration: Paul here describes a person (and, of course, is describing himself) who calls out in the anguish of his spirit, "O wretched man that I am! Who shall deliver me from the body of this death?" (Rom 7:24). This is a person who has come to have such a detestation of himself by reason of sin that he is no longer simply under the conviction of sin, but he *hates* sin and abhors himself because of sin. "Who shall deliver me from the body of this death?" There is the overwhelming desire for deliverance from the power of sin, from the defilement of sin, and from every attachment of sin to his person.

Then again, it is utterly impossible for an unregenerate man to say, "I thank God through Jesus Christ our Lord" (Rom 7:25). Paul is yearning for complete deliverance from the presence of sin and from all the defilement of sin, and he has the confidence of faith and hope. "I thank God through Jesus Christ." That is not the language of the unregenerate man. It is utterly impossible for the unregenerate man, however much he may be convicted of sin, to give expression to this exuberant and triumphant thanksgiving of praise to God: "I thank God through Jesus Christ our Lord."

Finally, there is that in which Paul describes himself: "So then with the mind I myself serve the law of God; but with the flesh the law of sin" (Rom 7:25). That can never be said of an unregenerate man—never! However high may be his attainments, however close he may be to the threshold of faith, he can never say, "I myself with the mind serve the law of God," because he is still under the dominion of sin. And being under the dominion of sin, he is characterized by the carnal mind that is enmity against God, which is not subject to the law of God, neither indeed can be.

I want you to place these two side by side and see how utterly contradictory they are, the one as the description of the unregenerate man and the other as the description of Paul himself: on the one hand, "The mind of the flesh is enmity against God, not subject to the law of God and cannot be" (Rom 8:7); on the other hand, "So then with the mind I myself serve the law of God; but with the flesh the law of sin" (Rom 7:25). There is, indeed, that with which we shall presently deal—the conflict, the antithesis within himself—but, nevertheless, what is most characteristic of this person, what characterizes his inner man, what characterizes his mind, is delight in the law of God. "I delight in the law of God after the inward man . . . with the mind I myself serve the law of God" (Rom 7:22, 25).

We are confronted here, you see, with this all-important consideration: Paul, in verses 14 to 25, is describing himself, in respect to his own experience, as a man in the same category as the person in Romans 6. He died to sin, the old man has been crucified, the body of sin has been destroyed, and sin no longer exercises dominion over him. Focus attention on these truths. This person whom he is describing here in Romans 7 (and, of course, first of all he is describing himself) is the person in the category of Romans 6.

So you have your questions, and everyone who has studied this great epistle of the apostle with any intelligence is perplexed by what seems to be a contradiction. How can the person who is in that category of having died to sin—whose old man has been crucified, whose body of sin has been destroyed, and who is no longer under the dominion and power of sin—how can he say, "I am carnal, sold under sin" (Rom 7:14)? How can he be in this condition of conflict, which he describes in verses 15 and following?

> For that which I do I allow not: for what I would, that do I not; but what I hate, that do I. If then I do that which I would not, I consent unto the law that it is good. Now

> then it is no more I that do it, but sin that dwelleth in
> me. For I know that in me (that is, in my flesh,) dwelleth
> no good thing: for to will is present with me; but how to
> perform that which is good I find not. . . . O wretched
> man that I am! (Rom 7:15–18, 24)

You see, you seem to have a contradiction between that which the apostle teaches in chapter 6 and that which he teaches in chapter 7. What is the solution?

My friends, you must remember that the person whom Paul describes in chapter 6 is the person, indeed, who has died to sin—he no longer lives in sin, Christ has mastered him, he has come under the dominion of the Lord and Savior, and sin no longer exercises its dominion over him. *But* there is still sin *in* him. And there is a radical difference, you see, between living in sin and being under the dominion of sin on the one hand, and having sin in us on the other hand.

In Romans 7, Paul makes that very same distinction with the use of another term. In chapter 6, the language used to describe living in sin is being under the dominion of sin, being the old man, and being governed by the body of sin. But in chapter 7, you notice, he changes his language and describes the person who is still living in sin, who is still under the power of sin, who is still the bondslave of sin, and who is still the old man, as being "in the flesh." "When we were in the flesh, the motions [or passions] of sin, which were by the law, did work in our members to bring forth fruit unto death" (Rom 7:5). And yet, in the very same passage, the apostle recognizes that the flesh is still in him: "I know that in me (that is, in my flesh,) dwelleth no good thing" (Rom 7:18). So you see that there is this radical distinction between being in the flesh and the flesh being still in the believer. Just as in chapter 6 there is the radical distinction between *living* in sin and having sin *in us*, so now the distinction is between being *in* the flesh (that is, being completely governed and directed and controlled by the flesh) and finding that the flesh is in him (and the flesh *in him* is just the same thing as sin dwelling in him). The person who has made the transition to newness of life still finds sin dwelling in him.

So you have the distinction between living in sin and still having indwelling sin, and that's the person whom Paul is describing in this epistle as the true believer. He no longer lives in sin, he's no longer the bondslave of sin, but sin still indwells him. He's no longer in the flesh, but he still has the flesh. And he says, "I know that in me (that is, in my flesh,) dwelleth no good thing" (Rom 7:18). "It's no longer I that do it, but sin that dwelleth in me" (Rom 7:17). So you see that we are faced inevitably with this conclusion: the apostle Paul is describing himself as the person who has still flesh in him and who has sin indwelling. Now you have the solution, therefore, of the apparent contradiction in this passage.

The question we are discussing is this. How can the apostle Paul describe the experience of a true believer in these terms: "I find then a law, that, when I would do good, evil is present with me" (Rom 7:21); "I know that in . . . my flesh dwelleth no good thing: for to will is present with me; but how to perform that which is good I find not" (Rom 7:18); "With the mind I myself serve the law of God; but with the flesh the law of sin" (Rom 7:25)? The question is not only understandable, my friends, but it is inevitable! And that is the great mistake that a great many people make in interpreting the Christian life. So long as there is indwelling sin in any degree or proportion, there must be the contradiction that Paul describes in this chapter. In another epistle, he states this conflict in these terms: "The flesh lusteth against the Spirit, and the Spirit against the flesh: and these are contrary the one to the other: so that ye cannot do the things that ye would" (Gal 5:17).

The characteristic of the believer is that he has died to sin, that he is a new man in Christ Jesus, that holiness and righteousness and truth are the most distinctive features of his character. But if there is still sin in him, he cannot be at peace with it. To be at peace with sin would be a complete contradiction of the very nature of that regeneration by the Holy Spirit that takes place at the very inception of the believer's life. It would be a contradiction of that union with Christ by the virtue of his death and the power of his resurrection. Consequently, you have here an honest description of what a believer *must* be until he is made perfect in holiness, until all sin is completely eradicated and he is completely conformed to the image of Christ. It *cannot* be otherwise because sin and holiness are contradictory. You have, in the believer, holiness after the pattern of the Savior himself created anew in Christ Jesus, but you still have indwelling sin, and between these two there is not simply *conflict* but there is *contradiction*. Therefore, the experience of the honest, exercised, sincere, and humble believer is just the experience of the contradiction that Paul describes in this passage.

To think otherwise about this would simply mean that the believer is completely conformed in his whole being to the image of Christ, and that is not characteristic of the believer in this life; it has not yet been manifested what we shall be (1 John 3:2). We are not yet completely conformed to the image of God, to the image of the Savior, and therefore wherever there is sin and shortcoming in any degree whatsoever, there must be the conflict and the contradiction that the apostle Paul describes in this passage.

And so there must be, by the nature of the case, the exclamation of self-detestation, "O wretched man that I am! Who shall deliver me from the body of this death?" (Rom 7:24). Is this not true the more a believer is sanctified? The more sanctified a believer is, the more sensitive he is to the contradiction of sin; and the holier he becomes, the more his experience becomes that which is delineated for us in this particular passage. And that necessarily so! The nearer we come to the majesty of God, the nearer we come to the vision of his holiness; and the nearer we come to conformity to that holiness, the greater is our detestation for everything that is inconsistent with it. And it is just the truth that what a believer at one stage of his life may even have gloried in, he comes in the progress of his sanctification to regard as an abomination in the sight of God. What at one period he might have regarded as virtue, he now regards as detestable vice.

That is the experience of Job: "I have heard of thee by the hearing of the ear: but now mine eye seeth thee. Wherefore I abhor myself, and repent in dust and ashes" (Job 42:5–6). Self-abhorrence. It was the reaction of Isaiah when he saw the Lord high and lifted up and his train filling the temple and the seraphim crying, "Holy, holy, holy, is the Lord of Hosts: the whole earth is full of his glory" (Isa 6:3). The reaction of the prophet was, "Woe is me! for I am undone; because I am a man of unclean lips, and I dwell in the midst of a people of unclean lips" (Isa 6:5). This passage, my friends, is perhaps the most eloquent rebuke and the most eloquent witness against that self-complacency that is the very antithesis of godliness.

Oh, my friends, if you are satisfied with your attainments, with your social-political decency, or with your respectability in the world (even as a professing believer), you're not in the path of honesty and you're not in the path of true sobriety. For honesty looks facts in the face and sobriety will reckon with reality; and the reality is that wherever there is lack of conformity to the image of the Savior, there is sin, and all sin is detestable. And sin becomes more and more detestable to the person who is sanctified in the Holy Spirit and who is more and more sensitive to the demands of holiness and to the grand goal of perfection that God has set before his people: that they will be "conformed to the image of his Son, that he might be the firstborn among many brethren" (Rom 8:29).

But it would not at all do justice to the delineation that we have in this particular passage if we failed to take account of the triumphant note that the apostle Paul gives us in this passage. Oftentimes in Christian interpretation, a certain contrast is drawn between the person in Romans 7 and the person in Romans 8: that you have in Romans 8 the victorious, triumphant believer, whereas you have in chapter 7, at the very best, the downtrodden and defeated believer. Oh, my friends, there is no note of triumphant confidence in Romans 8 that surpasses the note of triumphant confidence that you have in Romans 7. "O wretched man that I am! Who shall deliver me from the body of this death? *I thank God* through Jesus Christ our Lord" (Rom 7:24–25). There is no exultation, no triumphant note, in all the epistles of the apostle Paul that excels the confidence and the hope expressed in that word: "I *thank* God through Jesus Christ our Lord." That thanksgiving did not end the conflict for the apostle because he immediately proceeds, "So then with the mind I myself serve the law of God; but with the flesh the law of sin." But it is that triumphant note, my friends, that we must never overlook. It is the note of triumph, the note of faith, and the note of assured hope.

My friends, remember this, that the precondition of that triumphant note is just the complaint of the preceding verse: "O wretched man that I am! Who shall deliver me from the body of this death?" It is only in the context of the self-detestation and the self-commiseration expressed in verse 24 that there can be, in truth and sincerity, the triumphant exultation of verse 25, because it is only into the wretchedness and misery of our sinful condition and situation that Christ comes. "This is a faithful saying, and worthy of all acceptation, that Christ Jesus came into the world to save sinners" (1 Tim 1:15).

My friends, until we have something of the conviction of the apostle Paul, until we have something that corresponds to this exclamation of self-detestation, "O wretched man that I am," Christ cannot come into our situation with the note of triumph expressed in this: "I thank God through Jesus Christ our Lord." It is only in a sinful and a wretched situation that Christ has relevance and significance. Let us therefore emulate rather than commiserate with the apostle when he says, "O wretched man that I am! Who shall deliver me from the body of this death?"

For it is *precisely* into the situation that he there describes that Christ comes in all the glory of his person, in all the perfection of his finished work, and in all the efficacy of his heavenly ministry.

And he comes with the assurance that one day this conflict will be forever terminated, that this contradiction will be no more, because the grand goal to which the whole of the redemptive process moves is that we might be conformed to the image of God's Son, that he might be the firstborn among many brethren. Let us beware of shortcuts to the attainment of that grand goal, the shortcuts that self-righteousness and self-complacency too often provide. Let us have the honesty, let us have the candor, let us have the sensitivity of the apostle. And then we shall be on the path of attainment that is the expression of the apostle's triumphant confidence: "I thank God through Jesus Christ our Lord."

Oh God and Father of our Lord Jesus Christ, hear us in the complaint that our misery constrains and do thou grant us a visitation of thy almighty power and thy efficacious grace, so that we shall be able to join with the apostle, "I thank God through Jesus Christ our Lord," to his glory. Amen.

5

The Father's Love

He that spared not his own Son, but delivered him up for us all, how shall he not with him also freely give us all things?

—ROMANS 8:32

The death of Christ upon the accursed tree is the supreme exhibition of the love of Christ. Christ "loved the church and gave himself for it" (Eph 5:25). Christ laid down his life for the sheep because he loved them with such intensity that no obstacle could quench his love (John 10:15). But as we are thinking of the death of Christ upon the accursed tree, we must not so focus attention upon the love of *Christ* that we overlook the action of God the Father. It is not as if the Son of God gave himself to this undertaking while the Father turned away his face until the ordeal was ended and then received Christ into the bosom of his love again. No, the events of Gethsemane, the events of the arraignment before the High Priest and before Pilate, and the events of Golgotha, were events in which God the Father was *intensely* involved. Calvary is also the supreme exhibition of the *Father's* love.

And it is upon the love of God the Father that the emphasis

falls in this particular text. Only of the Father is the Lord Jesus Christ the Son, and thus only of the Father can the apostle be speaking when he says, "*He* that spared not *his* own Son." There are four features of the text upon which we will dwell: first, the uniqueness of the person; second, the extremity of the sacrifice; third, the particularity of the provision; and finally, the guarantee of grace.

So, first, we have *the uniqueness of the person*. Jesus called God his own Father (John 5:18), which means that no other but the Father stood in this relation to Jesus the Son. Likewise, Paul, in Romans 8:32, calls Jesus "his own Son," meaning that no other stands in this unique relation to the Father.

God the Father, of course, has many sons by adoption, but the revelation that God has given us does not permit any confusion to exist between the sonship of the only begotten and the sonship of the adopted. The highest privilege bestowed upon men is to be adopted into the family of God, to be heirs of God and joint heirs with Jesus Christ. God will bring to glory all the sons whom he has appointed to that destiny. They will be conformed to the image of God's own Son "that he might be the firstborn among many brethren" (Rom 8:29). But however high is the privilege bestowed in adoption, there is no confusion in the Scripture between the uniqueness of the sonship that belongs to the only begotten and the sonship that belongs to the adopted. No other but the eternal Son is the Father's *own* Son. His is an ineffable and incomparable sonship, as we have discovered in our studies of the last two days. When the Son of God came into the world, there was no suspension of this unique sonship, this eternal sonship. The glory of the Word made flesh, which the disciples beheld, was the glory of the only begotten from the Father, and the revelation of the Father dispensed by him was revelation dispensed by the only begotten. How eloquently John 1:14 and 1:18 testify to these facts!

Since there was no suspension of this ineffable fatherhood or sonship, there was no suspension of the love that the Father bore to the Son or that the Son bore to the Father. As incarnate, Jesus said, "The Father loveth the Son" (John 3:35; 5:20), and he also said, "I love the Father" (John 14:31). These very simple statements point to an infinitude of reciprocal love—love not constrained by ignorance nor quenched by knowledge, but love that is drawn out by the exclusive and exhaustive knowledge that the persons have of each other.

The Son came to do the Father's will. He came because he loved the Father, and the Father sent him because there was no other who could fulfill such a mission. And throughout all the stages of Jesus's messianic task, until his work reached its climax in his death upon the cross, the love of God the Father flowed out to him with increasing satisfaction and delight. That is Jesus's own witness: "Therefore doth my Father love me, because I lay down my life, that I might take it again" (John 10:17). It is, of course, necessary to distinguish between that infinite love that flows out from the Father to the Son because of the intrinsic relationship that they sustain to one another and the love of complacency that flowed out with increasing intensity to the Son because of his fulfillment of the Father's commission. So, in the agony of the garden and the abandonment of Calvary's tree, our Lord was the unique object of the Father's love because he was the Father's own Son fulfilling the Father's unexampled commission.

Second, we have *the extremity of the sacrifice*. He "spared not his own Son, but delivered him up" (Rom 8:32). I am not suggesting that God the Father sacrificed the Son; Christ sacrificed himself in the strict sense of that word. Our attention, in this case, is drawn to a negative and a positive: what the Father did not do and what he did.

First, the negative: he spared not. Sparing applies to suffering that may be inflicted. For example, parents spare their children when they do not inflict the full measure of the chastisement due, and judges spare criminals when they do not pronounce a sentence commensurate with the crime committed. This is the opposite of what God the Father did! Suffering was inflicted by God the Father upon his own Son, and the Father did not spare. He did not alleviate the stroke, did not withhold one whip of the full toll of judgment due to the sins of those on whose behalf his Son suffered. Do we hesitate with such a thought? Let us remember the words of the prophet, "The Lord hath laid on him the iniquity of us all. . . . It pleased the Lord to bruise him; he hath put him to grief" (Isa 53:6, 10).

Oh, think of this incomparable conjunction; there is no such conjunction elsewhere, even in God's counsel. The Father loved the Son with infinite and immutable love because he did not cease to be the only begotten Son, and the infinite love necessarily flowed out from the very relationship that he essentially and immutably sustained to God the Father. And furthermore, every detail of the suffering endured by the Son constrained the love and delight of God the Father because it was all endured by the Son in obedience to the Father's will and, in the performance of the Father's will, the Son committed no sin. He was "holy, harmless, undefiled" (Heb 7:26), and in his own witness, his meat and drink was to do the will of the Father who was in heaven (John 4:34). *But*, despite his infinite and immutable love, the Father did not lighten the stroke that fell upon his own well-beloved Son. So, you have this incomparable conjunction of the full toll of judgment executed upon the person who was the object of infinite and immutable love and who, in the very performance of his undertaking, is necessarily drawing out the complacent delight of God the Father because of the perfection of his obedience and performance. The strokes fell upon him with unrelieved intensity, with all the weight deserved by the sins that he bore.

Now what does this mean? In this we see the marvel of the Father's love to the people whom he had chosen. It was the person uniquely related to the Father as the well-beloved Son and uniquely loved by the Father with infinite and immutable love whom the Father did not spare. The reason is that if he had spared him, if any of the judgment had been left for the people of God to bear, then all whom the Father had chosen would have been consigned to perdition. The Father loved his people with such invincible love and purpose that he executed the full toll, the full stroke, of *their* condemnation upon his own Son. *That* is the Father's love. Do you stagger with amazement? Does your mind reel with amazement? Oh, let that not be the amazement of bewilderment, but may it be the amazement of believing and adoring wonder!

In understanding the extremity of the sacrifice, there is also the positive: he delivered him up. The Father delivered him over to nothing less than the curse and consequence of sin. Jesus was made a curse and he was made sin (Gal 3:13). He was brought into the closest relation as was possible for him to come to sin, without becoming himself sinful. And it is that which the apostle Paul brings to our attention in the expression, "He was made sin for us" (2 Cor 5:21)—he was not simply the sin-bearer, he was *made sin*. Paul points us to the intimacy of the relationship that Jesus sustained to sin: he identified with it as closely as he could without becoming himself implicated in its defilement. And the condemnation of sin is preeminently God's wrath. It is the wrath of God that will burn in the place of woe and that will constitute hell essentially. "The breath of the Lord, like a stream of brimstone, doth kindle it" (Isa 30:33).

Here again we have this unheard-of conjunction: infinite love and divine wrath. The Son bore the stroke of the Father's wrath, and there was no amelioration. Don't be deceived by the widespread current of thought that denies the real doctrine of propitiation. The essence of sin's curse and judgment is the wrath of God. So, if Jesus bore sin and if he bore our curse and if he was made sin, then the vicarious bearing of the wrath of God belongs to the very essence of his atoning accomplishment. How cramped the understanding and how narrow the perspective of those who think that the infliction of wrath is inconsistent with the exercise of infinite love. Oh, my friends, the truth is that it was just *because* the Son was the object of this immutable, infinite, and unique love that he could at the same time be the subject of the wrath of God. The opposite of love is not *wrath*, it is *hate*. There is no inconsistency between the infinitude of love that flowed forth to him and the execution upon him of the full toll of divine condemnation for sin and, therefore, the full toll of divine wrath, divine indignation, and divine displeasure.

The condemnation of sin is also abandonment. That was the cry of the Son of God from the accursed tree: "My God, my God, why hast thou forsaken me?" (Matt 27:46; Mark 15:34). It was only because the Son was the object of the Father's unique and immutable love that he could be thus abandoned. No other would be equal to it. The lost in perdition will be abandoned eternally, but not one of them will ever be able or have occasion to say, "My God, my God, why hast thou forsaken me?" The abandonment of Christ on Calvary's tree was abandonment in pursuance of the commission given him by the Father, and it was abandonment with the unparalleled effect of *ending* that abandonment. And because it was abandonment with this result, it was abandonment with inimitable agony and reality.

Octavius Winslow stated, "Who delivered up Jesus to die? Not Judas for money, not Pilate for fear, not the Jews for envy, but the Father for love" (Octavius Winslow, *No Condemnation in Christ Jesus* [London: 1857], 358). The determinate purpose of the Father's love was the explanation for the spectacle of Christ's death. But the love that the Father bore to the Son did not diminish the severity of the ordeal that creates this spectacle—the ordeal of the cross and the abandonment vicariously born. Oh, may I draw your attention again, my friends, to the marvel of this conjunction and the full reality of this experience.

Another aspect to this giving up on the part of the Father is the giving up of the Son to all that the arch-enemy and his agents could do against him. Did not Jesus say to his adversaries, "This is your hour, and the power of darkness" (Luke 22:53)? And did he not speak in prophecy? "Many bulls have compassed me: strong bulls of Bashan have beset me round. They gaped upon me with their mouths, as a ravening and a roaring lion. . . . For dogs have compassed me: the assembly of the wicked have inclosed me: they pierced my hands and my feet" (Ps 22:12–13, 16). If there had been restraint placed upon the power of the enemy, then Jesus himself would not have vanquished him and "spoiled the principalities and the powers" (Col 2:15). And if he had not vanquished the full power of the enemy and bound him to the triumphal chariot of his cross, if he had not executed full judgment upon the god of this world and cast him out, then the powers of darkness would have proven too strong for the people of God. Here, my friends, is further proof of the Father's love that he gave up his own Son to the malignity, hate, power, and ingenuity of the Prince of Darkness. Therefore, he gave him over to the contradiction of what he, the Son of God, was in his own spotless purity and love.

In summary, we need to think much of the Father's love. It is indeed necessary to think much of the love of Christ and appreciate more and more Paul's word,

> For the love of Christ constrains us; because we thus judge, that if one died for all, then all died. And that he died for all, that they who live should not henceforth live unto themselves, but unto him who died for them, and rose again. (2 Cor 5:14–15)

But we cannot afford to stop short of the holy of holies of the Father's love, that love which has the emphasis in this text. It is then that we shall get to the fountain of the whole plan of salvation, and it is then that we shall have a deeper appreciation of Christ's own love. For it is only as the ordeal of Gethsemane and Calvary is viewed in the perspective of damnation vicariously born, damnation executed with the sanctions of unrelenting justice, that we shall be able to apprehend the wonder and taste the sweetness of love that surpasses knowledge (Eph 3:19). This love will be eternally explored by the saints of God but will be eternally inexhaustible. Oh, how necessary it is that we should appreciate that which stands in back of the whole spectacle of Calvary: God the Father's *love* and God the Father's *action* in pursuit of the determined purpose of that love.

Third, we have in this text *the particularity of the provision*: "He that spared not his own Son, but delivered him up *for us all*" (Rom 8:32). Who are these people for whom God delivered him up? They are the "all" defined by the context. It is an elementary principle of hermeneutics that we must always observe the universe of discourse. So, when Paul says, "for us all," he has in mind those of whom he is speaking in the context. Paul has been speaking of those "called according to . . . purpose" in verse 28, and that purpose is defined in terms of full knowledge and predestination in verse 29. He is addressing those for whom he can challenge, "If God be for us, who can be against us?" and he proceeds to the protestation, "Who shall lay any thing to the charge of God's elect?" (Rom 8:31, 33). It is simply exegetically monstrous to try to extend the denotation of the "all" in our text beyond the denotation provided by the universe of discourse in the context.

But the point of importance here is that within the circle of those concerned there is no restriction or exclusion. That's the emphasis of the "all." "He that spared not his own Son but delivered him up for us *all*." Jesus was delivered up *for us all* if we are within the circle of those defined in the context of Romans 8.

Now, each person has his or her own individuality. No two persons are identically the same, not even identical twins—they have their own distinguishing marks, and the parents soon discover that. This particularity is true also in sin, misery, and liability: "All we like sheep have gone astray; we have turned every one to his own way" (Isa 53:6). And we cannot place this manifold of guilt in any one category. Oh, there is indeed the one characterization that "all have sinned, and come short of the glory of God" (Rom 3:23), but within that characterization there are as many categories of sin as there are individuals. And when God saves, he does not save in the mass; he deals with each individual in his or her own particularity. It is this that the apostle is emphasizing in our text in reference to the giving up of God's own Son. The Father contemplated those embraced in Christ's vicarious undertaking in the distinctness of their sin, their misery, and their liability.

If we are sensitive to the enormity of our own sin and to the particularity of our own sin and guilt, then it may be difficult for us to entertain this talk. It might be easier for us to think of the Father's love and provision if we were submerged in the mass and if he did not contemplate us in our own individuality and in the particular aggravations of our own sin.

But we dare not think of the Father's provision in that fashion. For if we were submerged in the mass and forgotten in the mass, there would be no salvation at all. A mass salvation will not do me any good in the wretched particularity of my own sin. And we dare not think of salvation even once-for-all accomplished in that way. Salvation can only be "for us" if it is salvation in all the particularity of our need—in all the enormity of *my* particular guilt and in all the loathsomeness of *my* particular corruption.

Paul expresses this in reference to the love of Christ: he "loved *me* and he gave himself up for *me*" (Gal 2:20), and in our text he expresses it in terms of the Father's love. When you think it over with a little more maturity, my friends, that very truth becomes supremely precious. It alone inspires the confidence needed in the gravity of our own individual sin and in the enormity of our own individual guilt: God the Father gave up his own Son to the wrath and curse and condemnation that *your* sins deserved, that *my* sins deserved. That is what constrains again the marvel of believing apprehension.

There is no case, therefore, that falls outside the scope of the Father's provision. Let us ever bear in mind that the Father knew each of us in all the loathsomeness of our beguilement, in the enormity of our guilt, in the wretchedness of our misery, in the particularity of our purpose, and in all the intensity of our need. And he loved with an everlasting love nevertheless. He loved us with such intensity that he gave none other than his own well-beloved and only begotten Son that he might bear our sin and the full judgment that the holiness and justice of God demand for our sin. He loved with a love so great, so invincible, and so purposeful that he gave over his own Son to face death for every one of the sons to be brought to glory so that they would never taste one drop of this damnation. Oh, they will taste much of the bitterness of sin and, with their increasing sanctification, they will taste more and more of its bitterness, but they will never taste one drop of the damnation of that sin. "There is therefore now no condemnation to them who are in Christ Jesus" (Rom 8:1).

Oh, let us exclaim, in the language of wonderment, the marvel of the Father's love. Eternity will not scale its heights; it will not fathom its depths. This, like the love of Christ himself, surpasses knowledge. And as the greatness of God is incomprehensible, so is the greatness of his love. It will fill us *increasingly* with amazement. Let it not be the amazement of bewilderment, but let it be the amazement of believing and adoring and loving wonder.

Finally, we have *the guarantee of grace*: "How shall he not with him also freely give us all things?" All that precedes in the text leads up to this rhetorical question, and the interrogative confronts us with the unthinkableness of the opposite. The purpose is to enforce the assurance that all things necessary to, yea, all things securing and furthering, the glorification of the people of God will be freely and infallibly bestowed. It is the argument, of course, from the greater to the less: if the Father did not spare his *own* Son but delivered him up, how shall he fail to bring to fruition and final realization the end for which he was given up?

It is well to take account of this very brief expression, "with him also." This phrase attaches itself very closely to the "for us all" of the preceding clause. The Father gave the Son to undergo for our benefit all that had been stated in both the negative and positive implications. "Shall he not *with him* . . . give us *all things*?" See something of the contrast between "the Son" and "things." What was the Father's greatest gift? What was the most precious donation for us? It was not "things." However precious his calling (when God the Father calls into the fellowship of his Son), however precious his justification (when God the Father freely justifies by faith), however precious his adoption (when he brings into his own family the sons to be brought to glory), however precious his sanctification, however precious ultimate glorification, these are not the greatest gifts of God. It is not even the security with which the apostle closes this particular chapter that is God's greatest gift.

All of these are favors bestowed, graces dispensed, and the design of God the Father's counsel, but the incomparable *gift* is the giving up of his own Son. Not only was he given *for us*, but he is also given *to us* in all the plenitude of his grace, power, truth, and love. Let us not miss, therefore, that richness of the prepositions: *for* us, *with* him. The thought is that so great is the gift, so marvelous are its implications, and so far-reaching are its consequences, that all gifts of lesser magnitude are infallibly certain of free bestowment. That is the apostle's argument from the greater to the less: if he did the greater, if he did that which is incomparable, shall he not freely give us all things?

Are we thinking of the enormity of our sins and the question of pardon? Are we simply appalled by the offense that is offered to the majesty of God by our sins so that we are overwhelmed with the enormity of their guilt? The Father will blot them out with a thick cloud (Isa 44:22), because these very sins in all the enormity of their being and liability he laid upon his own Son. Let us always get back to the assurance of the fact that it is God the Father who forgives, and he forgives because of that which he did in not sparing his own Son but delivering him up for us all.

Are we thinking of the temptation so subtle and overpowering that we dread to fall before the tempter's devices and stratagems? Do we tremble before the iniquity that is perfectly devised by the great arch-enemy or his human instruments, or before the slanders that will be circulated because people hate the people of God (John 15:19; 17:14; 1 John 3:13)? Remember, my friends, that God gave up his own Son to bring to naught the Prince of Darkness. He has been cast out and is no longer the victor. "Now is the judgment of this world," said Jesus, "now shall the prince of this world be cast out" (John 12:31). And it is just because God the Father gave him up to the full power of the arch-enemy that Christ executed upon him this fatal wound.

Are we thinking of the last enemy, death, and the grim struggle that may be ours when death assails us? It is natural to dread death because death is unnatural. We dread what we may have to face. Remember, the Father gave his Son to die in order that he might take the sting out of death. And that is the consummation of the people of God as they contemplate confrontation with the last enemy. It is not without significance that the writer of the Epistle to the Hebrews reminded his readers that it was the Lord Jesus Christ who delivered them from the fear of death because he brought to naught him who had the power of death, that is the devil (Heb 2:14). Oh, there is reality in death and perhaps that reality is being accentuated in our day and generation, but whatever our situation may be as we are thinking of death, let us remember that Christ said, "O death, where is thy sting? O grave, where is thy victory? The sting of death is sin; and the strength of sin is the law. But thanks be to God, which giveth us the victory through our Lord Jesus Christ" (1 Cor 15:55–57). And he could say this just because he was delivered up by God the Father to the full power of the great arch-enemy, who had the power of death.

Are you thinking of the spotless perfection that must be ours if we are to enter the portals of glory? Are you thinking of the awful discrepancy that there is between your present condition and that which is entailed in your hope? Remember, beloved, what the Father inscribed on the Son's commission: "This is the Father's will which hath sent me, that of all which he hath given me I should lose nothing, but should raise it up again at the last day" (John 6:39). In this conference, surely I bespeak the feelings of everyone. Have we not been laid prostrate in the dust? Have we not felt our utter desperation before the reproof of God's Word? Have we not felt the awful discrepancy between our attainment and our obligations?

I want to bring to you the encouragement: "He that spared not his own Son, but delivered him up for us all, how shall he not with him also freely give us all things?" (Rom 8:32). And the determinate purpose of his love will not rest until everyone to whom Christ is precious will be presented spotless "before the presence of his glory with exceeding joy" (Jude 24) and will attain to the highest conceivable destiny that God himself could devise for sinners: that they will be "conformed to the image of his Son, that he might be the firstborn of many brethren" (Rom 8:29). In the pilgrimage to that glorious consummation, let us find ourselves constantly in this assurance of God the Father's love, that "he that spared not his own Son, but delivered him up for us all, how shall he not with him also freely give us all things?"

Oh God, do thou be merciful to us. Meet our insufficiency with the abundance of thy provision. Meet our unbelief with the power of thy grace. And grant that we may be able more and more to abound in faith, in love, and in hope, that we may put on the Lord Jesus Christ and make no provision for the flesh, but that we may lay hold upon all the promises that are yea and amen in Christ. And out of his fullness, may we all receive grace upon grace. In his name, amen.

6

Be Ye Transformed

I beseech you therefore, brethren, by the mercies of God, that ye present your bodies a living sacrifice, holy, acceptable unto God, which is your reasonable service. And be not conformed to this world: but be ye transformed by the renewing of your mind, that ye may prove what is that good, and acceptable, and perfect, will of God.

For I say, through the grace given unto me, to every man that is among you, not to think of himself more highly than he ought to think; but to think soberly, according as God hath dealt to every man the measure of faith.

—ROMANS 12:1–3

Oh God, who art holy, holy, holy, Lord God of Hosts, who dwellest in light that is unapproachable and full of glory, who art light and in whom there is no darkness at all, praise and honor and glory belong unto thy great and holy name. It is a good thing to extol thy grace, for this is an exercise to which there can be no restraint. Thy glory is above all the earth. Thy righteousness is like the great mountains. Thy judgments are a great deep. oh Lord, thou preservest man and beast. How precious is thy grace! All thy works shall praise thee, oh Lord, and thy saints shall bless thee. They shall abundantly utter the memory of thy great goodness and shall sing of thy righteousness.

We would, oh Lord, draw nigh unto thee in confession, in humble supplication, for we have sinned. We have all turned aside from the right way, we have together become unprofitable, and there is none that doeth good, no, not even one. Our throat is an open sepulcher; with our tongues we have used deceit; the poison of asps is under our lips. Our feet are swift to shed blood. Destruction and misery are in our ways, and the way of peace we have not known. There is no fear of God before our eyes. And it is this confession that becomes us. Blessed forever be thy great and holy name, that we may come to thy throne of grace to confess our sin because thou hast said that if we confess our sins, thou art faithful and just to forgive us our sins and to cleanse us from all unrighteousness. Oh, how precious is thy grace, that we may come with confidence to obtain mercy and find grace to help in every time of need.

Do thou, oh Lord, impress upon us the claims of thy holiness so that we may take the place that belongs to us, that we may smite upon our own breasts and utter the suppliant cry of the penitent, "God, be merciful to me a sinner." Oh Lord, our God, do thou grant that we might also know the claims of thy holiness upon us for our life and conduct. May we not think that the claims of thy holiness upon us have respect simply to those exercises of worship in which we are engaged in thy house. But do thou grant that thy fear may be in our hearts and, therefore, that we may have an all-pervasive sense of thy presence, a continuous sense of our dependence upon thee, and a continuous sense of our responsibility to thee—so that in every detail of life we may realize how indispensable it is that the forces of redemptive and regenerating and sanctifying grace may be operative in us, so that we may bring, by the operation of thy Holy Spirit in our hearts, every thought into captivity to the obedience of Christ.

Do thou, oh Lord, make us a sanctified people. Do thou make us a consecrated people so that we shall live in our daily life and walk and conversation in a way that becomes the gospel of Christ and does honor to thee, the God of truth, and to Christ, the Savior and the King. May he be the Lord of our life, for none of us lives to himself and none of us dies to himself—whether we live, we live unto the Lord, and whether we die, we die unto the Lord. Therefore, whether we live or die, we are the Lord's. And may we understand the meaning of Christ's death and resurrection. For it was for this purpose that he died and rose again, that he might be Lord both of the dead and the living.

Do thou grant unto us, oh Lord, that we may be instructed aright in thy Word, that we may not be led astray with the error of the wicked, that we may not have our minds corrupted from the simplicity that is in Christ, and that we may not have our minds imbued with the vain philosophy of this world. May we not be conformed to this world but be transformed by the renewing of our minds, so that we may prove what is that good and acceptable and perfect will of God.

Grant, oh Lord, that in every situation of life, we may have respect to truth and justice and honor, that whatsoever things are true, whatsoever things are lovely, whatsoever things are of good report, if there be any virtue, if there be any praise, may we think on these things. For, oh Lord, we confess that it is as we think in our hearts, as we meditate in the deepest recesses of our minds, that we are. And do thou, oh Lord, grant even to each one of us that, in the particular situations in which we are placed, in the various employments of life, we may bear witness to Christ Jesus as Savior and as Lord.

Do thou, oh Lord, remember us as a branch of thy visible church, and do thou graciously establish and further the interests that pertain to the church of Christ here and throughout the whole world. May we always have jealousy for the purity and the honor and the peace of thy church throughout the whole world. May we recognize, indeed, that the church is the bride of Christ, his body, the fullness of him that filleth all in all. And grant that we may constantly have in mind the advancement of thy church and of thy kingdom to the very ends of the earth.

Have mercy, oh Lord, upon the nations of the world. Do thou cause righteousness and praise to spring forth before all the nations, and do thou grant that there might speedily be fulfilled that which thou has promised, that thy people Israel might turn again to the Lord and might see the glory of the Redeemer. Do thou hasten the day, oh Lord, when the fullness of the Gentiles will come in and when all Israel will be saved. Oh, grant that we may have constant concern for the conversion of all Jews and Gentiles. And have mercy, oh Lord, upon the nations in their political capacities. Grant, we pray thee, that wisdom may be given unto those who rule, so they may rule in thy fear and in justice and truth.

And now while we wait upon thee, grant us thy blessing, the unction and power of thy Holy Spirit in the understanding of thy Word, in the application of it to ourselves, and in the bringing forth of the fruit that is unto everlasting life, for Jesus's sake. Amen.

⁂

A great deal of thinking in the professing church of Christ has tended to regard the physical body as evil and as a hindrance to the attainments and exercises of the human spirit. The human body is regarded, as it were, as a weight that drags down the human spirit, and that it is our physical body that is the source of evil. In the Roman Catholic Church, for example, it is taught that sin began at the beginning of human history because bodily appetites crossed the line of reason or transgressed the dictates of reason. Of course, the implication is that sin really has its source and origin in the human body, that there is something in bodily appetite that tends to sin and is degrading.

That view of the human body is not biblical at all. The teaching of Scripture is very different, and we need to be warned against that very dangerous tendency that has appeared again and again in the history of the church, which regards this human body or human frame as essentially evil and as essentially degrading. The teaching of Scripture points in the very opposite direction. Have you ever noticed that in Genesis 2:7, which is an account of the origin of man, it is the human body that is mentioned first? It is the material, which entered into man's being, that is mentioned first: "The Lord God formed man of the dust of the ground, and breathed into his nostrils the breath of life; and man became a living soul [or a living creature]."

You find the teaching of Scripture to the same effect when it deals with the question of death. Death consists in the separation of the human body and the human spirit, so that the human body returns to dust. It disintegrates and returns to dust according to the Word, "Dust thou art, and unto dust shalt thou return" (Gen 3:19). If the body is essentially evil, then death would be a good thing, wouldn't it? Because it would separate the human spirit from this material entity that we call the body.

But the Scripture doesn't represent death as a good thing at all. The Scripture represents death as an evil, as the wages of sin, and as utterly abnormal. And remember that the final step in the redemption of God's people will be the destruction of death for them and the resurrection again from the dead, so that man would be both spirit and body in glory. Christ, we are told, "must reign until he places all enemies under his feet, and the last enemy that will be destroyed is death" (1 Cor 15:25–26). So, "when this corruptible will put on incorruption and this mortal will put on immortality, then will be brought to pass the saying that is written: Death is swallowed up in victory" (1 Cor 15:54). Yes, the great goal of the whole redemptive work is the destruction of the last enemy itself, and "the dead will be raised incorruptible, and the living will be changed" (1 Cor 15:52).

The body belongs to the human person, and a man is constituted as no other being in God's creation. He is given a physical body, and he is given a human spirit, and these are in perfect union the one with the other. There was no disharmony when God created man at the beginning. There was perfect harmony between body and spirit. That is the unique kind of being that man is. God created angels, but they don't have this physical entity that we call the body; they are simply spirits. But man is both body and spirit, and these in perfect union, the one with the other, as he was created.

Paul, in this epistle, has come to the point where he is dealing particularly with practical exhortation, the exhortations that bear upon practical life and upon the practical sanctification of believers. It is very important to notice that, when he begins these practical exhortations to believers, he begins with this: "I beseech you therefore, brethren, by the mercies of God, that ye present your *bodies* a living sacrifice" (Rom 12:1). You see, the apostle Paul was not carried away by that error of the wicked, by that vain philosophy that regarded the body as something evil or something that was to be crucified altogether. Not at all! Paul was imbued with the knowledge of the Word of God. Therefore, he regarded the body as of the greatest importance in the Christian life and in that process of sanctification. Consequently, he says: "I beseech you therefore, brethren . . . to present your *bodies*." (He means, of course, the physical body.) Paul was very concrete; he was very practical. And because he was very concrete and practical, he put in the forefront of practical exhortation that which is most concrete and practical—namely, the use of the human body: "That ye present your bodies."

What are they to be presented as? A living sacrifice. And we may very well be surprised to find in the New Testament such language as "living sacrifice" because it was in the Old Testament that sacrifices were offered and were a necessary part of the worship of God. There could not be any effective approach to God under the Old Testament except through sacrifice, except through the shedding of blood. We might be surprised to find that here, at the very beginning of practical exhortation, there is the place for sacrifice. But that's exactly what Paul says: "Present your bodies a living sacrifice." He is making allusion, without any doubt, to the sacrifices under the Old Testament.

You know, most of the sacrifices under the Old Testament were brought to the altar as living creatures. There were, indeed, meal offerings and certain offerings that were not living beings, but generally the sacrifices that were brought to the altar under the Old Testament were living beings. They were oxen, sheep, goats, or birds. But I think what Paul is particularly emphasizing here when he says, "a living sacrifice," is that there is a common thrust between the type of sacrifice that was made under the Old Testament and the type of sacrifice that we are to make under the New Testament when we present our bodies as a living sacrifice. For these animals that were brought to the altar under the Old Testament were always slain. Their blood was shed, they were offered upon the altar, and parts of their bodies were burned upon the altar. Whenever a living sacrifice was placed upon the altar, it was always slaughtered.

So, you hear a contrast. We're not to come to God with our bodies that they may be slaughtered. We're not to come to God with our bodies so that their life forces may be taken away. No, we're to present our bodies as a living sacrifice, and there's to be no slaughter. There's to be no shedding of the blood of our physical bodies when we present them to the Lord. It's a *living* sacrifice, and that is what we are to present to the Lord. I shall show you just in a moment what that means.

Paul characterizes this sacrifice that we are to make of our bodies as holy and acceptable: "holy, acceptable unto God, which is your reasonable service" (Rom 12:1). When he says "holy," he means that *the body* is to be holy; it's a characterization of the body. That means, you see, that of the human body there is such a thing as moral predication (if you understand what that means). Morality belongs to the human body. The human body is, indeed, material. But the body that is to be presented as a living sacrifice is a living body. It's a body that is animated by a spirit, and therefore it is to be holy.

Of course, implied is the very opposite, that sin is attributed to the human body. Apart from the forces of redemption and regeneration and sanctification, our bodies are sinful, and Paul characterizes the body of the unregenerate person as a sinful body, as a "body of sin" (Rom 6:6). It means, you see now, that the body is to be the very opposite: instead of being sinful, it's to be holy. And you remember what Paul says in the same epistle,

> Let not sin therefore reign in your mortal body, that ye should obey it in the lusts thereof. But present your members as instruments of righteousness unto God, and yield not your members as instruments of unrighteousness unto sin, but yield yourselves to God, as those that are alive from the dead, and your members as instruments of righteousness to God. (Rom 6:12–13)

That's what the body is to be, and that's what its members are.

Now let us ask the very practical question: how do we use the members of our body? Do we use them in the practice of sin? How do we use our tongues, how do we use our hands, how do we use our feet? Are our feet swift to be evil? Are our hands ready to be involved in the practice of iniquity? Are our tongues the tongues of deceit and falsehood? It's very practical, don't you see? Let not sin reign in your mortal body, but present your members as instruments of righteousness to God. In another epistle, Paul brings that to the sharpest focus when he says, "Know ye not that your body is the temple of the Holy Ghost which is in you, which ye have of God, and ye are not your own? For ye are bought with a price: therefore glorify God in your body" (1 Cor 6:19–20).

Holiness is to characterize the human body, and if holiness is to characterize it, it isn't to be characterized by the indulgence, by the dissipation, by the debauchery, and by the uncleanness that are so prevalent and that are so characteristic of us. How do we use our physical members? Do we use them for uncleanness? Do we use them for the practice of iniquity? That is, after all, the test of our status, of our standing, before God.

Then you notice that the apostle not only characterizes this body that is to be offered to God as holy but as *acceptable unto God*. There the apostle is pointing to that which is, after all, the regulating principle of the believer's life. What is the first thought that looms up in your mind when you are confronted with a decision, with a certain situation that demands action? Is it some purely material, worldly consideration that looms up first of all in our minds, some material advantage that you are going to get out of this or that course of action? No, if we are presenting our bodies a living sacrifice and holy, we are to present our very bodies as acceptable to God. And the first thing that looms up in the mind and thought of a believer when he is confronted with a certain situation is this: What is well-pleasing to God?

What is the will of God in this situation? If I'm going to choose one course of action rather than another, if I'm going to enter into one business rather than another, if I'm going to choose one vocation rather than another, what should be the first consideration? It must be what is well-pleasing or acceptable to God.

You see that governing principle of the believer's life is brought to bear upon the human body. What am I going to do with my hands? What am I going to do with my tongue? What am I going to do with my feet? What am I going to do with all the other various organs with which God has equipped my body? What are they going to be the instruments of? These are the questions that will determine what is well-pleasing to God, what is the will of God.

You young people, who may be choosing a vocation, who are going out into life with all its problems and sometimes with its very crucial decisions, I plead with you, my dear young friends, to lay that principle in the very forefront of your thought. What is well-pleasing to God? Now I know that I'm not yet answering the question, "What *is* well-pleasing to God?" But we'll come to that in just a moment. Nevertheless, let that always be paramount. And let it be paramount even in connection with the use of your human body, which is to be acceptable to God.

Then Paul characterizes that whole exercise of presenting our bodies as living sacrifices, holy and acceptable unto God, as our reasonable service. You could translate that by saying, "our *rational* service." Don't think that the use of the human body, or the purpose to which the human body is devoted, is an irrational thing. It's perfectly true that this human body is material and will, on the event of death, return to dust. These components of our bodies are material particles, but don't think that reason, the mind, and the spirit do not come into operation. Perhaps what Paul means when he says, "your reasonable service," is that it is a service to God that derives its character, meaning, and acceptableness with God because it enlists our mind and our reason. You can't deal (just to put it very practically) with your human body automatically or mechanically. The human body is the servant of the spirit, it's the servant of the mind, and therefore the mind, the reason, the intelligence comes into the fullest operation in connection with the presentation of our bodies as living sacrifices, holy and acceptable unto God.

But there is something more than that in this expression "reasonable service." For what Paul is speaking about here is not simply what we call *service* but the service of *worship*. Perhaps I could render the thought this way: "It is your reasonable service of worship." The word that Paul uses here means the service of worship; therefore, it is a *spiritual* service. Remember that the apostle Peter speaks of "spiritual sacrifices, acceptable to God by Jesus Christ" (1 Pet 2:5). The people of God, you see, are built up and made a priesthood to offer up spiritual sacrifices, that is, sacrifices that are indicted and impelled by the Holy Spirit. That is certainly implied when Paul says that this is your reasonable (or rational) service. It means, undoubtedly, that devotion to God in the fullest sense of the term, that is, spiritual devotion, enters into this particular exercise of presenting our bodies a living sacrifice, holy and acceptable unto God.

You will notice, of course, that the apostle Paul goes further in connection with his practical exhortation. He goes on in Romans 12:2 to bring in something that is, as it were, more inclusive: "Be not conformed to this world: but be ye transformed by the renewing of your mind, that ye may prove what is that good, and acceptable, and perfect, will of God." Now Paul turns to other aspects of our obligation, other aspects of sanctification. But it isn't as if he leaves entirely behind the thought that he expresses in the first verse; there's the closest relationship. "Present your bodies a living sacrifice, holy, acceptable unto God, which is your reasonable service. And be not conformed to this world" (Rom 12:1–2). That means that even our bodies are not to be used in a way that is conformed to the patterns and passions of this present evil world.

Now in this exhortation you'll notice that the apostle says something that they are not to do and something that they are to do. That's very simple. In every situation in life, if we do one thing, we don't do something else. And if we do that something else, we don't do the other thing. So, it is very practical and very simple, indeed, for Paul to present his exhortation in that form. "Be not conformed to this world, but be ye transformed"—one is negative, the other is positive.

When Paul says, "Be not conformed to this world," he says be not conformed, literally, to this age. In the Scripture there's a contrast always drawn between this age and the age to come. It's not because time is evil; God created time. Time is not evil, but it so happens that sin entered into *this age*, and sin very largely controls and determines this age. Paul calls Satan "the god of this age" (2 Cor 4:4), and he speaks of the rulers of this age that "crucified the Lord of Glory" (1 Cor 2:8). So "this age" is somewhat synonymous with what we would call "this present evil world" (Gal 1:4). When he says, "Be not conformed to it," he just means something like this: do not have your character and conduct patterned after the fashion of this present evil world.

Is that not practical enough? You young people know perfectly well, if you have had any Christian instruction and if you have any sensitivity or conscience with reference to Christian obligations, how difficult it is to practice what you may have been taught at your father's or mother's knee in reference to the Christian faith. How difficult it is to practice because of the pressure of this present evil world. You know, just as well as I do, what a pressure there is from the ungodly world around you. You're constantly required by this present evil world to suppress and, indeed, to eliminate your Christian convictions and the Christian instruction you have received. There's always the pressure from this present evil world to adopt its patterns, its fashions, and its customs, and that's exactly what the apostle Paul is saying here: "Be not conformed to this world."

I tell you, beware cultivating the patterns of this present evil world because they will bring you down to destruction. You know the commandments of God, and these are the patterns and the standards of the kingdom of God. And you know perfectly well what the contrast is between the commandments of God on the one hand and the commandments of this present evil world on the other. "If sinners entice thee, consent thou not" (Prov 1:10). Be not conformed to this world.

But there is something else. Paul is not only reflecting here upon the wickedness of this present evil world and the wicked patterns that this present evil world presents to us for emulation and cultivation. In the language that Paul uses here, he is thinking likewise of the fleeting character of this present evil age. Remember that this age is going to pass away, and if the patterns that we follow in this life of ours are the patterns that belong to this present evil age, then they will pass away. They will come down with terrific destruction upon our heads. They will tumble upon us, and they will tumble us into everlasting perdition—there's nothing less than that. Remember what John the apostle says: "All that is in the world, the lust of the flesh, the lust of the eyes, and the pride of life, is not of the Father, but is of the world. And the world passeth away, and the lust thereof: but he that doeth the will of God abideth forever" (1 John 2:16–17). I think there is something of that very same thought in the language that Paul uses here when he says, "Be not conformed to this world."

It's an instinct of human nature to want something that is abiding, that is permanent, that will endure. You don't pay very much attention, do you, to something that is going to pass away with the night. There is a desire in the human heart for something that is abiding. Let me tell you this: the patterns of this world belong to that which is going to be completely destroyed. They're *passing* fashions, and they will come to an end, to destruction. Do not pattern your life, therefore, after that which is passing away, for all that is in the world, and the lusts thereof, will pass away, but he that doeth the will of God abideth forever.

In contrast with that is the positive side of the apostle's exhortation. "But be ye transformed by the renewing of your mind, that ye may prove what is that good, and acceptable, and perfect, will of God" (Rom 12:2). The word he uses here is a word that is suggestive of what is abiding, what will continue. Remember what John said: "He that doeth the will of God abideth forever"; he's not going to be brought to naught. There you have a pattern that will continue, that will be as abiding as your very human person is abiding. "Be not conformed to this world, but be ye transformed." It's the same word that Paul uses when he says in another place, "We all, beholding as in a glass the glory of the Lord, are being transformed into the same image from glory to glory, even as by the Spirit of the Lord" (2 Cor 3:18). That is the pattern of the conformity that is here enjoined by the apostle when he says, "Be ye transformed." Be ye transfigured from the fashion, from the image, of this present evil world into that image that is none other than the image of the Lord of Glory himself, therefore ensuring its permanency.

This conformity that the apostle enjoins is a conformity that is directed to a certain end. Be transformed by the renewing of your mind, that ye may prove that will of God—the good and the acceptable and the perfect. Now we come to the very point with which we had been dealing earlier: the thing that should be uppermost in the thought of every one of us in every particular circumstance and situation of life is what is well-pleasing to God. Now the apostle comes to that: "that ye may prove what is that good, and acceptable, and perfect, will of God."

The word that Paul uses here for "prove" is a word that can mean "to test," "to prove," or "to approve." We're not going to test the will of God; we're not going to subject the will of God to examination to see if it is good. No, that's not the meaning. After all, we're not going to prove that the will of God is good. So, it must be that third meaning, that we may *approve*. I think the thought of the apostle can be expressed in this way: "that you may find out by experience how approved the will of God is."

Find out by experience. This is close to the thought that the will of God will never disappoint you. If a particular instrument is approved, then of course it stands up in every test; it stands up in every situation in which you use it; it doesn't disappoint you. If an automobile is approved, then it is supposed to stand up under all the conditions that are necessary for ordinary, reasonable driving. And that is, on the highest level, what is true with reference to the will of God. It will never disappoint us; it will never fail. You will never find the will of God to be wanting. We do the will of God, and if we find out by experience how approved the will of God is, we'll never be disappointed with the will of God. That's, I think, what Paul means: that ye may approve, that ye may find out how approved is, the will of God. And the will of God is simply that which he reveals unto us as his pleasure for us.

The apostle characterizes that will of God as the good, and the acceptable, and the perfect. It's most interesting to notice how Paul renders this in the original language. It can't very well be plain put that way in English, but there are, in the original languages of Scripture, certain ways of saying things that are most forceful. This is the way he says it: "That ye may prove [that is, find out how approved] what is the will of God," and he characterizes the will of God as that which is the good, and the acceptable, and the perfect.

People speak about the chief good, but what is the chief good of life, what is the highest good in human life? That has been the quest of people from the very beginning. What is, after all, the chief good for mankind or for an individual human being? Surely there is nothing that is closer to your interest than to know what is the highest good. You know perfectly well how relative some good things are. There are a great many things that are good and that just pass away. They're good for a little while, and then they're of no more use. Consequently, a great many of these good things of this life are relative. What is the *lasting* good? Here the apostle Paul tells us that it is the will of God that is supremely good, that is the highest and the chief good.

Then he characterizes the will of God also as that which is acceptable, well-pleasing to God. As I have said before, the governing principle of the believer's life is to be well-pleasing to God. The great question that ought to concern each one of us is this: When I am ushered before God's judgment seat, will that which I have done in this life be approved of God or will it be disapproved? Will it stand upon the test of his judgment? That's a very practical question, isn't it? This is what Paul says about the will of God: it is acceptable to him. We must believe that that which is the will of God and acceptable to him in this life meets with his approval in heaven. God doesn't give us a double standard. He hasn't one standard for us in this life and another standard for his own judgment in heaven. It's the standard that applies to this life that will be applied at the judgment seat of Christ. Remember this: the will of God is acceptable to God, and it will stand the test of his judgment. Every man's work shall be tried and tested. If that which we are doing in this life is in accordance with the will of God, it will stand the fires of divine judgment.

Finally, the apostle characterizes the will of God as perfect. Human laws are necessary, and it is necessary for us under all normal circumstances to obey human laws. But, after all, we must remember that human laws are not perfect. There may arise a situation in which it will be necessary for you to transgress a human law (even though ordinarily it's a good law) because the law of God requires you to do otherwise. In contrast with the imperfection that attaches to humanly devised law, the law of God is perfect. It's perfect, and therefore it is a law that meets every situation. Remember this: it is never necessary to transgress a law of God. It may be necessary in a particular situation to transgress a law that has been established by man, but it is never necessary to transgress a law that is established by God, and the reason is that "the law of the Lord is perfect" (Ps 19:7).

People will say sometimes, "It's really necessary for me to transgress a certain law of God. I don't like to do it, but I can't get out of it." It's often done with reference to the Sabbath and unnecessary Sabbath labor. "Well," people will say, "I have to live, and the employer requires that I do this on the Sabbath Day." And, of course, it's quite obviously not a work of necessity or mercy. But, after all, my friends, we don't *have* to live, but we do *have* to obey the law of God, because the law of God is perfect. There is never a situation in life in which God places us under the necessity of transgressing *any* of his commandments.

That's what Paul has in mind in Romans 12:2, that the will of God is not only good, it's not only acceptable to him, but it is perfect. And it is perfect because it is holy and just and good and is simply the transcript of God's own perfection (Rom 7:12). If we impugn the perfection of God's law, we impugn the perfection of God himself, because the law of God is simply the character of perfection of God coming to expression for the regulation of our thought and our word and our action. "Prove what is that good, and acceptable, and perfect will of God."

In the two preceding verses of this chapter, as we found, the apostle Paul is giving exhortations that obviously apply to all without any distinctions whatsoever. There is no differentiation in the way that the exhortations of the first two verses bear upon believers, because all believers, without any difference whatsoever, ought to "present their bodies a living sacrifice, holy, acceptable unto God, which is their reasonable service" (Rom 12:1), and all believers must be exhorted to "be not conformed to this world, but be transformed by the renewing of their mind, that they may prove what is that good, and acceptable, and perfect, will of God" (Rom 12:2).

But you will notice that at verse 3 Paul makes a very significant change. He proceeds, "For I say, through the grace given unto me, to every man that is among you, not to think of himself more highly than he ought to think; but to think soberly, according as God hath dealt to every man the measure of faith." It is quite apparent that the apostle Paul in this particular verse, and in the verses that follow, is going to deal with the *differences* that exist among believers. That's quite apparent because even in verse 3 he says, "according as God hath dealt to every man [that is, to each one] the measure of faith" (Rom 12:3). They don't all have the same measure. There's a difference, a distribution, on the part of God.

And then he confirms this by saying:

> For as we have many members in one body, and all members have not the same office [that is, don't all have the same function]: So we, being many, are one body in Christ, and every one members one of another. Having

then gifts differing according to the grace that is given
to us, whether prophecy, let us prophesy according to
the proportion of faith; or ministry, let us wait on our
ministering: or he that teacheth, on teaching; or he that
exhorteth, on exhortation: he that giveth, let him do it
with simplicity; he that ruleth, with diligence; he that
showeth mercy, with cheerfulness. (Rom 12:4–8)

There is the distribution of offices, the distribution of gifts, in the church of God.

I take it that that is why the apostle Paul says at the beginning of verse 3, "For I say, through the grace of God given unto me" (Rom 12:3). He is no doubt appealing there to the particular office that was given unto him in the church of Christ. It is in terms of that office, or by virtue of the authority with which he was invested in connection with that office, that he proceeds to give exhortations to the believers in *their* various offices, in their various differences. The grace that Paul speaks of here is very likely the same grace that he refers to elsewhere when he says, "Unto me, who am less than the least of all saints, is this grace given, that I should preach among the Gentiles the unsearchable riches of Christ" (Eph 3:8). And when Paul—in this chapter and in other epistles and other parts of this epistle—assigns to each one in the church of God his own particular place and prescribes for the church of God the various offices that are to be exercised in the church of God, he does so in pursuance of his apostolic authority. If any other ordinary believer in the church of God would speak as the apostle Paul speaks in some of his epistles, it would be downright presumption. But Paul is conscious of his apostolic authority, the authority delegated to him by the great head of the church. He is prescribing for the church in all ages that government and discipline, as well as that ministry, by which the church of God is to be carried on and governed to the very end of the age. Consequently, there was a necessity that Paul at this point should make some allusion to the authority with which he was speaking. That is why he says, "For I say, through the grace given unto me, to every man that is among you, not to think of himself more highly than he ought to think."

You see the difference at this point between what you have at the beginning of verse 3 and that which you have at the beginning of verse 1? For at the beginning of verse 1, the apostle Paul based his plea upon the tender compassions of God, saying, "I beseech you therefore, brethren, by the mercies of God, that ye present your bodies a living sacrifice." Of course, that kind of plea is not by any means abrogated or suspended at the third verse. But the apostle now finds it necessary to introduce an allusion to his own particular office in the church of God and to the grace that was given to him in order that he might perform that office, so he says, "For I say, through the grace given unto me, to every man that is among you . . ."

When we are thinking of the differences that exist among believers and of the different offices, the different graces, and the different gifts that God bestows upon the various members of his church, what is the most important consideration that has to be urged upon the members of the church of Christ? What is the paramount virtue, what is the paramount grace, that people must exercise when they are thinking of the different functions and offices that particular individuals perform in the church of Christ? It is humility. That is what Paul alludes to here: "To every man that is among you, not to think of himself more highly than he ought to think."

There is always the danger that when a person is endowed by God with particular gifts, he or she is liable to become so absorbed in the gifts he or she possesses that he or she will consider himself or herself more important than others. There's always that danger—the danger of becoming inflated with pride, the danger of self-assertiveness, the danger of overbearingness in the church of God. The apostle John spoke of a certain person who loved to have the preeminence (3 John 9). There's always that danger, and it will appear sometimes in very subtle and deceitful forms—it might even appear under the garb of humility! Beware the danger of self-assertiveness, overbearingness, and of being unwilling to recognize one's particular place in the body.

You see how utterly inconsistent, and even inconceivable, it is in the human body for the hand to boast itself against the foot, or for the eye to boast itself against the ear, or for one part of the body in any way whatsoever to boast itself against some other part of the body (1 Cor 12:14–21). That, you see, is what the apostle is pleading, for we have many members in one body and all members have not the same office, so "we, being many, are one body in Christ, and every one members one of another" (Rom 12:5).

So, instead of exalting oneself, instead of self-assertiveness and overbearingness, we ought to recognize our mutual dependence and interdependence, that we are members one of another. If one member is honored, all the other members rejoice with it. Or if one member suffers, all the others suffer with it (1 Cor 12:26). That is what is done in the human body. If you have a toothache, your whole body suffers. It's not simply your tooth that aches; your whole body suffers (even though it may not even be a very important ailment at all). Likewise in the church of Christ! Or, if you have a particular member in your body that's particularly useful or strong, your whole body contributes to that strength, and your whole body rejoices in the strength. If a person has a very strong arm, the whole body rejoices in that strength and contributes to the strength of that particular arm. That's what Paul is urging: that we should recognize our mutual interdependence and dependence, the one upon the other, and that we should understand that the whole body is not one member.

It is very frequently in connection with *office* in the church that this vice of pride, of self-assertiveness, and of overbearingness appears. And it has become, of course, a very great vice of the Christian church that certain persons have tried to elevate themselves to positions of particular preeminence in the government of the church. Don't let us think that because we are Presbyterians that we are immune to that vice. It has frequently appeared in the history of Presbyterian churches and even of doctrinally orthodox Presbyterian churches. Certain persons in their self-assertiveness and their overbearingness have arrogated to themselves an authority that is precisely the contradiction of that which the apostle Paul enjoins in this particular passage: "To every man that is among you, not to think of himself more highly than he ought to think."

You know the great example of this vice is what has occurred in the church of Rome. For there you have one man who has presumptuously arrogated to himself supreme eminence in the church on earth. He has claimed for himself to be the Vicar of Christ and has even claimed for himself that when he speaks *ex cathedra* (that is, officially), he speaks infallibly, that he is, as it were, the very voice of God himself. Now that, of course, is the extreme application, the extreme development, of that particular vice against which the apostle Paul is warning us in Romans 12:3: "To *everyone* that is among you, not to think of himself more highly than he ought to think" (author's translation).

But there is another vice, and perhaps it is the companion vice to pride that so frequently appears, even in the church of Christ. It appears because out of the fear of self-exaltation or pride, people don't think soberly. That's the next virtue that the apostle Paul enjoins in our text: "Not to think of himself more highly than he ought to think; but to think soberly [literally, 'but to think, so as to think soberly'], according as God hath dealt to each one a measure of faith" (Rom 12:3). So what is this vice? It's the vice of a false humility (or a false modesty) whereby a person whom God has placed in the church of Christ and to whom God may have given certain gifts (not perhaps very prominent gifts, but certain gifts) is not willing to take the place that belongs to him or to her. It is an underestimation of the grace of God, and that is likewise a vice. If we are not to think more of ourselves than we ought to think, we nevertheless ought to think according to the grace that God has given to us and act accordingly.

There is a vocation that God gives to each individual in the body of Christ, and that person is to take his position and exercise the grace that God has given to him or to her in that particular position and, therefore, to think soberly. There is the danger, oftentimes, of people failing to exercise the function or the office that God has assigned to that person in the church of God, sometimes because of false modesty or false humility, sometimes perhaps because of unfaithfulness, sometimes even because of laziness, and sometimes because of fear of man. And that is the other vice, in addition to pride, that Paul warns against in this verse: the vice of not thinking soberly. If God has given a measure of faith, if he has given a gift, he has given it to be exercised.

You must remember that there is a certain responsibility devolving upon us in the church of Christ. We're not to sit by idly. It's perfectly true that God has not appointed women, for example, to office in the church of Christ. According to his own institution, he has appointed men and has endowed them with certain gifts. In the last analysis there are only two offices in the church permanently: the office of elder and the office of deacon. And these two offices are, according to the institution of Christ, always exercised by men, so that ruling in the church of Christ is the function of men not of women.

But nevertheless, there are certain functions that women, just as well as men, have to discharge in the church of Christ. They are members of the body of Christ, and therefore they have to discharge their responsibilities and function, always in the place that God has assigned them but nevertheless *in that place* and according to that measure of faith. That is what the apostle Paul is enjoining in this particular passage. When he says, "But to think soberly, according as God hath dealt to everyone the measure of faith" (Rom 12:3; author's translation), he does not simply mean "to every *man*." He doesn't say every man as distinguished from a woman, but he speaks to *each* one, that is, to the woman as well as to the man. And as you proceed to examine this passage, you will find that the gifts that the apostle mentions and that God has distributed include *every* member of the church of Christ:

> Having then gifts differing according to the grace that is given to us, whether prophecy, let us prophesy according to the proportion of faith; or ministry, let us wait on our ministering: or he that teacheth, on teaching; or he that exhorteth, on exhortation: he that giveth, let him do it with simplicity; he that ruleth, with diligence; he that showeth mercy, with cheerfulness.
>
> Let love be without dissimulation. Abhor that which is evil; cleave to that which is good. (Rom 12:6–9)

Consequently, just in one word, we have to appreciate more and more what I have been stressing on these few visits to you: the unity of the body of Christ. The church is the body of Christ, that is, the *visible* church is the body of Christ. Each member has to exercise his or her function; otherwise there is mutilation in the body. If a certain organ is not exercised, it becomes atrophied and perhaps diseased, and the whole body is afflicted with that disease. If that is true in our physical body, it is also true in the body of Christ. If a person doesn't exercise the gifts and the graces that God has given to him or to her, then there is to that extent a certain disease, a certain affliction, in the body of Christ.

As you know, in the fourth chapter of the Epistle to the Ephesians, Paul likewise emphasizes how the members of the body of Christ are to mutually support one another and mutually encourage one another, so that, "in the unity of the Spirit and the bond of peace," we may all come "in the unity of the faith, and of the knowledge of the Son of God, unto a perfect man, unto the measure of the stature of the fullness of Christ" (Eph 4:3, 13).

Oh God, do thou bless our meditation on thy holy Word. Mix it with faith in our hearts and grant that it may bring forth the fruit of love and of good works in our lives, for Jesus's sake. Amen.

7

Put on the Lord Jesus Christ

And that, knowing the time, that now it is high time to awake out of sleep: for now is our salvation nearer than when we believed.

—ROMANS 13:11

Sleep is a great blessing, for it is God's provision for rest and recuperation after we have expended our energies. Oftentimes it is God's provision for the regaining of health when we are ill. Remember that the disciples said to Jesus with reference to Lazarus, "If he sleep, he shall do well" (John 11:12). The ability to sleep well is the sign of health and contentment, and oftentimes restlessness, when we should be asleep—I don't say always, but oftentimes—is due to a lack of trust in God, a lack of that godliness with contentment that is great gain (1 Tim 6:6). That is why the psalmist said, "I will both lay me down in peace, and sleep: for thou, Lord, only makest me to dwell in safety" (Ps 4:8).

But any good thing out of place is an evil. To be asleep, for example, when our house is on fire may end in tragedy. To be asleep when we ought to be at work is sloth. And to be asleep when we ought to be engaged in prayer and worship is godlessness. That is why the wise man said: "Love not sleep, lest thou come to poverty" (Prov 20:13), "Drowsiness shall clothe a man with rags" (Prov 23:21), and "Go to the ant, thou sluggard; consider her ways, and be wise" (Prov 6:6).

There is also, of course, the sleep of moral and spiritual apathy, the sleep of *spiritual* sloth. That is the kind of sleep that is referred to in our text: "And that, knowing the time, that now it is high time to awake out of sleep." It is the sleep of spiritual indolence and spiritual indifference. You will notice that Paul is here speaking not to unbelievers but to believers, for only to believers could he say that "now is our salvation nearer than when we believed" (Rom 13:11). He reckons them with himself as being believers, and he is speaking about some kind of salvation that is nearer than when they believed. This is to remind us that even believers need oftentimes to be aroused from spiritual indolence and from carelessness, indifference, and listlessness.

What is the reason that the apostle presses home in this text for the arousing of believers from their spiritual sleepiness or slothfulness? Simply stated, the reason that the apostle urges his fellow believers that it is high time to awake out of sleep is the calendar. It is well to look at the calendar, isn't it? That's exactly in essence what the apostle Paul is urging in this text: the calendar, that is, the calendar of events and the passage of time. Time has meaning, and that is why it is so ungodly to be asleep when we should be awake, that is why it is wrong to be asleep when we should be in *prayer*, and wrong to sleep when we should be at *work*. Time is precious. There is a time for everything. There is indeed a time to sleep, and it is a great blessing (we all know that very well). But there is a time to be awake, and it is just because time has significance that sleepiness out of place is something that contradicts our Christian faith.

It is a particular aspect of time that the apostle Paul has in view in this text because he's saying, "And that, knowing the time," that is, the *appointed* time. Paul is reminding his readers that time is running out—that the whole expanse of time is moving to an appointed season. He first says, "Knowing the time, that now it is high time to awake out of sleep," and then he specifies what he has in mind: "For *now* is our salvation nearer than when we believed."

What salvation does the apostle have in mind in this text when he says, "Now is our salvation nearer than when we believed"? If you look at expositors, you will find various views expressed, but, according to the teaching of the New Testament, I don't think there is any other alternative but this: the apostle Paul is here referring to the salvation that would be completed at the coming of Christ, at the glory of his appearing. The word *salvation* is used quite frequently in the New Testament in that sense.

Of course, it is also used with reference to the salvation that believers have in their possession here and now, but that salvation could not be spoken of as "nearer than when we believed" because it is in our actual possession *when* we believe. That is the salvation Paul has in mind earlier in this epistle when he says, "I am not ashamed of the gospel of Christ: for it is the power of God unto salvation to every one that believeth" (Rom 1:16). And again, a little later on, he says, "With the heart man believeth unto righteousness; and with the mouth confession is made unto salvation" (Rom 10:10). There he is thinking of the salvation that comes into a person's possession by faith, not a salvation that is future, but something that we possess here and now. But the word *salvation* is quite often used by Paul, and in other places in the New Testament, in the sense of the future salvation that will be completed and consummated at the coming of Christ.

The word *redemption* is used oftentimes in this sense also. Redemption is certainly used with reference to what is completed in the finished work of Christ, which the people of God enjoy here and now, but it is also used with reference to the redemption that will be completed and consummated and perfected at the coming of Christ. Jesus used *redemption* in that sense when he said to his disciples with respect to his second coming, "Be ye not afraid, lift up your hearts because your *redemption* draws nigh" (Luke 21:28). And it is in that sense that the apostle uses the word *redemption* earlier in this epistle when he says that we are "waiting for the adoption . . . the redemption of our body" (Rom 8:23).

Likewise, the word *salvation* is quite often used in the New Testament in that sense. Of course, it is very important to recognize the unity that there is between the salvation now in possession and the salvation that will be completed and perfected at the coming of Christ. There's a unity and there's a continuity, but we must remember that it is at the coming of Christ that that salvation will be perfected.

So, when Paul says, for example, in the Epistle to the Philippians, "Work out your own salvation with fear and trembling. For it is God that worketh in you both to will and to do of his good pleasure" (Phil 2:12–13), Paul is not talking about the salvation that believers have now in their possession by faith. That salvation is not worked out; it's a gift of grace, and there's no working of ours in connection with it. He's instead thinking of the salvation that *would be* completed, and it is that salvation that he enjoins believers to work out. Or again, when the apostle says in the First Epistle to the Thessalonians, "God hath not appointed us to wrath, but to obtain salvation by our Lord Jesus Christ" (1 Thess 5:9), the context clearly indicates that he is referring to the salvation that will be perfected and completed at the coming of Christ.

In the Epistle to the Hebrews, when the writer is referring to the angels, he says, "Are they not all ministering spirits, sent forth to minister for them who shall be heirs of salvation?" (Heb 1:14). They're *heirs* of salvation! And you can't speak of heirship except with reference to something in the future. They're not heirs of the salvation they have now in possession because it is already in possession, but they are heirs of a salvation that is yet to be revealed. And again, in the same epistle, he says, "Christ was once manifested to bear the sins of many; and unto them that look for him shall he appear the second time without sin unto salvation" (Heb 9:28). This clearly indicates that it is *the salvation* that will be manifested when Christ will come. Christ will be manifested the second time, without sin, unto salvation—that is, unto the complete, perfect salvation that will be bestowed upon the people of God when Christ will come again.

The apostle Peter likewise uses this word *salvation* in that very same sense when he says that believers are "kept by the power of God through faith unto salvation ready to be revealed in the last time" (1 Pet 1:5). The salvation *ready to be revealed*!

And it is unto that terminus, unto that goal, that they are being kept by the power of God through faith.

It is that salvation, therefore, that Paul must have in view in this text when he says, "Now is our salvation nearer than when we believed" (Rom 13:11). He is thinking of that great event in the future when the salvation of the people of God will be completed. And it is *that salvation* that is nearer than when we believed.

There are certain lessons that we must derive from the exhortation of the apostle: that, knowing the time, it is now "high time to awake out of sleep." The first lesson is that this salvation is the hope of the people of God.

Here we are touching on something that I feel needs a great deal of emphasis and is oftentimes sadly overlooked. And when it is overlooked, it reflects very seriously upon the vitality and the genuineness and the liveliness of our faith. This salvation is the hope of the people of God. Death is not the hope of the people of God. Death, after all, is an enemy. It is perfectly true that at death believers are made perfect in holiness as respects their spirits and are translated into the very presence of Christ, so that Paul could say that to depart and to be with Christ is far better (Phil 1:23) and that to be absent from the body is to be present with the Lord (2 Cor 5:8). Death should not be something to fill the people of God with terror. It's perfectly true that death for a believer is a blessed event: "Precious in the sight of the Lord is the death of his saints" (Ps 116:15). But death is not the great hope of the believer at all. We have a serious deflection from the Christian hope, and therefore from the Christian faith, when we are thinking of death as the great hope of the church or as the great hope of the believer. Not at all! It's this *salvation* of which the apostle here speaks! It is for this that they are groaning and waiting because the whole expectation of a true believer is gravitating towards that glory that will be manifested when Christ will come again the second time, without sin, unto salvation. That *is* the expectation; that is the *goal* of the believer.

And if a believer does not have this as his goal, it is because there has been in his case or her case a deflection from the teaching of the gospel, the teaching of the New Testament. You notice, for example, that earlier in this very epistle where the apostle says that not only does the creation groan, but "ourselves also, who have the firstfruits of the Spirit, even we ourselves groan within ourselves, waiting for the adoption, to wit, the redemption of our body" (Rom 8:23). That's the resurrection hope. When he speaks of the adoption, the redemption of the body, he is thinking of that glorious consummation that will be realized when Christ will come again the second time, without sin, unto salvation.

You find that very same type of expectation reflected by the apostle in the Second Epistle to the Corinthians when he says,

> For we know that if our earthly house of this tabernacle were dissolved, we have a building of God, an house not made with hands, eternal in the heavens. For in this we groan, earnestly desiring to be clothed upon with our house which is from heaven. If so be that being clothed we shall not be found naked. (2 Cor 5:1–3)

The clothing that the apostle has in view is, of course, the clothing with the resurrection body; that's what he groans for. "Not that we would be unclothed"—he has no particular desire in itself to die—"but clothed upon, that mortality might be swallowed up of life" (2 Cor 5:4). This mortality that is swallowed up of life is that same immortality that the apostle Paul speaks of in the First Epistle to the Corinthians when he says,

> This corruptible must put on incorruption, and this mortal must put on immortality. So when this corruptible shall have put on incorruption, and this mortal shall have put on immortality, then shall be brought to pass the saying that is written, Death is swallowed up in victory. (1 Cor 15:53–54)

And again, in the Epistle to the Philippians, he says, "For our citizenship is in heaven; from whence also we look for the Saviour, the Lord Jesus Christ: Who shall change our vile body, that it may be fashioned like unto his glorious body, according to the working whereby he is able even to subdue all things unto himself" (Phil 3:20–21). This is what Paul, in his Epistle to Titus, calls "the blessed hope": "Looking for that blessed hope, and the glorious appearing of the great God and our Saviour Jesus Christ" (Titus 2:13). That's the hope and expectation of a true believer, and there's something radically wrong with our faith and radically wrong with our hope if we do not gravitate in expectation, in expectancy, and in hope towards that great event when Christ will descend from heaven with a shout, with the voice of the archangel, and with the trumpet of God.

Having established very clearly from the teaching of the New Testament that this salvation is our great hope, the next aspect of the text that we need to take into account is that Paul says, "Now is this salvation nearer than when we believed." It's near. You are perhaps not aware of the currents of thought that are abroad in the world at this present time that are really in direct contradiction to this emphasis of the apostle Paul. What Paul is saying is that there is a *date* in the *calendar* when it will arrive. And it's nearer than when we believed. If you are thinking, for example, of an event which is going to occur in the year 1970—let us say on December 25, 1970—you say that it's nearer than it was a year ago. And that's just because there is the lapse of time that makes the future lapse of time shorter. That's all there is to it. When Paul therefore says, "Now is our salvation nearer than when we believed," he is saying that there is a day in the calendar of events when this event will occur. And since it is a day in the calendar of events, it is nearer than it was a year ago or two years ago or twenty years ago or a thousand years ago.

There is tremendous significance in the fact that there is a day coming in the calendar of events when this salvation will be realized, when Christ will come down from heaven. "In a moment, in the twinkling of an eye . . . the trumpet shall sound, and the dead shall be raised incorruptible, and we shall be changed" (1 Cor 15:52). It means that history is moving to a terminus, that time is moving to its end—and it's rapidly moving to its end.

No one knows the day or the hour. Jesus himself said in the days of his flesh, "But of that day and hour knoweth no man, no, not the angels who are in heaven, neither the Son, but the Father" (Mark 13:32). That is to say, as regards his human knowledge, Jesus was expressing his ignorance regarding that day. It was not given to him in his human nature and knowledge to know when that day would occur. We don't need to suppose that he is ignorant of it now, even in his human nature, but in any case, no *man* knows, and not even the angels of heaven know, when this day is to occur. But Paul is here, in Romans 13, reminding believers that as far as their lifespan is concerned, or was concerned, "it was nearer than when they believed."

And that is true also of us. We know not how far distant this great event may be, but it's going to come some day in the calendar of events. There will be calendars in that day. And there will be the first of January until the thirty-first of December in that particular time. Things will be going on as Jesus himself told us, "marrying and giving in marriage . . . and they knew not until the flood came, and took them all away; so shall also the coming of the Son of man be" (Matt 24:38–39). We must remember that. Events will be going on according to the regular routine of this world's history until then; suddenly, in a moment when no man knows, Jesus will come "in the clouds of heaven with power and great glory" (Matt 24:30). "The day of the Lord will come as a thief in the night; in which the heavens shall pass away with a great noise, and the elements shall melt with fervent heat, the earth also and the works that are therein shall be burned up" (2 Pet 3:10). It's going to come suddenly indeed, but it's going to come in the calendar of events. For all we know, it may be a thousand years distant or two thousand years distant—God has not revealed it to us—but it still can be said with reference to each believer, "Now is that salvation nearer than when he or she believed."

There is significance to that fact because what transpires between death and resurrection is *not* reckoned in the calendar of time. All that remains for us is what remains of our earthly pilgrimage. That is why it is of significance to say, "It is nearer than when we believed." The Scripture makes it very plain that as far as the history of this world, there is no significance to what will transpire between death and the resurrection for the believer.

This period has great significance for the believer himself, indeed, but as far as the calendar of events in this world is concerned, it is not reckoned. God has appointed that man should die and afterwards there is the judgment (Heb 9:27), and that period that intervenes is not reckoned in terms of time, however long it may be in terms of our calendar. Just as we may say that now is our death nearer than when we believed, so we can rightly say with equal significance, "Now is *this salvation* nearer than when we believed." And that is what the apostle is urging here as the reason why it is high time to awake out of sleep. This is the appointed season, the appointed time in God's ordination and plan that we are to know (Rom 13:11).

You see that there is a definite connection between what precedes in this passage and what succeeds in this passage in relation to that necessity of awaking out of sleep. When Paul says at the beginning of verse 11, "And that," he is pointing back to what goes before. And he is saying, in effect, "All the more so is this necessary *since* you know the times, *since* you know the appointed season, *since* you are aware that this salvation on the part of God is appointed in his determinate purpose." And what is it that is all the more necessary? It is just that which Paul says from the eighth verse on:

> Owe no man any thing, but to love one another: for he that loveth another hath fulfilled the law. For this, Thou shalt not commit adultery, thou shalt not kill, thou shalt not steal, thou shalt not bear false witness, thou shalt not covet; and if there be any other commandment, it is briefly comprehended in this saying, namely, Thou shalt love thy

neighbour as thyself. Love worketh no ill to his neighbour: therefore love is the fulfilling of the law. (Rom 13:8–10)

It is all *that* which the apostle Paul has in mind when he says in verse 11, "And that." All the more so must you take heed to these exhortations of the preceding verses since you know the appointed time.

Then you have in very close relationship to that the succeeding verses:

The night is far spent, the day is at hand: let us therefore cast off the works of darkness, and let us put on the armour of light. Let us walk honestly, as in the day; not in rioting and drunkenness [that is, not in excess and drunkenness], not in chambering and wantonness [that is, not in sexual excesses and debauchery], not in strife and envying. But put ye on the Lord Jesus Christ, and make not provision for the flesh, to fulfil the lusts thereof. (Rom 13:12–14)

So you see that the whole preceding context in this passage and the whole succeeding context and all the exhortations that are involved in these verses from verse 8 to the end of the chapter are bound up in what Paul says in verse 11: "Now is our salvation nearer than when we believed." It shows us that the significance for practical living in this world, for practical godliness, is the great truth respecting the consummation of the kingdom of God and the consummation of the whole time process. Time is moving rapidly on. The night is far spent; the day is at hand. And it is for that reason, in this particular context, that it is all the more necessary that we should awake out of our spiritual sloth and attend to those things that are the marks and the injunctions and the criteria of our Christian faith and of our Christian hope.

We are drawing near the close of another year, and it is well for us to take the lessons that accrue to us from the passage of time. Time is not endless; it is moving toward its consummation. The night is already far spent—that is to say, the whole temporal order is already far spent. The ages that are past have run their course, and we are in what the New Testament calls *the last days*, that is to say, the age that will have its termination in nothing less than the consummation of the whole of history, of the whole time process. And is it reasonable that we should be asleep? When a person is asleep, of course, he is not alive to his environment, to what is going on. Is it compatible with our Christian faith and hope that we should be, as it were, indifferent to the events that are transpiring, to the significance of what the time is?

Oh, my friends, we are here in our text pressured into the presence of eternal reality: "Now is this salvation nearer than when we believed." It is well for us to take heed so that we realize the necessity of casting off the works of darkness and putting on the armor of light (Rom 13:12), that we may show our affinity with that salvation that will be manifested in its completeness when Christ will come in his own glory and in the glory of the Father with the holy angels (Luke 9:26).

We are living in days, my friends, in which the vices that the apostle Paul condemns in this passage are particularly manifest in the world and, sad to say, are particularly manifest in many instances even within the church of God. The works of darkness—chambering, sexual excesses, debauchery, drunkenness, riotings—all these things are the manifestations of darkness, and they are the things upon which the extreme judgment of God will be executed on the day when the full light will be manifested. How utterly inconsistent for the people of God to have any business with that which is characteristic of this present evil world upon which the judgment of God will be executed in its greatest extremity, without any amelioration, when the day of his judgment will arrive.

There is the exhortation, my friends, that is brought to bear upon us, and let us take it to heart. "The night is far spent, the day is at hand: let us therefore cast off the works of darkness" (Rom 13:12). Let us manifest ourselves to be the children of light and the children of the day (1 Thess 5:5), the children who will be manifested in that great salvation, which Christ will bestow upon his own church and upon his own people when he will come again the second time, without sin, unto salvation.

Oh God, we pray thee that thou wouldst quicken us to a realization of the great issues that devolve upon us and with which we are confronted as we are hastening on to that judgment seat where Christ will manifest himself in his glory and where he will bestow upon his people according to his grace and minister unto all his enemies that judgment that is equitable but that is also everlasting. And do thou grant unto us that we may take heed unto those things that are ours now, so that we may awake out of sleep and that we may cast off the works of darkness and put on the armor of light, and all for Jesus's sake and in his name. Amen.

8

Let This Mind Be in You

Let this mind be in you, which was also in Christ Jesus: Who, being in the form of God, thought it not robbery to be equal with God: But made himself of no reputation, and took upon him the form of a servant, and was made in the likeness of men: And being found in fashion as a man, he humbled himself, and became obedient unto death, even the death of the cross. Wherefore God also hath highly exalted him, and given him a name which is above every name.
—PHILIPPIANS 2:5–9

The first mystery of being is the mystery of the Trinity. That is not a mystery that came to be. The revelation of this mystery came to be because all revelation is temporal and given to temporal creatures, but the truth of this mystery, the mystery of the Trinity, is eternal. It is the mystery of God's eternal being in three persons.

The second mystery is that of the incarnation, and that is the mystery of godliness, the mystery of Christianity. It is that to which Paul refers when he says, "Great is the mystery of godliness" (1 Tim 3:16). This is a mystery that came to be, one that had a beginning in history. The Son of God became in time what he eternally was not. He did not cease to be what he eternally was, but he began to be what he was not. It is with this mystery that Philippians 2:5–9 is concerned. The salient features of this passage and its three headings are, first, the dignity possessed; second, the humiliation undertaken; and third, the exaltation bestowed.

In reference to the dignity Christ possessed, there are two aspects: the dignity of *his being* and the dignity of *his station*. The dignity of his being is announced in the words "being in the form of God." The dignity of his station in the words "equal with God" or "on an equality with God."

This expression "the form of God" does not mean anything less than Godhood. We are not to be misled by the meaning we today attach to the word *form*. In the Greek language (and in the English language more than three hundred and fifty years ago) the word *form* points to the essence of a thing. In this case it means the reality and fullness of Godhood, the sum of those perfections and attributes that belong to God and by reason of which he *is* God. So, when it is said of Christ Jesus that he was in "the form of God," that has richer meaning than to say simply that he was God. The accent falls, you see, upon the fullness of his Godhood, upon his being originally, natively, and essentially God in the full possession of all that is distinctive of God in his glory and majesty. That is the dignity of his divine identity, the dignity of unabridged deity.

There have infiltrated from time to time into the church thoughts that bring Christ down to a lower level than that of full deity (or full divinity). For example, the notion that Jesus is less than fully divine is fanatically peddled today by the so-called Jehovah's Witnesses. It is precisely that heresy in any and every form that Paul's assertion in Philippians 2:6 directly condemns. It is one thing to not believe in the full deity of Christ, but let us not try to peddle it as biblical. That profanity has no support whatsoever in Scripture. And let us not be deceived by an illusory learning that knows not of what it speaks. Jehovah's Witnesses do peddle an illusory learning, which may very easily lead some people astray. The apostle could not have used any expression that would more clearly articulate the completeness of Jesus's Godhood than to say, "Who, being in the form of God."

Let us also consider the dignity of his station. He is "equal with God" or "on an equality with God." This equality is not an accession either by robbery or attainment. Jesus Christ did not consider his being "on an equality with God" something he had gained or something he was to gain; it was not something of precarious tenure. Rather, it was the consequence of his being, and continuing to be, in the form of God, and therefore it was also his natively, essentially, and immutably. I think the thought of the clauses can be very well paraphrased, "Being in the form of God, and therefore not considering his being on an equality with God a prize or booty but an inalienable possession, he made himself of no reputation." I am quite convinced that this is the direction of thought that is in accord with Pauline language in Philippians 2.

Here, in respect to the dignity possessed, we have a combination of terms that only the mystery of the Trinity (the first mystery of being) can explain. Christ Jesus is identified with God and therefore on an equality with God. He is identified with God and yet distinguished from God—distinguished from God and yet not on a lower status. He possesses the fullness of Godhood and yet is not the only one who is God. How eloquently Paul bears witness to the identity and the differentiation that belong to the glorious mystery of the Trinity. It is oftentimes in unsuspecting ways that we find the witness of Scripture to that great and ultimate mystery of being.

Second in Philippians 2:5–9, we have the humiliation undertaken. Christ Jesus did not undertake divine being and station. Divinity was his natively and essentially. But he did take humiliation upon himself. The apostle is very careful to call our attention to this contrast, and therefore peculiar emphasis falls at this point upon the voluntary action of the person who is the subject of this text. *He* made himself of no reputation. *He* took the form of a servant. *He* humbled himself. There is sustained progression. And this, of course, is a series of events that happened in time and had no actuality prior to the fullness of time.

When we read that he made himself of no reputation, a literal rendering would be "he emptied *himself*." But here I want to be very emphatic and very denunciatory: there is not one whit of good reason for a literal translation at this particular point. Usage elsewhere and the context here require the figurative rendering, which is well given in our reading, "He made himself of no reputation," or an alternative, "He made no account of himself." Versions that have adopted a literal translation have imposed upon English readers a rendering that has ignored the demands of good translation and interpretation and have introduced a question into the minds of English readers that neither the context nor the particular passage concerned warrant or require. The thought is simply that Christ Jesus did not make his own self the all-absorbing and exclusive object of interest, concern, and attention; he became absorbed in concern for others. He made no account of himself, and if you know the Greek, you see that the emphasis falls upon *himself*. "Made no account *of himself*." That, of course, is the leading lesson of the whole passage: "Let this mind be in you, which was also in Christ Jesus."

What was this voluntary undertaking? There are three observations in connection with the humiliation undertaken. First, he became man. Verse 8 says, "And being found in fashion as a man," or "made in the likeness of men." That was humiliation. It would have been humiliation under the most ideal of human and earthly conditions because of the great discrepancy between the Creator and the creature, an unbridgeable discrepancy. It was not into an ideal world that the Son of God came; it was into a world of sin, of misery, and of death. And he came in the likeness of sinful flesh, in the likeness of sin-cursed humanity (Rom 8:3). Although he himself was without sin, "holy, harmless, undefiled, and separate from sinners" (Heb 7:26), nevertheless, he came into the closest relationship to sinful humanity that it was possible for him to come without thereby becoming himself sinful.

Then second, he took the form of a servant. Just as in verse 6 the word *form* points to the fullness and reality of his deity, so now *form* is very significantly repeated in connection with his servanthood and underlines the reality and fullness of that servanthood. It was not simply that he *became* a servant! He became a servant with all the subservience and obligations that subjection to the will of another entails. That is the magnificent emphasis in the word *form*.

It is true that Jesus devoted himself to the service of men. That is reflected on in the preceding statement: that he made no account of himself. He became preoccupied with the service and interest of others. Of course, it is the practical lesson of the whole passage: "Let this mind be in you, which was also in Christ Jesus" (Phil 2:5), and, "Think not every man of his own things, but every man also of the things of others" (Phil 2:4). But it is not his service of men that defines the expression "the form of a servant," not at all. Although he himself said indeed and emphasized that he came "not to be ministered unto, but to minister, and to give his life a ransom for many" (Matt 20:28), and although he said, "I am among you as he that serveth" (Luke 22:27), it is not his service of men that defines this expression "the form of a servant." Jesus did not subject himself to the will of men. To have taken the form of a servant in reference to being under the authority of any human will or any creature will, would have contradicted the dignity of his mission, the dignity of his being, and the dignity of his station.

It was to God the Father that he was a servant, and this expression "the form of a servant" must be fully understood in reference to his service in doing the will of God the Father. It was to the will of the Father that he surrendered himself in the fullness of subjection and obligation. He came down from heaven not to do his own will but the will of him that sent him (John 6:38). This great lesson is certified to us in the Old Testament, eloquently inscribed in the Isaianic passages: "Behold *my* servant, whom I uphold; mine elect, in whom my soul delighteth . . . Behold, *my* servant shall deal prudently, he shall be exalted and extolled . . . By his knowledge shall *my* righteous servant justify many" (Isa 42:1, 52:13, 53:11). So, it is therefore *Jehovah's* servant. It was this office of unreserved commitment to the Father's will that he voluntarily undertook, and because it was the Father he served, there was humiliation but no degradation.

We must not overlook the contrast that we find again in this passage. Christ Jesus was on an equality with God, and this equality was natively, essentially, and unalterably his. It was the dignity of station coordinate with his "being in the form of God." But in his humiliation, he took the form of a servant and therefore became subject to God, and it is subordination, remember, in the fullness and the reality of subjection. On the one hand there is equality and therefore no subordination. On the other there is servanthood and therefore subordination in all the reality and fullness of its meaning.

Well, beloved friends, we must come hither if we want even a glimpse of the mystery of godliness. There is no analogy that is the solitary instance of such conjunction. There is no analogy in heaven, earth, or hell; there is no analogy in the whole of history; there will be no analogy throughout the endless ages of eternity. Here is something that belongs solely and uniquely to him, "who, being in the form of God, thought it not robbery to be equal with God: but made himself of no reputation" (Phil 2:6–7).

Thirdly, in connection with the humiliation undertaken, he became obedient unto death, even the death of the cross. Now that is the *extent* of his humiliation according to this passage. Death, for our Lord, was an act of obedience, and it was the grand climax of his commission as a servant, as the Lord's servant. It was not mere death; it was the accursed death of the cross. It was death in the unspeakable anguish of damnation vicariously born, death in the experience of that which is reflected in the most mysterious cry that ever ascended from earth to heaven: "My God, my God, why hast thou forsaken me?" (Ps 22:1; cf. Matt 27:46; Mark 15:34).

My friends, let us appreciate it. It would have violated all divine propriety and shaken the foundation of God's throne and justice and judgment if this were not damnation vicariously born, for Jesus was "holy, harmless, undefiled, and separate from sinners" (Heb 7:26), and he was unalterably in the form of God and "thought it not robbery to be equal with God" (Phil 2:6). In the very ordeal of laying down his life on the accursed tree, he was rendering the supreme act of obedience to the Father in his capacity as the servant. In fact, it is the very expression "form of a servant" that points to this so eloquently, because we are here advised of the full extremity to which his office as a servant constrained him. This obedience to the Father unto death is an obedience that has no parallel and never will have a parallel or repetition or duplication. Here again, you see, we are advised of the absolute uniqueness of that which belongs to the mystery of godliness.

These are the lowest depths of humiliation conceivable. And it is no blasphemy to say (in fact, it is absolute truth to say) that God himself could not conceive of or devise a humiliation lower than that to which our Lord subjected himself. For he who humbled himself was in the form of God and on an equality with God, and that, of course, bespeaks the highest dignity of unalterable being and station. But he humbled himself to the accursed death of the cross, where no lower depths were possible. For the cross bespeaks the whole curse and judgment of God upon sin. It is humiliation inimitable, unrepeated, and unrepeatable. Again, let us be reminded that it was self-humiliation. Christ Jesus undertook not only to *be humbled*, but to *humble himself*, and humiliation was an action in his capacity as the servant.

Here, my friends, is convergence with no similitude: the will of the Father that the servant be humbled and the will of Christ Jesus to humble himself, the will of the Father that he should be humbled to the lowest depths of humiliation conceivable and the will of the servant that he should humble himself to the lowest depths of humiliation conceivable.

Now, third, in addition to the dignity possessed and the humiliation undertaken, we have the exaltation bestowed. Again, you see the eloquent contrast: Christ Jesus possessed divine dignity, undertook humiliation, but now *God* has highly exalted him. That is the action of the Father, and again there are three features to particularly note in connection with the exaltation bestowed.

First, the exaltation is the reward of this lowest conceivable humiliation. The "wherefore" at the beginning of verse 9 establishes that connection. Here is obedience that merited reward, and it is the only obedience that has that intrinsic quality, at least the only obedience among men that has that intrinsic quality of *meriting* reward. The obedience of the saints will be rewarded; "each will receive his own reward according to his own labor" (1 Cor 3:8). But, in the case of the saints, this is the reward of grace not of merit. In the obedience of Christ, we have obedience that divine propriety must reward. It is an obedience that merits reward, and, as we shall see, this reward is correspondingly in the opposite direction from the humiliation undertaken.

Second, the exaltation is the guarantee that Christ Jesus perfectly fulfilled the commitment given to him by the Father. In Paul's teaching, of course, this is but the echo of our Lord's own prayer as recorded in John 17: "I have glorified thee on the earth: I have finished the work which thou gavest me to do. And now, O Father, glorify thou me with thine own self with the glory which I had with thee before the world was" (John 17:4–5). You cannot but detect in the very words of our Lord in that prayer the very sequence that is expressed in our text by the word *wherefore*, "*wherefore* God also has highly exalted him."

Third, the exaltation is the highest conceivable. "God also hath highly exalted him, and given him the name which is above every name" (Phil 2:9). You can see the marvel; oh, how marvelous! May we catch something of the matchless glory of the mystery of godliness. The incarnation would have been humiliation even in a sinless world! We might therefore think that humiliation would be inseparable from the human nature of our Lord in that bliss whither he has ascended. We might think that a certain element of humiliation permanently attaches, therefore, to the incarnation. But the truth is that now no humiliation attaches to him in his glorified humanity!

Yet if the distance between the Creator and the creature is so great, how can it be that no humiliation belongs to the incarnate Christ in his exalted glory? The reason is the uniqueness of the commission that he undertook and the perfection with which it was accomplished. Super-eminent and transcendent glory attaches now to his very incarnation because only as incarnate could he have fulfilled this unique commission and only as incarnate could he have perfectly fulfilled the office of servant. He is exalted "far above all principality, and power, and might, and dominion, and every name that is named, not only in this world but also in that which is to come" (Eph 1:21)—not only in this age but also in that which is to come.

The apostle has here delineated for us the great pivots of the mystery of godliness. It is high and heavenly doctrine and, for that reason, of little appeal to dull minds and darkened hearts. It is the mystery that angels desire to look into (1 Pet 1:12). They are not partakers of the specific benefits of redemption because they don't need them. But they desire to look into these things, and their bliss is greatly enhanced, indeed, by the redemption that Christ has wrought. But it is also, my friends, the delight of enlightened and humbled souls. They love to explore the mysteries that bespeak the glories of their Redeemer.

There is a direct line from these high and exalted themes to the most elementary duties of the Christian vocation. Oh, what folly when people speak of doctrine as being impractical. Of course, we may make what we conceive to be doctrine very impractical, but it isn't because *doctrine* is impractical. This is the great lesson that is emblazoned on this text, as on many others, if we had the time to educe them. There is a direct line from these great themes to the most elementary duties of the Christian vocation. The humiliation of Christ is here appealed to in support of considerate and unselfish regard for others. "Think not everyone of his own things, but everyone also of the things of others. Let this mind be in you, which was also in Christ

Jesus" (Phil 2:4–5). And you see, it is therefore on the supreme example of our Lord that the basic virtues of the Christian life are nurtured. That is the great lesson of our text, as of numerous others.

It is significant that what was *unique* in Jesus's undertaking is also the *pattern*. There can be no repetition or duplication of what he has done, and to have the mind of Christ is not mimicry of his action—that would be blasphemy. Rather, to have the mind that was in Christ Jesus is to be animated in *our* vocation and in *our* relations to others by that mind that was exemplified by him in his inimitable commitment, that commitment that has no analogy or similitude in the whole of history or throughout eternity. Our Lord's incomparable self-humiliation accords to the humble-mindedness required of us—the highest sanction. And with that I must leave it: "it is enough for the disciple to be as his master, and the servant as his lord" (Matt 10:25). It is just the uniqueness and inimitableness of the Lord's own actions and the uniqueness of his commitment that gives added sanction to our actions and commitment in our very humble and common-sphere activity.

Oh God, do thou grant unto us that we, beholding as in a glass the glory of the Lord, may be transformed into this same image from glory to glory, even as by the Spirit of the Lord. We confess, oh Lord, our utter bankruptcy, the utter corruption of our hearts, the defilement that permeates our whole being, and that our only appeal is to him who is holy, harmless, undefiled, and separate from sinners, who is the advocate at thy right hand, and who is the great intercessor, able to be touched with the feeling of our infirmities because he was in all points tempted like as we are, yet without sin. May we be constrained by his love, may we be captivated by his glory, and may we glory in him and be able to say with thy servant, "God forbid that I should glory, save in the cross of the Lord Jesus Christ, by whom the world is crucified unto me, and I am to the world." In Jesus's name and for his sake, amen.

9

The Lordship of Christ

Therefore let all the house of Israel know assuredly, that God hath made the same Jesus, whom ye have crucified, both Lord and Christ.

—ACTS 2:36

It is apparent that Peter is speaking in this text of what occurred in the resurrection and ascension of Christ. In Acts 2:31, the reference to the resurrection is quite explicit, "He seeing this before spake of the resurrection of Christ, that his soul was not left in hell [that is, he was not left in the grave], neither his flesh did see corruption." And in verse 34, the reference to the ascension is equally clear, "For David is not ascended into the heavens: but he saith himself, 'The Lord said unto my Lord, Sit thou on my right hand.'" When we read verse 36, therefore, in that sequence and in that context, there are questions that arise. In order to answer these questions, very important distinctions have to be made.

The first question is this: how could Jesus be made Lord and Christ by the resurrection when lordship belonged to him in virtue of creation? For he, equally with the Father and the Holy Spirit, was engaged in creation. We read of him, "All things were made by him; and without him was not any thing made that was made" (John 1:3). And again, "By him were all things created, that are in heaven, and that are in earth, visible and invisible, whether they be thrones, or dominions, or principalities, or powers: all things were created by him, and for him: And he is before all things" (Col 1:16–17). Because he was, equally with the Father and the Holy Spirit, the Creator of the heavens and the earth, he exercises all-inclusive providence. For in that text I was just quoting, we not only read that by him all things were created, but that by him all things consist—that is to say, all things are held together by him and in him.

When Jesus became man, that lordship that belonged to him by virtue of his creative activity was not suspended. We have a very significant witness in the Epistle to the Hebrews when we read, "Upholding all things by the word of his power, when he had by himself purged our sins, sat down on the right hand of the Majesty on high" (Heb 1:3). Even when he was making purification for sin, the import is that he was upholding all things by the word of his power in that identity of the brightness of the Father's glory and the express image of his being. How could he be made both Lord and Christ by the resurrection and ascension so long subsequent to the events of creation?

The distinction, you see, is all-important. The lordship of which Peter speaks in Acts 2:36 is the lordship given to Jesus as the God-man, as the Christ. It is a lordship that was not his as Creator because he was not then the God-man. He became the God-man when he became incarnate. And this particular lordship of which Peter speaks, bestowed upon Jesus as the God-man, as the Savior, as the Redeemer, as the Christ, did not belong to him in his creative activity. You see the one kind of lordship belongs to him in virtue of his deity as the Creator and as the Sustainer of all. But the other kind of lordship is in virtue of the new relationship that he came to sustain to us and to creation as Savior and Redeemer, a new relationship that began to be his when he was begotten by the Holy Spirit in the womb of the virgin. That is the distinction, and it's all-important that we should appreciate that distinction between the lordship that belongs to Christ in virtue of creation (which was not suspended in any way when he became man) and between another lordship with which he is invested by reason of his being the God-man.

Let us pose another question: Even when we are thinking of the lordship that belongs to Christ as the God-man, as the Mediator, as the Savior, and as the Redeemer, how can Peter say that he was *made* Lord in the resurrection and ascension? Was he not Lord and Christ prior to his death upon the cross, prior to his resurrection, and prior to his ascension forty days after the resurrection? Of course he was! It was Peter himself who made the confession at Caesarea Philippi prior to Jesus's death, "Thou art the Christ, the Son of the living God" (Matt 16:16). And Peter received the benediction, "Blessed art thou, Simon Bar-jona: for flesh and blood hath not revealed it unto thee, but my Father who is in heaven" (Matt 16:17). Likewise, Jesus manifested his lordship in his works of mercy and of power. Remember that when he stilled the storm upon the sea, he not only stilled the wind but he stilled the waves, and therefore manifested his omnipotence, his lordship, over the works of creation

(Matt 8:26; Mark 4:41). How can Peter therefore say that by the resurrection and ascension he was *made* Lord?

We have to make yet another distinction. Even within the sphere of that lordship that was bestowed upon him as the God-man, it is necessary to appreciate that there are stages of realization. It was only by the resurrection and ascension of Christ that the lordship he sustains as the God-man came to its fullest expression and exercise. It could not be fully realized before then because there were limitations placed upon him in his humiliation. That, of course, is most evident in the fact that he had to die. He was under the dominion of death for a period, and that shows, you see, what a limitation was placed upon him in terms of his humiliation. It was therefore only when his humiliation ended, and the limitations imposed upon him by reason of his humiliation lifted, that this lordship could come to its fullest exercise and its fullest manifestation. It was by the resurrection that Jesus began his exaltation, and his exaltation was further exemplified in his ascension to the right hand of power. You can see, therefore, the difference very evidently: death had dominion over him for three days and three nights, he was crucified through weakness (2 Cor 13:4), but none of that dominion of death and none of that weakness applies to him in his resurrection and his exaltation to the right hand of the power of God.

So you see how important it is to appreciate these distinctions, especially the distinction between the lordship that belongs to Christ in virtue of his deity as the Creator and the lordship of Christ as the God-man in its stages of realization. It is this that Peter has in mind: the fullest realization of Christ's lordship and messianic dignity by his resurrection and ascension. That is why he says, "Therefore let all the house of Israel know assuredly, that God hath made that same Jesus, whom ye have crucified, both Lord and Christ."

But with these distinctions in mind, and particularly taking account of the lordship with which Peter is dealing in this text, we may proceed to note, first of all, the contrast; second, the agent; and third, the investiture itself.

First of all, then, we have the contrast. Peter says, "Know assuredly, that God hath made the same Jesus, whom ye have crucified, both Lord and Christ" (Acts 2:36). See the contrast between the action of the people ("whom ye have crucified") and the action of the Father ("God hath made . . . both Lord and Christ"). It's a very striking contrast and one that Peter is very fond of instituting. You have it again later on in one of his other speeches as recorded in Acts 3:13–15:

> The God of Abraham, and of Isaac, and of Jacob, the
> God of our fathers, hath glorified his Son Jesus; whom
> ye delivered up, and denied him in the presence of Pilate,
> when he was determined to let him go. But ye denied
> the Holy One and the Just, and desired a murderer to
> be granted unto you; and killed the Prince of life, whom
> God hath raised from the dead; whereof we are witnesses.

You see the contrast between the action of ungodly men and the action of God.

And again, in Acts 5:30–31, you have the same contrast: "The God of our fathers raised up Jesus, whom ye slew and hanged on a tree. Him hath God exalted with his right hand to be a Prince and a Saviour, for to give repentance to Israel, and forgiveness of sins." The judgment of this world with respect to Christ was to crucify him: "We will not have this man to reign over us" (Luke 19:14). And remember Acts 4:27–28: "For of a truth against thy holy child Jesus, whom thou hast anointed, both Herod, and Pontius Pilate, with the Gentiles, and the people of Israel, were gathered together, for to do whatsoever thy hand and thy counsel determined before to be done." There is a contrast between the judgment and the action of man on the one hand and the judgment and action of God on the other. "This same Jesus, whom ye have crucified, God has made both Lord and Christ" (Acts 2:36).

Now we might think that this is just a contrast applied to the Lord himself nineteen hundred years ago when he was crucified on Calvary, but, oh, it is still relevant. This is still the judgment of unbelief, and there can still be a contrast between our judgment and the judgment of God with respect to him whom God has highly exalted. For if we do not yield to Christ unreserved commitment, if he is not our Lord and our Christ, then our judgment also is "we will not have this man to reign over us." That's the issue. And it's as relevant today as it was over nineteen hundred years ago when they crucified the Lord of Glory. What are our alignments? Is our supreme jealousy Jesus's honor? Is the yoke we wear Jesus's yoke? Is the scepter to which we pay allegiance Jesus's scepter? The point is, do we yield to him that unreserved commitment so that he is Lord for us in every detail of our lives and in every detail of his claims? It is certainly relevant to us. The question is to whom do we yield unreserved commitment? Is Christ *our* Lord?

Second in the text we come to the agent. Of course the agent here is God the Father, for the name God very frequently applies to God the Father as his personal name (not by any means implying that Jesus is not also God; it's just a matter of distinguishing names). When we read in this text, "Let all the house of Israel know assuredly, that *God* hath made this same Jesus," *God* refers to God the Father. And in the teaching of the apostle Paul, Jesus was raised "by the glory of the Father [or *through* the glory of the Father, as it is more recently]" (Rom 6:4). Again, in the Epistle to the Ephesians, we read:

> What is the exceeding greatness of his power toward us who believe, according to the working of his mighty power, which he wrought in Christ, when *he* raised him from the dead, and set him at his own right hand in the heavenly places, far above all principality, and power, and might, and dominion, and every name that is named, not only in this world, but also in that which is to come. (Eph 1:19–21)

Who is the subject in this passage? You have to go back to verse 17: "the God of our Lord Jesus Christ, the Father of glory" is the person who is referred to when we read at verse 19, "What is the exceeding greatness of *his* power for us who believe." And it is the frequent witness of the New Testament that God the Father raised up Jesus, that it was by the exceeding greatness of the Father's power that he broke the bands of death "because it was not possible that he should be holden of it" (Acts 2:24).

There is a contrast even in this instance between the action of God the Father in the resurrection and ascension of Christ and the action of God the Father in the humiliation of Christ. It is a very striking contrast and a very different type of contrast from the one that we discovered a little bit earlier between the action of men and the action of God in the judgment exercised. This contrast is very eloquently brought to our attention repeatedly in Scripture, for example, "The Lord hath laid on him the iniquity of us all," and, "It pleased the Lord to bruise him; he hath put him to grief" (Isa 53:6, 10). It is God the Father who is in view; it pleased *God the Father* to bruise his own Son and put him to grief. And when we listen to the witness that we find in Zechariah, it is God the Father who is speaking: "Awake, O sword, against my shepherd, and against the man who is my fellow, saith the Lord of hosts: smite the shepherd, and the sheep shall be scattered" (Zech 13:7). Yes, mystery of mysteries, but mystery that is of supreme preciousness—that God the Father bruised his own Son because he made him sin "that we might be made the righteousness of God in him" (2 Cor 5:21).

But see now the contrast: "Let all the house of Israel know assuredly, that God hath made that same Jesus . . . both Lord and Christ." *Now* there is glorification on the part of God the Father, and glory in accord with the Savior's own prayer, when he said, "Father, the hour is come; glorify thy Son. . . . I have finished the work which thou gavest me to do. And now, O Father, glorify thou me with thine own self with the glory which I had with thee before the world was" (John 17:1, 4–5).

I spoke a little while ago about the importance of distinctions. Oh, appreciate this distinction that is at the very center of the gospel: the distinction between the action of God the Father in Jesus's humiliation and the action of God the Father in his exaltation. This is the wisdom of God; this is the love of God. And how marvelous are the arrangements of the economy of salvation! Because it is in these marvelous distinctions and these marvelous arrangements in the economy of salvation that you will get glimpses of the glory that is unspeakable. "God hath made that same Jesus, whom ye have crucified, both Lord and Christ" (Acts 2:36). And it is with all the splendors of the Father's glory that he is invested with this dominion.

And that brings us to the third aspect of the verse, the investiture: "both Lord and Christ." This is lordship, may I remind you, in contrast with what was intrinsic in his deity as Creator. There are just two things that I want to mention with respect to this investiture. The first is that it is the highest conceivable exaltation in the realm of history. God the Father himself could not conceive of an exaltation that is higher in the realm of history than that which he bestowed on his own Son when he raised him from the dead and set him at his right hand. You remember how Paul expresses that in Philippians 2:9–11:

> Wherefore God also hath highly exalted him, and given him a name which is above every name: That at the name of Jesus every knee should bow, of things in heaven, and things in earth, and things under the earth; and that every tongue should confess that Jesus Christ is Lord, to the glory of God the Father.

And again, he was set at God's right hand "far above all principality, and power, and might, and dominion, and every name that is named, not only in this world, but also in that which is to come" (Eph 1:20–21).

I said a little while ago, oh, marvel at the arrangements of the economy of salvation, the economy of redemption. The height of Jesus's exaltation is another aspect. Think of it and you'll get glimpses of the glory that is unspeakable. The *highest conceivable* glory is bestowed upon God's own Son just *because* he descended into the lowest death and humiliation in accordance with the wisdom and love of God the Father and in accord with the full consent of his own love and will and power.

The second aspect of this investiture of which I want to say just a word is this: it is universal. It is not only the highest conceivable exaltation, but it is universal: "Far above all principality, and power." It is impossible for us to say how this universal dominion, with which Christ is invested and which he exercises as the God-man, the Savior, the Redeemer, and the only Mediator between God and man, is related to that dominion that belongs to him in virtue of his deity as Creator. Of course, the dominion that is his in virtue of his deity as Creator is universal—it's just as universal as the dominion of God the Father and God the Holy Spirit. When Scripture says, "Upholding all things by the word of his power" (Heb 1:3) and "In him all things consist" (Col 1:17), there's universality there.

But here in Acts 2:36, there is another universality that belongs to him as the God-man. How they are related we cannot say. There's incomprehensible mystery attached not only to the person of Christ but also, in this particular case, to the two distinct aspects of his universal dominion and lordship. And just as we cannot unravel the great mystery of the two natures of the person of Christ—Godhood in all its fullness, manhood in all its reality—so we cannot unravel the mystery of this two-fold dominion that Christ exercises.

But it is necessary for us to appreciate both. And although we cannot unravel all the mystery that is associated with these two types of dominion—universal dominion exercised by him as Creator and as the God-man—I think this we can say, that the dominion that he exercises as God, as Creator, equally with the Father and the Holy Spirit, undergirds that lordship that he exercises as the God-man, as the Mediator, as the Savior, and as the Redeemer. The one undergirds the other; there's no conflict. How marvelous is this great truth, that the person who is exalted now through the exercise of universal dominion is the eternal Son of God in full possession of his Godhood, who, nevertheless, exercises it in his unique capacity as the God-man, Mediator, and Redeemer. And how marvelous that our very nature should be exalted to the very throne of history! Oh, how marvelous that Christ is truly king! And it is in the full reality of his manhood, of his glorified humanity, that he exercises universal sovereignty.

My friends, two words in conclusion. Do you feel something of the greatness of Christ's lordship? Do you believe that he is the Lord exalted to the Father's side? Doesn't that imply the demand of recognition, the demand of faith, the demand of whole-souled commitment to him? Oh, there are some young people here. In the days of your youth give your heart to the Redeemer; recognize the commitment that you owe to him.

And the second word by way of conclusion, application, and exhortation is this: you are Christ's. Remember that the person who wields the scepter of this creation, who owns all details in this land, so that not a sparrow falls to the ground without his knowledge, so that the very hairs of your head are all numbered, is none other than your Savior, your King, your Lord, and your Christ. How precious! When he will come again the second time, when he will be seen on the clouds of heaven in great power and glory, manifesting to the whole universe the universal sovereignty that belongs to him as Lord, he will then appear as *your* Savior and you will not be ashamed. May you long for that day when his universal lordship will be fully manifested and fully vindicated.

Oh God, thanks be to thee for the marvel of the economy of redemption, the marvel of the economy of salvation, that in it thy glory is reflected, the glory of the Father, Son, and Holy Spirit. And it is in that glory that belongs to the Father and the Son and the Holy Spirit in the economy of salvation that we have salvation and that we have the hope of everlasting life, through Jesus Christ. Amen.

10

The Priesthood of Christ

Seeing then that we have a great high priest, that is passed into the heavens, Jesus the Son of God, let us hold fast our profession. For we have not an high priest which cannot be touched with the feeling of our infirmities; but was in all points tempted like as we are, yet without sin.
—HEBREWS 4:14–15

If you examine these words carefully, you will notice that the teaching of these two verses is directed toward the fulfillment of the exhortation, "Let us hold fast our profession" (literally, "let us hold fast the confession," that is, the confession of the faith). In this epistle we have repeated warning against the danger of defection from the faith, defection from the confession. Some of these warnings against apostasy, against departure from the living God, are among the severest that we find in the whole of Scripture. You find this epistle just strewn with such warnings: In the third chapter at the twelfth verse: "Take heed, brethren, lest there be in any of you an evil heart of unbelief, in departing from the living God." And chapter 4 begins with the same thought, "Let us therefore fear, lest, a promise being left us of entering into his rest, any of you should seem to come short of it" (Heb 4:1).

Then in Hebrews 6:4–6, you have this very severe warning:

> For it is impossible for those who were once enlightened, and have tasted of the heavenly gift, and were made partakers of the Holy Ghost, and have tasted the good word of God, and the powers of the world to come, if they shall fall away, to renew them again unto repentance; seeing they crucify to themselves the Son of God afresh, and put him to an open shame.

Perhaps the most severe and most solemn warning of all you find in Hebrews 10:26–31:

> For if we sin willfully after that we have received the knowledge of the truth, there remaineth no more sacrifice for sins, but a certain fearful looking for of judgment and fiery indignation, which shall devour the adversaries. He that despised Moses's law died without mercy under two or three witnesses: Of how much sorer punishment, suppose ye, shall he be thought worthy, who hath trodden under foot the Son of God, and hath counted the blood of the covenant, wherewith he was sanctified, an unholy thing, and hath done despite unto the Spirit of grace? For we know him that hath said,
>
> > "Vengeance belongeth unto me,
> > I will recompense, saith the Lord."

And again,
"The Lord shall judge his people."
It is a fearful thing to fall into the hands of the living God.

The opposite of this defection, the opposite of this apostasy, the opposite of departure from the living God, is to hold fast the confession.

That word *confession* refers to the confession of the faith of Jesus. It is that to which we are directed, for example, at the beginning of the third chapter: "Wherefore, holy brethren, partakers of the heavenly calling, consider the Apostle and High Priest of our profession [that is, of our confession], Christ Jesus" (Heb 3:1). This confession is the confession of that faith which finds its fullness, its very center, in the Apostle and High Priest of our confession, Christ Jesus.

We use the word *belief* in two distinct senses (and the Scripture does the same). These senses are inseparable but they are also distinct. Belief can refer to that which is believed in truth or it can refer to the exercise of belief. The moment we are called in this text to "hold fast the confession" (Heb 4:14; author's translation), both ingredients are in mind: holding fast the faith and keeping faith, abiding in confidence with respect to God himself and particularly with respect to the Savior. We can't keep faith without holding fast the faith; and if we hold fast the faith, we must also keep faith. In the text there are two things with respect to this holding fast the confession. The first is *the validation*, and the second is *the encouragement*.

First, there is the validation. You ask the question, "What is it that induces, that grounds, and that demands this holding fast, this perseverance in the faith and in faith itself?" And the answer is in the text: the exaltation of Jesus the Son of God. Look again at verse 14: "Seeing then that we have a great high priest, that is passed into the heavens, Jesus the Son of God." It's the exaltation of the Lord Jesus Christ that is particularly in view.

When we think of the exaltation of Jesus, we most frequently think of his kingly office, of the sovereignty with which he is invested as King of kings and Lord of lords—invested with that principality and power "far above all other principality and power and might and dominion and every name that is named not only in this world but also in that which is to come" (Eph 1:21). We think of him as given the name that is above every name (Phil 2:9); we think of him as head over all things to his body the church (Eph 1:22). And there comes into our thought inevitably the exercise of this kingly office. It was with that aspect of Jesus's exaltation that we were dealing at the noonday service when Peter said, "Therefore let all the house of Israel know assuredly, that God hath made that same Jesus, whom ye have crucified, both Lord and Christ" (Acts 2:36). It is altogether important for us that we should appreciate this sovereignty—universal sovereignty, incomparable sovereignty, sovereignty than which there is nothing higher.

But, you see, it is not the kingly office that is in the center of thought in this text. This is very important and very precious. "Seeing then that we have a *great high priest*, that is passed into the heavens." I fear that this is far too frequently overlooked when we are dealing with the exaltation of Christ, when we are dealing with his investiture with lordship, with universal sovereignty. We overlook the fact that it is not only as King of kings and Lord of lords that he is invested with that sovereignty, but in his very office as the Great High Priest. Our Great High Priest has passed through the heavens, and it is in that capacity that he is exalted far above all powers.

Now this is particularly relevant because kingly rule and kingly sovereignty in all the dignity that it invokes, in all the sovereignty that it embraces, would only be terror were it not for the high priestly mediation. This, my friends, must strike a chord of deepest distress in the heart of every true believer. I say it again, that the kingly rule, exalted in all that sovereignty that is universal and that is surpassingly glorious, would only fill a contrite soul with terror were it not that Christ was exalted as the priest upon his throne, because it is the priestly office that speaks of atonement and reconciliation and propitiation.

Go back to Hebrews 2:17: "Wherefore in all things it behooved him to be made like unto his brethren, that he might be a merciful and faithful high priest in things pertaining to God, to make reconciliation for the sins of the people." Our version is in distinct error in this text; it has translated a certain word as *reconciliation*. The King James translators way back in the beginning of the seventeenth century made a mistake, as well as other translators. And this is a grave mistake. It should read, "to make *propitiation*." It is indeed very true that he made reconciliation, but the focus of thought here is that he made *propitiation*, and propitiation is that which is directed to the wrath of God and to the removal of that wrath. That is what makes the priestly office of the Redeemer supremely precious: that he made propitiation for our sins. That is the thought that is in the forefront of our text: a Great High Priest, one who made atonement, one who removed guilt, one who made reconciliation for iniquity and made propitiation for wrath, for the holy wrath and indignation of God.

My friends, does this not strike a chord, the deepest response in your bosom, that you could not derive any real comfort from the kingly authority of the Savior were it not that he is a *priest* upon his throne. By the inspiration of the Holy Spirit, the writer of this epistle was guided to pen that all-important truth: "We have a great high priest, who is passed into the heavens." And as John says in 1 John 2:2, he is not only the one who made propitiation once-for-all but the one who is the abiding propitiation, because he is the embodiment of that which he wrought on behalf of his people in order to remove from them the holy wrath of God, so that there is now no condemnation to them who are in Christ Jesus (Rom 8:1). That is the emphasis of the text regarding his exaltation.

Our version speaks of Jesus's exaltation saying that he has "passed into the heavens," but it is literally saying that he "passed *through* the heavens." This is similar to the witness later in this epistle that he was "made *higher* than the heavens" (Heb 7:26), and to the witness of the apostle Paul that he "ascended . . . *far above* the heavens" (Eph 4:10). It's not simply that he has passed into the heavens (although that is true), but the thought that is emphasized in the text is the exaltation of Christ *far above* all that has been created. You see, I spoke this morning of this exaltation as universal, and this very thought is essential to its very universality: that he is exalted far above, that he has passed *through* the heavens. And that is simply my point: the universality of his rule and dominion—and oh, how precious is that universality of dominion—belongs to him in his high-priestly office.

Now there is another ingredient in the exaltation of Christ in his priestly office, in all the sovereignty that is his in his identity as the Great High Priest. It is not only making a propitiation, not only the making of atonement for sin, not only the making of an end of sin and reconciliation for iniquity, but it is what is defined later on in this epistle: "Wherefore he is able also to save them to the uttermost that come unto God by him, seeing he ever liveth to make intercession for them" (Heb 7:25). He makes intercession. Christ ever lives to make *intercession* for them, and therefore he is able to save to the uttermost. Don't you see, my friends, how things pan together? The universality of his dominion and his capacity as the high priest make it certain that "he is able to save to the uttermost." Doesn't this strike another chord in the breast of every exercised and sensitive believer? How precious is the exaltation of Christ in his priestly office as the great intercessor. "We have an advocate with the Father, Jesus Christ the righteous" (1 John 2:1).

This is the validation. All this, you see, is directed to holding fast the confession. How can there enter into the human mind departure from the living God, apostasy from the faith, defection from the confession of the Great High Priest of our own confession, who is exalted far above all heavens? Don't you see, my friends, the contradiction between defection from the faith, apostasy from the faith, departure from the living God, and the exaltation that is the validation of holding fast and persevering?

But now, in the second place, we come to the encouragement, and that is given to us in verse 15: "For we have not an high priest which cannot be touched with the feeling of our infirmities; but was in all points tempted like as we are, yet without sin." Just as the exaltation of Christ grounds and validates the believer's holding fast, here is something that encourages the believer in the onward course of his perseverance: we do not have a high priest who cannot sympathize with our infirmities, who cannot have compassion on us in our infirmities, but we have one who was in all points tempted like as we are yet was without sin.

When thinking of the priestly office of Christ, I think very often we just focus attention on the things I have mentioned: his making of propitiation, his offering up of sacrifice for sin, and his intercession. However intelligent a Christian you may be, might I ask you if that is not in line with your thought in connection with Christ's priestly office? But don't you see that there's another all-important ingredient in the priestly office of Christ? Yes, the atonement that he makes and the intercession that he exercises as high priest are certainly in the forefront of thought in verse 14, but the other ingredient is that of compassion. It is that ingredient, after all, that is the encouragement because we do not have a high priest who cannot be touched with the feeling of our infirmities. As this compassion, this empathy, was an indispensable qualification of the high priest under the Levitical economy, so it is an indispensable ingredient in the exercise of Christ's high-priestly office.

There are three things which I want to mention in connection with the priestly office of Christ described in this passage. The first is that the people of God have very peculiar trials and tribulations. You will find that no two believers are in identically the same situation. There's a peculiarity, a particularity, to the trials and temptations and tribulations of each child of God. I suppose that sometimes you are disposed to say, "Well, there's no one who's just in the same category that I am. My trial is just peculiar to myself. I don't believe there is anybody else in the world who has just the particular complexion to trial and temptation and tribulation that I have." And there's an element of truth in that; there's no exact duplicate. In fact, that trial and tribulation that you have today is not identical with that which you had yesterday. There's always a new ingredient, there's always a new circumstance, and there's always a new context. When you are passing through a trial or temptation, it is peculiar to you. For example, you may have a husband who is a godly man and who has all the sympathy in the world, but he just can't entirely enter into the peculiarity and the particularity of your temptation and trial, even in that element of relationship. So, there's an element of truth in the conclusion, "My place is just different; it belongs to myself and it doesn't belong to anybody else."

But, my friends, "we have not an high priest who cannot be touched with the feeling of our infirmities; because he was in all points tempted like as we are" (Heb 4:15). What I have to draw to your attention now, beloved, is that you have a forerunner! Whenever you think there is a trial or tribulation or temptation that nobody else can understand because of its particularity, remember that that is not true of the Great High Priest. He was tempted in all points like as you are. He was your forerunner, and you can go to him and derive from him the fullest understanding and the fullest sympathy. And it is the sympathy of none other than of him who is the God-man, who is the Great High Priest far above all principality and power and might and dominion (Eph 1:21), who passed through the heavens (Heb 4:14), far above all heavens (Eph 4:10).

You see, this is something indispensable in the perseverance of the saints, that they know that when they go to this Great High Priest, they go to one who has perfect understanding, perfect sympathy, and perfect compassion, because he passed through that himself. He was tempted in all points like as we are. Oh, what a marvelous thing! You think nobody has ever passed through anything like that with which you struggle. Oh, remember the Great High Priest who has trodden the path before you, and go to him. Oh, it is necessary to repeat: with him you have perfect understanding and perfect sympathy and perfect compassion.

The second thing I want to say about this is that in his exalted glory there is no suspension of his sympathy. That is implied, of course, in all that I said, but it needs to be emphasized particularly now: there's no suspension; sympathy is not now beneath him. Go back to Hebrews 2:18, "For in that he himself hath suffered being tempted, he is able to succour them that are tempted." He is not being tempted now, he is not suffering now, he is now glorified with the glory which he had with the Father before the world was (John 17:5), but nevertheless, although he is forever removed from the arena of conflict, temptation, trial, and suffering, oh, my friends, he has taken to heaven with him a heart that was forged in the furnace of temptation. That's the point of Hebrews 2:18, and also our text, "We have not an high priest who cannot be touched with the feeling of our infirmities; because he was in all points tempted like as we are" (Heb 4:15).

And because he has a heart in heaven that was forged in the furnace of temptation and trial and suffering, he ministers to the tempted who resort to him in their weakness and desperation.

And he ministers to them in all the tenderness of compassion. He still speaks to your heart as he spoke to his disciples, "Peace I leave with you, my peace I give unto you: not as the world giveth, give I unto you. Let not your heart be troubled, neither let it be afraid" (John 14:27).

The third and final observation I want to make about this encouragement that we have in Hebrews 4:15 is that which is concerned with the qualification at the end of the verse. He was tempted "in all points . . . like as we are, *yet without sin.*" *Without* sin. There was no sin in him to which temptation could appeal, and there was no sin issuing from the temptation. He said himself on one occasion, "The prince of this world cometh, and hath nothing in me" (John 14:30). There was no defilement in him to which sin could appeal, and there was nothing issuing from him in that character of sin.

You might think that this is an interference with the efficacy of his compassion. How can he have properly trodden the path of temptation and trial when he is not in the same category as I am? I'm sinful and weak, I fall too frequently to temptation, but he never fell—he had no sin in him, he had no sin issuing from him. And you might think that's an interference with the compassion, with the efficacy of his fellowship. My friends, it is the other way—try to get hold of that. Oh, it is just because "such an high priest became us, who is *holy, harmless, undefiled, and separate from sinners*" (Heb 7:26), just because he was a Great High Priest without sin, that he can now exercise, in his exalted glory, an high-priestly compassion that is the *indispensable* ingredient to the efficacy.

The apostle John quotes this in another way, but in a way

that is pretty close to the thought of the text, "And if any man sin, we have an advocate with the Father, Jesus Christ the righteous" (1 John 2:1). He's our righteous advocate and, in this connection, he's our righteous Savior, Jesus. And that righteousness, that spotless righteousness, that he was holy, harmless, undefiled, and separate from sinners, is indispensable to the very compassion he exercises and indispensable to the efficacy of that compassion that he bestows upon you in your trials and temptations. Oh, think of it: "Seeing then that we have a great high priest, that is passed into the heavens, Jesus the Son of God, let us hold fast our confession" (Heb 4:14).

We now say and demonstrate that there is lament on defection from faith and there is lament on apostasy. For there are many who at one time seemed warm and ardent in the faith whose love has waxed cold (Matt 24:12), who have made shipwreck of faith. Here, my friends, is an exhortation that comes to us with all urgency, with an urgency that has never been surpassed in the history of mankind. So, let us hold fast the confession. When we pass through trials in all their particularity and peculiarity, oh, let us have resort to the Great High Priest, the spotless mediator, as he exercises this marvel of compassion to the utmost of efficacy just because he is holy, harmless, undefiled, and separate from sinners, and because he passed through all these temptations without sin.

This belongs to him; it belongs to the very exercise of his priestly office. And let us take to ourselves the encouragement that belongs to those who are tempted: that he was likewise tempted. And let us have resort to him, even if it be but to touch the hem of the garment of his compassion. If we just but touch the hem of the garment of his compassion, there is a virtue there that will sustain us, so that we shall hold fast the confession, that our faith will not be extinguished because Christ is sufficient in all the glory of his exaltation, in all the efficacy of his intercession, and in all the reality of his compassion.

Bless to us, oh Lord, thy Word. Bless to us our meditation upon it. May it be written upon our hearts as with the point of a diamond, and may we meditate upon the law of the Lord. Oh, let us behold the glory of the Redeemer, and beholding as in a glass his glory, may we be transformed into the same image from glory to glory, so that, notwithstanding all our infirmity, notwithstanding all our weakness, notwithstanding all our sinfulness and our sin, notwithstanding all our weakness in falling before temptation, nevertheless, one day we will be spotless after the image of Christ as the firstborn among many brethren. And all for this great Savior, amen.

11

The Cost of Discipleship

Then said Jesus unto his disciples, "If any man will come after me, let him deny himself, and take up his cross, and follow me."
—MATTHEW 16:24

Oh God, who dwellest in thy holy temple, who art high and lifted up, but who also dwellest with the humble and the contrite, do thou grant unto us that we may have a profound sense of thy glory and of thy presence. May the knowledge of the Lord captivate our minds and our hearts, and may we have an all-pervasive sense that thou art the Lord God Almighty—Father, Son, and Holy Spirit. Grant us thy presence in thy sanctuary in accordance with thy promise that where two or three are gathered together in thy name, there thou art in their midst. May we, oh Lord, have the experience of this inestimable grace. And may the words of our mouth and the meditations of our heart be acceptable in thy sight, oh Lord, our strength and our Redeemer. Amen.

One of the evils in the professing church of Christ, particularly apparent in our day, is the tendency to cheapen the gospel. Now the gospel is free, but the gospel is not cheap. And the gospel is cheapened when the conditions and demands of discipleship are torn down. Our Lord himself, in the days of his flesh, never concealed the cost of discipleship. He never tried to enlist disciples by suppressing what discipleship would involve. On one occasion he said to a certain person who said, "I will follow thee wheresoever thou goest," "Foxes have holes, and birds of the air have nests; but the Son of man hath not whereupon to lay his head" (Matt 8:19–20; Luke 9:57–58). And to another, who made what was apparently a reasonable request, "I will follow thee, but suffer me first to go and bury my father," he said, "Let the dead bury their dead, but follow thou me" (Matt 8:21–22; Luke 9:59–60). No, Jesus never suppressed the cost of following him, and there is no text in the Scripture nor word from the lips of our Lord that brings out the conditions of discipleship more forcefully than this particular word: "If any man will come after me, let him deny himself, and take up his cross, and follow me."

A disciple, of course, is one who follows Christ. Just as a disciple in the human sphere is a person who has a master and who follows that master, so, with reference to Christ, a disciple of Christ is just one who follows him and who is absolutely committed to him. There are always certain restrictions in the human sphere, for no one man may ever commit himself entirely, without reservation, to another man. It would be blasphemy;

it would be a substitution of what is a divine prerogative for a human prerogative. But with reference to Christ, the following involves total self-commitment. It is that kind of following of which Jesus speaks in this text, and it is that kind of following that constitutes a disciple. When Christ is our master and our Lord, then he is our master and our Lord without any reservations or without any qualification.

Now these words of our Lord, "If any man will come after me, let him deny himself," are frequently misunderstood. To deny oneself is not simply to deny oneself certain things. It is true that if we have denied ourselves, we shall desist from certain things, and our abstinence from certain things will, of course, be the proof that we are disciples of Christ. Discipleship means repentance, and repentance means turning from sin unto God. And if we turn from sin unto God, we turn from *specific* sins. We don't know what repentance is if we simply turn from sin in general because there never is, in this world, something that is general without the particulars. If we truly repent, we turn from specific sins, we abhor certain specific sins to which we ourselves have been addicted, and we abhor ourselves because of these particular sins. Repentance manifests itself in a very concrete and practical way by turning away from specific sins and idolatries. We turn to God from idols to serve the living God and to wait for his Son from heaven (1 Thess 1:9).

And if we turn from *specific* sins, we also turn from those things that, though they may not be sinful in themselves, become the occasion of sin to us. Jesus said to his disciples, "If thy right eye offend thee, pluck it out and cast it from thee. It is better for thee to enter into life with one eye than having two eyes to be cast into hell" (Matt 5:29). Now an eye is a precious gift of God, but if such a precious thing as our right eye becomes the occasion of stumbling, then we are to pluck it out and cast it from us. Not that we are to be guilty of self-mutilation, but the great truth is that however precious a thing may be, if—because of our weakness and sinfulness—it becomes the occasion of sin to us, then we are to turn from it.

But we are not getting to the heart of this text if we think that the text means that we are to deny to ourselves certain things. In fact, we may deny ourselves certain things, and that very self-denial becomes the means of cultivating self-righteousness. And self-righteousness is the very opposite of self-denial. Don't let us be deceived: there are lots of people in the world and in the professing church for whom Christianity, to a very large extent, consists in a few things from which they abstain, things that in themselves are not sinful at all but that are made, as it were, the criteria of godliness. If they abstain from just a few things, of which you know perfectly well, they think they are a very devoted and a consecrated Christian. My friends, this is a great deception of the Devil. In the days of the apostle Paul, he wrote that there would come in the last days deceivers, and one of their doctrines would be commanding people to abstain from meat, which God has commanded to be received with thanksgiving. And Paul calls that doctrine the doctrine of demons and the propaganda of seducing spirits (1 Tim 4:1–3). My friends, don't be deceived by that prohibitionism that is abroad in the world and that is so frequently identified with Christianity. It's a doctrine of demons, and it's the work of seducing spirits.

The great truth that this text does teach is that to deny ourselves means a renunciation of our own selves. Denying ourselves will certainly be a renunciation of sin, it will certainly be a renunciation of specific sin, and it certainly will be the renunciation of things that are not sinful in themselves if they become the occasion of sin for us. But what this text says, what this solemn Word of our Lord says, is that we must deny *ourselves*. We cannot appreciate this truth unless we realize what lies back of it. What lies back of that truth on the part of our Lord is an indictment against human nature. It is an indictment against human nature in its fallen state, of course, but nevertheless it is an indictment against our *person*. And it is to the effect that our *person* has so identified with sin that the first requirement is the denial of our own selves. Have you ever thought of it, my friend, with sufficient seriousness, that the first thing we have to be saved from is from our own selves?

Now sin is enmity against God; that's the essence of sin. It's the contradiction of God, and it's the contradiction of God all along the line of his perfection. But nevertheless, where there is that rebellious character, there is always something that goes along with it: the enthronement of our own selves in the place of God. That's it. Sin is first of all directed against God, but when it is directed against God we put *ourselves* in the place of God and worship and serve the creature rather than the Creator (Rom 1:25). The indictment that our Lord brings against us in this particular text is this: sin has taken such possession of us, the tangle of iniquity has so wrapped itself around us, that we ourselves are identified with that which is the contradiction of God and of his glory. Our own selves have become so identified with that which is the contradiction of God, that the first thing that has to be done, if we are to be disciples of the Savior, is that we must be saved from ourselves.

And that will manifest itself in our own exercise and engagement in this: that we deny ourselves. If Christ is our Savior and Lord, he saves us from ourselves, and therefore there must be that radical transformation that our Lord here calls self-denial. It means an abandonment of our own self-confidence and self-worship. It is the renunciation of our own self as the center of our all-absorbing interest, affection, and attention. Nothing less is the intent of our Lord; we cannot reduce this requirement to any lower terms than that.

Now you find the expression of such self-denial in many places in Scripture, but perhaps there is no place where it is put into such practical, concrete form as the confession of Job, the man of God: "I have heard of thee by the hearing of the ear: but now mine eye seeth thee. Wherefore I abhor myself, and repent in dust and ashes" (Job 42:5–6). And why did Job abhor himself? Because he got a vision of the matchless glory of God. And when he got a vision of the matchless glory of God, he saw his own self in the light of that glory, and he was prostrate in sackcloth. Oh, my friends, let us realize how subtle is iniquity; it is identified with our own person. The first thing that we have to be saved from is our own selves. And the first thing in the exercise of practical repentance is that we deny ourselves.

Now the second condition that Jesus lays down in this text for a disciple is that he must "take up his cross." Remember that to be a follower of Christ is to be a follower of him in total self-commitment. And so the two conditions that Jesus prescribes for being his disciple are self-denial and taking up our cross and following him.

Now that Word of our Lord has also been oftentimes misinterpreted, and it has been misinterpreted by well-intentioned, well-meaning people. Quite often some particular trial is called a person's cross. I don't know, are you accustomed to that terminology? In any case, I am accustomed to that notion that a particular trial is the cross of that person, and so taking up the cross is interpreted as submissive and patient endurance of that particular affliction. It is perfectly true that oftentimes there is one particular trial or temptation that torments a child of God. And, of course, it is perfectly true that if we have taken up our cross and followed Christ, we shall prove that fact by our patient and submissive endurance of any particular trial that God has suddenly pleased to call into our lot. That is perfectly true.

But there is no good ground for supposing that that is what our Lord means in Matthew 16:24 by the phrase, "take up his cross and follow me." There's something far more basic in our Lord's mind than simply that this person has to bear patiently the afflictions that God in his providence has sovereignly imposed on him or her. You see, this endurance is something that belongs to a *believer*, but Jesus is here dealing with something that belongs at the very *inception* of the Christian life, not simply with something that comes subsequently in order to test and prove the true believer.

Another line of thought that has oftentimes been applied to the condition of taking up one's cross is that Jesus is here referring to his own cross and that we are to take up and bear the cross of Christ. Now, in itself, there's a great deal of truth in that principle. And it is perfectly true that if we are Christ's disciples, then we are to embrace the cross of Christ for what it is. We are not to be ashamed of it, we are to reckon the cross of Christ as the price of our redemption, and we are to bring everything into captivity to that redemption that Christ wrought when he died upon the accursed tree. And it is perfectly true that every believer has, in a mysterious sense, died with Christ and has risen with him in his resurrection to newness of life. The cross of Christ must be always central in the faith, love, and hope of the believer, because it is the price of redemption and because the shedding of Jesus's blood binds a believer to the Savior—binds him to Jesus even in the requirement that he should deny himself and take up his cross.

But there is an obvious objection to that interpretation of taking up one's cross. Jesus is not here talking about his own cross. There's a very important distinction. Jesus doesn't say, "If anyone will come after me, let him take up *my* cross and follow me." Not at all! "If anyone will come after me, let him deny himself, and take up *his* cross" (Matt 16:24). There is a distinction between the cross that we bear and the cross that Christ bore. And we will very gravely distort the meaning of this text if we understand it to mean the cross of Christ, because, after all, although the cross is the price of our redemption, although we identify ourselves with it as that which wrought our redemption, nevertheless, we do not really bear the cross of Christ.

You see, it would be blasphemy to say that we bear the cross of Christ. *Christ alone* bore his cross, and we do not bear it at all in the sense that Jesus means in this instance. Don't you see that he alone went to Calvary; he alone bore the unparalleled and unspeakable agony of Calvary's accursed tree? We do not participate at all in the bearing of Christ's cross; he bore it all alone. "He hath trodden the winepress alone; and of the people there was none with him" (Isa 63:3). It can be very prejudicial to the uniqueness of the cross of Christ to represent our relation to it as a *bearing* of it. One of the greatest heresies that has been promulgated in the church of Christ is representing us as participating with the Redeemer in the bearing of his cross and the making of expiation and of reconciliation.

What then is the meaning of this particular condition of discipleship? It's not difficult to find the meaning if you study the context very carefully. Our Lord is here speaking of something that occurs at the inception of the believer's life, at the very beginning of discipleship. "If any man will come after me"—that is, follow me—"let him deny himself, and take up his cross." Of course, it isn't something that terminates at the beginning. If we take up our cross, then we continue to bear it; we don't lay it down. That's implied in the very figure that Jesus uses: let him take up his cross and follow me, that is, follow me *bearing* his cross. We are not to think of this as something that occurs just once-for-all and then is repudiated any more than we can think of self-denial as something that takes place once-for-all and then is repudiated. So, it is something that continues indeed, but, at the same time, it is something that occurs at the very inception of the believer's life.

So what is it? Just what is indicated by the context? The cross stands as the most reproachful and shameful of deaths. In the Near East at that particular time in the Roman empire, a criminal who was to be crucified had to bear his cross to the place of crucifixion. It is to that custom that our Lord is here clearly referring, which is a clue to the meaning. The cross is the symbol of death, and so if we are to follow Christ, we must be prepared to suffer death itself for his sake. That's what he means. But when he refers to the cross, he is also referring to the most reproachful, the most shameful, the most ignominious, and perhaps the most painful form of death. To be Jesus's disciple we must be prepared to die for his sake, and die not with all the glory of heroism, but die for his sake with all the associations of shame and reproach and ignominy and pain. That's what Jesus means. It is death with all the shame and dishonor that *this* world attaches to a death upon the tree.

There is confirmation of this interpretation in the context because Jesus proceeds, "For whosoever will save his life shall lose it: and whosoever will lose his life for my sake shall find it" (Matt 16:25). This verse refers to the saving of our own natural life in contrast with the loss of life eternal. It is therefore the losing of our natural life, the temporal life that we now possess, that is associated with crucifixion, and therefore associated with all that shame and ignominy that crucifixion implies.

Now, Jesus did not say, and he did not mean, that everyone who is a disciple must actually die a shameful death for his sake. And, of course, it is not at all Christian to crave martyrdom or to invite persecution unnecessarily. No, we ought to take all lawful endeavors to preserve our own life and the lives of others, but the point here is simply that we must take up the cross and therefore be prepared to endure all sorts of reproach—reproach to the extent of the most shameful and painful death—for the sake of Christ. That's it; be prepared. That is to say, our self-commitment to him will manifest itself in that preparedness to take all cost if his glory and his honor require it. If we prize our life (that is, our natural life) more than Christ's honor and will compromise his truth and glory rather than part with life, then we are not Christ's. That's the simple issue. We're not his if we'll compromise truth and justice and honor in order to preserve our life at the expense of Christ's glory.

That demand to take up our cross often comes to us in the form of the alternative between our means of livelihood and the truth and honor of Christ. How often do you hear the alibi, "I don't believe what I'm doing is right. I don't believe this type of business, in which I am engaged, is really right. I have to do many things that I don't believe are ethical, but I simply have to do it in order to live." Have you not heard that repeatedly? And if you have come to any years of understanding, have you not oftentimes been confronted with that very situation? You're required in terms of your earthly vocation, as you say, to do certain things that are not straight, that are not compatible with the principles that govern the Christian faith. Perhaps you're tempted, or perhaps you have even succumbed to the temptation, to say, "I don't like it. I don't believe it sits quite straight. I don't believe it's quite right. But nevertheless I just have to do it because I have to live."

Don't you see the fallacy? Hasn't it become very concrete and practical in that form? What have you said? "I have to live." What Jesus says is: "You *don't* have to live *at all*! If you have to live at the expense of conscience, it's better to die." That's just what Jesus is saying. If you have to live at the expense of a guilty conscience, if you have to live at the expense of the honor of

Christ, of fidelity to his commandments, then it's better to die. My friends, we *don't have to live*, but there's something that we *must* do, and that is honor Christ. *His* glory, the demands of *his* kingdom, and the commitment that belongs to *him* as Lord and Savior, is a commitment that demands of us that we shall *never* compromise truth, justice, and honor for the sake of a livelihood or for the sake of our own worldly advancement.

Now, that's the truth, and there it comes to us in a very concrete and practical and searching way: "If any man will be my disciple, let him take up his cross and follow me." That means nothing less than this: if we are Christ's disciples, we shall have to say in every concrete situation of our life, in every emergency in which we are placed, "Here is the gibbet for my execution, and it is the *only* alternative when the honor of Christ and loyalty to him demands it." Jesus is saying *nothing less* than that. Oh, my friend, I say it with all tenderness, but I must say it as the ambassador of Christ: we don't *have* to live, but we do *have* to be faithful to Christ. Otherwise, we are not his disciples.

My friends, where would we be if Christ had acted on that principle of preserving his life above all else? He wouldn't have gone to Calvary. He would have compromised before Pilate. He would have compromised before the High Priest. And he wouldn't have been the faithful witness. If Christ had acted on this principle—that is, the principle upon which so many of his professed followers act—there would be no redemption; Christ would never have gone to Calvary. Here is the great truth of what we are and what we shall be in the kingdom of our Lord and Savior, Jesus Christ.

Perhaps we have begun to see something of the exacting

character of Christ's demands. We are too ready to tone it down. Awareness of our own infirmity and the infirmity of others is too ready to lead us to make accommodations, to make certain reservations, and to try to make apologies for why we can evade the clear course and implications of Jesus's statement: "Let him take up his cross." But, my friends, however plausible that kind of argument may be, however much we may try to accommodate the Word of our Lord to our infirmity, to our weakness, and to our sinful lusts, there is no possibility of evading the simple course of that which Jesus here describes. When we try to accommodate the Word of Jesus to our weakness or to the weakness of others, whenever we begin to tamper with the stringency of the Word of him who is the truth, who is the faithful witness, and who went to Calvary's accursed tree that the Scripture might be fulfilled, we are guilty of iniquity. And we show by it that we are not following Christ. When Christ is our Lord, then we don't quarrel with his words; we take them in their simple meaning and in their simple directness. Jesus was supremely honest, and he was supremely honest because he was the truth. And it is the severity of that honesty and truth that will break upon us with awful avenge if we fail in this radical reach with our own selves and with the love of the world, which our own selves so frequently exemplify.

What is it in this particular situation and text that gives urgency to the severity of Jesus's words, to the conditions of discipleship that he here prescribes? Our Lord himself tells us in this very context: "For the Son of man shall come in the glory of his Father with his angels; and then he shall reward everyone according to his works" (Matt 16:27). Those are the words of

Jesus. The issues at stake are ultimate. If the issues at stake were simply those that belong to the span of this life, if it were simply a temporal perspective that Jesus had on this occasion, then it would be foolish to make things so severe and so stringent. But it was *not* the short span of life in this world that came within the perspective of our Lord when he spoke these words; it was the perspective of final reckoning, in the perspective of the judgment that he himself is ordained to execute. And as we view the present in the light of the final judgment, we see the grandeur—I say the grandeur and nothing less than the grandeur—of this particular word of our Lord.

It's severe, isn't it, that we have to part with life itself if the honor and glory of Christ demand it? It's severe indeed, and we don't like it. It's entirely contrary to the ethics and the philosophy of this world. But, my friends, I tell you that this is the severity of pure honesty and pure goodness. It is the severity of everlasting love because it is the severity of him who spoke in the light of the eternal reckoning of his final judgment, and the severity that takes account of that which will stand ultimate then in the pure light of judgment that is irrevocable. It was because Jesus was jealous for that kind of discipleship, that would be weighed in the balances and not found wanting, that he spoke these words: "If any man will come after me, let him deny himself, and take up his cross, and follow me." For he says, "Whosoever . . . shall be ashamed of me and of my words in this adulterous and sinful generation; of him also shall the Son of man be ashamed, when he cometh in the glory of his Father with the holy angels" (Mark 8:38). Jesus spoke these words of awful severity because he was, in his whole outlook, determined by *that* viewpoint that is based in the reality of ultimate issue. So, it is the severity of goodness, of honesty, and of truth, and it is the severity of eternal love.

My friends, may we have written upon our hearts, as with the point of a pen, the requirements that Jesus, as the faithful witness and as the first begotten from the dead (Rev 1:5), enunciates in this particular text: "If any man will come after me"—if any man will be my follower, if any man will be a Christian—"let him deny himself, and take up his cross, and follow me." That is the person of whom Jesus will not be ashamed when he cometh in the glory of his Father with the holy angels. May our reckonings, my friends, be the reckonings that are dictated by eternal issue, by the issue of right, ultimate, unerring, and irrevocable judgment. And when our thinking is dictated by these issues, then we shall add our "amens" to the Word of our Lord, and we shall be ready to say, "Here is the gibbet for my crucifixion if the honor and glory of my Redeemer demands it."

Oh God, thou the Redeemer who art exalted at the right hand of power, to thee we come imploring thy grace, that thy Word may be written upon our hearts, that it may bring conviction to our consciences, and that by thy Spirit there may be generated in our hearts that faith by which we shall count all things as loss for the excellency of the knowledge of Christ Jesus our Lord. May we be able to say in truth, with all its implications for life and for death, that to us to live is Christ and to die is gain. And may we be able to reiterate with thy servant that we know nothing among men save Jesus Christ and him crucified.

May we know, oh Lord, what it is to be captives to a crucified, a risen, an exalted, and a coming Lord, and may we have the joy of those who are the bondservants of Jesus Christ. Have mercy upon us, oh Lord, and wash away our sins. Bind us to the Savior in all the efficacy of his finished work, in all the glory of his person, and in all the perfection of his high-priestly, kingly ministry at thy right hand, that we may know him as the Lord of Glory, as the one who is exalted far above all might and dominion and power, and who will come again to receive his people unto himself and will give them a kingdom that will be everlasting.

Oh Lord, bless our meeting together, seal thy Word upon our hearts, and seal us to the Savior in the bond of complete and total commitment, that we may know none save Jesus Christ and him crucified. In all the emergencies that arise in this life and in every situation in which we are placed, may the honor of Christ be paramount and may we count him to be, indeed, the chiefest among ten thousand and altogether lovely. For his name's sake, amen.

12

Lazarus and the Rich Man

And he said unto him, "If they hear not Moses and the prophets, neither will they be persuaded, though one rose from the dead."
—Luke 16:31

The account that our Lord gives of the rich man and Lazarus regards what we call *the intermediate state*—that is to say, the state between death and the resurrection. In this account, our Lord draws the veil aside and gives us some insight into the issue of everlasting bliss and irrevocable woe in the irreversible beyond. A great many questions arise in connection with this account that our Lord gives, and we may not be able to solve all the difficulties of interpretation that arise in connection with this particular passage of Scripture. But there is a great danger that we may sometimes allow the difficulties, which encompass the interpretation of certain passages of Scripture, to blind our vision to the perfectly apparent lessons that the passage conveys. There are difficulties in Luke 16:19–31 simply because we know so little about this intermediate state, but these should not by any means obscure the perfectly obvious lessons that this passage is intended to convey.

There are three subjects in this passage around which I shall try to gather a few of the pertinent thoughts and lessons: the contrasts, the irreversible states, and the rich man's alibi.

First of all, we have the contrasts intimated in this passage. In respect to life in this world, there is the contrast between the luxurious splendor of the rich man and the poverty and physical misery of Lazarus. The rich man was clothed in purple and fine linen and fared sumptuously every day. This earthly life was for that rich man the bed of luxury; in this life he received his good things. The destitution of Lazarus is apparent from the facts that he was laid at the rich man's gate, that he was full of sores, that he desired to be fed with the crumbs of morsels that fell from the rich man's table, and that the very dogs came and licked his sores.

We are not to suppose that this poor man got none of these discarded portions of food that fell from the rich man's table. There would seem to be no purpose of his remaining at the gate of the rich man unless he received some of those morsels. But whether he received of those morsels or not, his poverty is emphasized by the fact that it was on *such* fare that he desired to be fed; it was in *that* way that he sought to satisfy his hunger. And you must remember: how great must have been the destitution of that poor man when his ambition respecting food was to be fed with the crumbs that were cast out from the rich man's table. A man must be destitute, indeed, if he is satisfied with such despised fare.

It is difficult to be certain whether the licking of the sores by the dogs is to be regarded as an amelioration of his suffering or as an intensification of that suffering, whether we are to regard it as an act of kindness on the part of the dogs or as an indication that the man was so helpless that he could not even protect himself from that particular kind of molestation. In any case, the action of the dogs emphasizes this poor man's extremity. His sores were exposed; they were not bound up; he was not cared for by others who could alleviate his misery and minister to his needs. It is all summed up in the fact that he was the companion of dogs. It may even be that the dogs were at the rich man's gate for the very same purpose as the poor man was there—namely, that they also might eat from the morsels that fell from the rich man's table and that were cast out at his gate. If that is so, then this poor man had some competition for these morsels. And since he was apparently very ill and very much weakened, it would be hard for him, indeed, to compete with the agility that characterizes hungry dogs.

Oh, you see how graphic is this description that our Lord gives in order to portray the extreme wretchedness and poverty of this poor man, as far as life in this world is concerned. That is the express purpose of Jesus's portrayal: the total contrast between the sumptuous life of the rich man and the miserable and wretched physical condition of the poor man.

That contrast, however, which our Lord so graphically portrays, is only the prelude to another: the contrast of complete reversal. There are many details that notify that particular contrast. The reversal begins at the point of death—not that the event of death itself intimates any contrast, for we read that it came to pass that the poor man died and the rich man also died (Luke 16:22). You see, that is a very striking similarity, and that similarity is full of meaning: the poor man died and the rich man also died.

When we are informed that the rich man was buried and no reference is made to the burial of the poor man, we need not suppose that Lazarus had no burial. It's possible that he had no burial, but the absence of reference to the poor man's burial, when the burial of the rich man is expressly stated, may have the very purpose of accenting the despised condition of Lazarus compared to the pomp that would have attended the rich man's burial. There is still an intimation of contrast between the unostentatious way in which the corpse of the poor man was disposed of and the pomp and parade that would have attended the burial of the rich man.

Or it may be, as has been proposed by many, that the burial of the rich man is shaped in very sharp contrast with what is stated respecting the poor man, namely, that he was carried by the angels into Abraham's bosom. Note the sequences in both cases: "And it came to pass, that the poor man died, and was carried by the angels into Abraham's bosom," and then you read, "The rich man also died, and was buried" (Luke 16:22). You can visualize the retinue in the burial of the rich man; there was perhaps quite a great deal of parade in connection with the conveyance of his mortal remains to the tomb. And then, in contrast with that, remember that Lazarus was carried too—but he was carried by the angels into Abraham's bosom. The rich man's body was carried to the tomb, but Lazarus, as respects his spirit, was carried by the angels into Abraham's bosom.

Whatever the intended contrasts were in this particular case, we cannot but note that at the event of death (though not in the event of death itself), the total reversal begins to appear. The poor man was carried by the angels into Abraham's bosom. What corresponds to this in the case of the rich man? "And in hell he lifted up his eyes, being in torments" (Luke 16:23). The reference in both cases is to the disembodied spirit of the persons concerned. As to his body, Lazarus was no doubt buried or cast away in some particular place away from the proximity to the rich man's home. As to his body, Lazarus was laid away, and as to *his* body, the rich man was buried. But as to his spirit, the poor man went to Abraham's bosom, and as to *his* spirit, the rich man went to hell.

In the fact that Lazarus was carried by the angels into Abraham's bosom, we are reminded of something in the teaching of Scripture that is, indeed, very precious: it is that the angels are "ministering spirits sent forth to minister for them who are the heirs of salvation" (Heb 1:14). And the ministry of angels does not terminate at death. I suppose it would be very easy for us to think that this is simply a figurative expression: "and was carried by the angels into Abraham's bosom." But nothing would be more contrary to the total representation of Scripture. If angels are ministering spirits sent forth to minister to those who are the heirs of salvation, do you think that that ministry is going to terminate at the point of death? Oh, no, not at all. We may be perfectly assured that the guardianship that the angels dispense to the people of God in this life does not terminate at the event of death but ensures safe conduct of the disembodied spirit to its heavenly home. What love, what tenderness, what care that this bespeaks on the part of these angels, who are the emissaries of God. Not only does it bespeak the love and the tenderness and the care on the part of the angels but also the love and the tenderness and the care on the part of God himself, because they are but the instruments of *his* love and kindness.

Now, of course, it is quite difficult to determine what exactly is Abraham's bosom. We have very few references to such in the Scripture (in fact, I think this is the only explicit reference). But the figure that is used here is used elsewhere by our Lord when he says that many shall come from the east and from the west and from the north and from the south and shall recline with Abraham and Isaac and Jacob in the kingdom of heaven (Matt 8:11). The figure here is really that of reclining in the kingdom of heaven. When it is said that Lazarus was in Abraham's bosom, you must not try to visualize that in terms of the way in which a mother hugs her child to her bosom, but something after the analogy of that which happened at the Last Supper when John reclined upon the bosom of his Lord (John 13:23). It is a figurative expression of the intimacy of relationship that there was between Lazarus and the saints of God who had gone before immediately upon the dissolution of his life.

What a contrast between that and the rich man. He was in hell. And because he was there, he was in torments. It's rather remarkable that not only is it said that Lazarus was in a place that implies bliss, but he also is represented as being in the most intimate fellowship with the father of the faithful, and there is nothing said about the company of the rich man. Lazarus was in the bosom of Abraham, that is to say in the most intimate fellowship in the kingdom of God with Abraham and therefore with all the saints of God. But there is nothing said about the company of the rich man. He was in hell, and because he was in hell, he was in torments. And the whole plot is concentrated upon that particular contrast.

There is no good reason for regarding the word that is used here to designate the place of his abode other than just what we call hell—the place of woe, the place associated with torments—and if you read the text very carefully, you will find that that is the implication: "and in hell he lifted up his eyes, being in torments." His being in torments is the very necessary result or consequence of his being in hell. It was a place of unmitigated pain, and pain of the most agonizing character because the plural is used: "being in torments." The extremity of torment is emphasized by the very request that he addressed to Abraham. You may say, "Oh, how foolish, what a ridiculous request: to send Lazarus that he might dip the tip of his finger in water and place it upon the rich man's tongue because he was tormented in this way. What comfort would it be to have the momentary consolation of the touch of a cold finger upon his tongue? Oh, how momentary!" Well, you see how graphic it is! It represents how extreme was the torment of this man when such a momentary touch of comfort would be in complete contrast with his condition of unalloyed, unmitigated pain and torment in the place of woe.

There are, again, questions that arise in connection with this passage. It was as respects their disembodied spirits that they were in their respective abodes. It was the disembodied spirit of the rich man that was in hell, and it was the disembodied spirit of the poor man that was in Abraham's bosom. So, then, how could there be physical sensation? Did the rich man have a tongue when he was in his disembodied state in the place of woe? And how could Lazarus be conceived of as having a finger, which he could dip in water and place upon the tongue of the tormented rich man? You see how many questions we will naturally raise in connection with this account.

It is not well for us to presume to be wise on such questions since we know so little about the disembodied state. And what do we know, but that in the disembodied state there may be that which corresponds to physical sensation? The spirit indeed is disembodied—it is separated from the body—but what do we know about the way in which pain and torment will affect that disembodied spirit? We know nothing about it because we have no experience of disembodied spirits, and it is just an example of the foolish way in which we are so liable to raise objections when it would be well for us to bow in humility and acknowledge our ignorance. Our Lord was speaking not in ignorance but in knowledge. He was the person who himself had come down out of heaven. He was the person who himself had created heaven and earth. Who are we, in the puny compass of our minds, to call into question the reality or the veracity or the meaning of that which he has stated on this particular occasion?

We must not allow such details to interfere with the obvious truth being conveyed and portrayed by our Lord, namely, the unrelieved anguish of the rich man and his abode in the place of woe. It is a place where he is alert of his own identity and where he is in the experience of unalleviated torment. That is hell: a place of intense consciousness, where all comfort is absent and where anguish is manifold and unalloyed. The plot serves to aggravate this contrast between the opulence of the rich man in his former state and his abject misery in the present. "Son, remember that thou in thy lifetime receivedst thy good things, and likewise Lazarus evil things: but now he is comforted, and thou art tormented" (Luke 16:25).

That is the final contrast, and oh, how eloquent in that it means a complete reversal. It is a complete reversal, in the case of the poor man, from abject misery to unalloyed consolation in paradise, in fellowship with the saints of God, with Abraham, Isaac, and Jacob. And it is a complete reversal, in the case of the rich man, from all the opulence and wealth and consolation that he enjoyed in this life to the abject, unalloyed misery and anguish and pain in the place of woe. That is the lesson that we cannot escape, the apparent and obvious truth that our Lord means to convey to us by this particular account.

Now, second, we have the irreversible state. It is Abraham who is still speaking, and he says, "And in all these things between us and you there is a great gulf fixed, in order that those who would pass from us to you may not be able, neither may they pass from thence to us" (Luke 16:26).

Again, it is quite natural for us to raise some questions in connection with that statement. If a great gulf is fixed between the two abodes, how could there be any converse between them? How can they speak to one another at a great distance? It just shows the folly of our supercilious and superficial objections. What experience do we have of spatial conditions or of conditions of communication in the unseen, invisible world? We know so little about the unseen world of spirits that our present conceptions of space may help us very little indeed. There may be a great distance and yet be the freest communication. Can we not ourselves speak to each other at great distances? What do we know as to conditions in the unseen world? So, let us cease our objections.

Another question might be raised about the immutability of the states. What Abraham says is this: that "there is a great gulf fixed: so that those who would pass from us to you might not be able, neither may they pass from hence to us" (Luke 16:26). And the way that Abraham speaks would seem to indicate that there would be some desire on the part of persons to go from heaven to hell and others to go from hell to heaven. You may raise the question, would any people want to go from Abraham's bosom to the place of woe? Again, we know very little about the unseen world, but in any case it may simply be a rhetorical way of expressing the great truth that there is absolutely no commutation after death. It is noteworthy that Abraham makes a general statement. He does not simply say to the rich man, "You may not come hence," and he does not simply say that Lazarus may not go hence to hell. That is implied, but Abraham makes a general statement to the effect that the lifetime is the sphere of opportunity and that there is no commutation after death. It is one of the most conclusive evidences that there is no such thing as future probation. We are not able to understand a great many of the details of this passage, but we cannot miss the plain import that there is no passing over from the place of bliss to the place of woe, nor is there any passing over from the place of woe to the place of bliss. And these are the words of him who has the keys of death and hell (Rev 1:18).

Now, finally, we have the rich man's alibi. It has been said that the rich man in hell was not totally reprobate because he still had some altruistic sentiment; he still had some concern for the welfare of his five brethren. He did not wish for them to come into the place of torment. And so it will be said, "Oh, he wasn't completely reprobate after all; he wasn't completely depraved.

Therefore, the place of woe that is spoken of here cannot mean the place of total reprobation or total abandonment. And, after all, this is only a parable; there is some redeeming feature about that rich man after all. He was still altruistic." But when you examine the passage very carefully, you will find that we are not told that the motive of his request, respecting the sending of messengers to his five brethren, was the desire to do his brethren good. We simply do not know what the motivation of that particular request was, but we are not told that it sprang from some love in his bosom for these five brethren.

But we do know this: that the whole attitude of mind that underlay that particular request was one that was an assault upon the justice, wisdom, and goodness of God, because he was, in effect, requesting a method that was in direct opposition to the way that God had prescribed for escape from the wages of sin and the attainment of eternal life. In this very plea that one should go from the dead toward his brothers, the rich man is insinuating that if he had had some such opportunity, if he had received a message from the beyond or messengers from the dead, then he wouldn't have come into this place of torment. He is insinuating that he had not received sufficient warning or sufficient instruction, and that is a direct assault upon the justice and the wisdom and the goodness of God. His repeated insistence that a voice from the dead would be effective in the case of his brethren clothed the persistent perversity of his thought, because he is insinuating that *that* is the way whereby men can come to repentance, that *that* is the way whereby men may escape the place of torment. And, therefore, he has set himself in direct contradiction to the wisdom and grace and goodness of God.

There is not the slightest indication that the truth as expressed by Abraham—"they have Moses and the prophets" (Luke 16:29) —had any effect in bringing about a change of conception and attitude in the rich man's reprobate mind. You see that even in the place of woe there was the subtlety of attack upon the very integrity of God. When you go back to the beginning, what was the spear-point of Satan's temptation? It was attack upon the integrity of God when Satan said, "God doth know that in the day ye eat thereof, then your eyes shall be opened" (Gen 3:5). You find that same malignity, that same subtlety, in this very attitude of the rich man. In a subtle, apparently plausible way, he was pleading something that was a direct attack upon the integrity of God. By insinuating that he had not received sufficient opportunity, he was laying the blame for his condition at the very door of God. And that is the very height, the very essence, of blasphemy.

The great truth expressed in Abraham's reply to the rich man's plea is that of the sufficiency of the revelation that God has given: "They have Moses and the prophets; let them hear them," and again, "If they hear not Moses and the prophets, neither will they be persuaded, though one rose from the dead" (Luke 16:29, 31). Oh, what an eloquent emphasis upon this great truth. The rich man made his request to the wrong person; he made his request at the wrong time; he made his request in the wrong place; and he made his request with wrong, God-assaulting, God-contradicting content. But though the rich man made his request to the wrong person at the wrong time from the wrong place and in the wrong way, Abraham speaks the truth.

And the great truth that he is speaking is this: God has given us a sufficient revelation. We would express this in our context by saying, "God has given us the Scriptures." Abraham appeals to the Scripture that was in existence at that particular time: "They have Moses and the prophets." That is just as much as to say, "They have the Old Testament; let them hear it." Our situation is this: that we have Scripture in its entirety! This Word of God is living and powerful; it is the power of God unto salvation (Rom 1:16). It is the bearer and the path and the way of life. It is a complete misconception of the way that infinite wisdom and grace *have* ordained to desire or imagine any other way. And it is wickedness and presumption of the deepest kind to demand another way as the basis or as the means of repentance and faith. That is the wickedness that the rich man's plea discloses. And that is the wickedness that this account of our Lord reveals. Surely, that is the great lesson for our responsibility, for our duty, for our repentance, and for our faith. That is the message that this passage enforces.

Thus it is, as I said at the beginning, the issues of life and death, the issue of irreversible destiny, and the issues of everlasting bliss and of irrevocable woe that our Lord unveils to us in Luke 16:19–31. In connection with these subjects, he is enforcing this great message that we don't need emissaries from heaven or hell because we have God's own Word to inform us and warn us. If we reject God's testimony, emissaries from heaven or from hell will not bring us to repentance and faith and new obedience. The only basis of faith and repentance is the Word of God and that Word we now have in its completeness and its finality. "To the law and to the testimony! If they speak not according to this word, surely there is no morning for them" (Isa 8:20; ASV). There is no light of day that will dawn upon those who reject the testimony of the Word of God. It is the blackness of darkness forever that is the only alternative to the rejection of the sufficiency and the finality of that Scripture, of that revelation that God has deposited for us in his Holy Word.

Oh, it is very easy for people to say that no one has ever come back from the dead to tell us what is beyond. And it is very easy for us to resort to "them who have familiar spirits and to wizards who peep and who mutter" (Isa 8:19). It is very easy for us to lapse into the errors and the mystifications of what is called spiritism or spiritualism. My friends, that whole traffic—whether it be simply fraud or whether there be in it something of the sinister agency of the demonic world (and the latter I verily believe)—has written across its very brow the marks of the pit. "They have Moses and the prophets; *let them hear them.* . . . If they hear not Moses and the prophets, neither will they be persuaded, though one rose from the dead." Visitors from heaven or hell would not bring us a message that would have the *validity* or the *authority* or the *power* of the Word of God! In particular, such a message would have nothing of the validity or the authority or the power of him who is the speaker on this occasion: the Lord himself, who is the Word of God incarnate, who is himself the way, the truth, and the life (John 1:14; 14:6).

My friends, we have unveiled to us in this passage something of the great mystery that surrounds the intermediate state. What we have sufficiently unveiled in Luke 16 and also in other passages gives us the necessary warning and the necessary consolation. We are faced with the alternatives of irreversible destiny: everlasting bliss or irrevocable woe. And the way of escape from the wages of sin, which is everlasting death, that place of woe and of torment into which the rich man fell, is none other than obedience to the revealed will of God. "All Scripture is given by inspiration of God, and is profitable for doctrine, for reproof, for correction, for instruction in righteousness: that the man of God may be perfect, thoroughly furnished unto all good works" (2 Tim 3:16–17).

My friends, in conclusion, let us avoid the subtleties that emanate from the pit and that are the marks of the pit itself. Those subtleties often have a plausible appearance, but they do dishonor to the sufficiency and the finality and the perfection of that revelation that God has given us, that gospel that God has deposited for us in his Word, which is the power of God unto salvation. That is the great lesson. Let us learn it with humility; let us learn it with a persistence of faith. "To the law and to the testimony! If they speak not according to this word, surely there is no morning for them" (Isa 8:20; ASV).

Oh Lord our God, we pray thee that thou wouldst bless to us our meditation upon thy Word and cause it to take root downward and spring forth upward, that we may receive it in faith and love, lay it up in our hearts, and practice it in our lives, as we are confronted with the solemnities of life and of death, of time and eternity, of heaven and of hell. Oh grant unto us that we may be among those people who are in this life indeed poor and afflicted and oftentimes tormented, but who have the hope of an everlasting inheritance, the inheritance incorruptible and undefiled and that fadeth not away, preserved in heaven for them that believe. And thou, oh Father, Son, and Holy Spirit, accept all our praise in Christ forever. Amen.

13

This I Call to Mind

> *This I recall to my mind, therefore have I hope. It is of the Lord's mercies that we are not consumed, because his compassions fail not . . . The Lord is my portion, saith my soul; therefore will I hope in him.*
> —Lamentations 3:21–22, 24

The prophet Jeremiah lived in those days when Judah was carried into captivity. The book of Lamentations consists of the lamentations of Jeremiah connected particularly with the desolations of Zion. That is perfectly obvious from the preceding and the succeeding parts of this book. At the beginning of the first chapter, we read:

> How doth the city sit solitary, that was full of people! How is she become as a widow! She that was great among the nations, and princess among the provinces, how is she become tributary! She weepeth sore in the night, and her tears are on her cheeks: among all her lovers she hath none to comfort her: all her friends have dealt treacherously with her, they are become her enemies. Judah has gone

into captivity because of affliction, and because of great servitude: she dwelleth among the heathen, she findeth no rest: all her persecutors overtook her between the straits. (Lam 1:1–3)

And again at the beginning of the second chapter:

How hath the Lord covered the daughter of Zion with a cloud in his anger, and cast down from heaven unto the earth the beauty of Israel, and remembered not his footstool in the day of his anger! The Lord hath swallowed up all the habitations of Jacob, and hath not pitied: he hath thrown down in his wrath the strong holds of the daughter of Judah; he hath brought them down to the ground: he hath polluted the kingdom and the princes thereof. He hath cut off in his fierce anger all the horn of Israel. (Lam 2:1–3)

And yet again, at the beginning of the fourth chapter, there is a similar refrain:

How is the gold become dim! How is the most fine gold changed! The stones of the sanctuary are poured out in the top of every street. The precious sons of Zion, comparable to fine gold, how are they esteemed as earthen pitchers, the work of the hands of the potter! (Lam 4:1–2)

These are Jeremiah's lamentations, but they are the lamentations of Jeremiah because of the Lord's indignation against

Zion, against the people of his possession. We read that "the Lord's portion is his people" and that "Jacob is the lot of his inheritance" (Deut 32:9), but now Jacob has gone into captivity and is trodden down: "Our gold is become dim." The Lord's indignation is perfectly apparent even at the beginning of our chapter. "I am the man that hath seen affliction by the rod of his wrath" (Lam 3:1).

Jeremiah was so identified with the welfare of Zion in his interests, in his affections, in his aspirations, and in his hopes, that mourning and weeping now took hold of the inmost recesses of his being. That is the portrait that we have in this particular book. Can it be otherwise with us today? It is one thing to read this book of Lamentations as a commentary on the past, but it also has relevance for us. "These things happened . . . for our admonition, upon whom the ends of the ages are come" (1 Cor 10:11). "All Scripture is given by inspiration of God and is profitable for doctrine, for reproof, for correction, and for the instruction which is in righteousness, that the man of God may be perfect, thoroughly furnished unto every good work" (2 Tim 3:16–17).

So, the book of Lamentations has a great lesson for us. Our interests, affections, aspirations, and hopes must likewise be identified with that to which the Old Testament Zion corresponded: the church of Christ. If we do not identify ourselves—in our interests, affections, aspirations, and hopes—with the church of Christ, then we do not identify ourselves in our faith and affection with him who is the head of the church. You can never separate Christ from his church or the church from Christ. Christ is meaningless apart from his interest in the church; it was for the sake of the church that he came into this world. "Christ loved *the church* and gave himself for it; that he might sanctify and cleanse it by the washing of water by the word to present it to himself a glorious church" (Eph 5:25–27).

And, as we can never think of Christ apart from the church or the church apart from Christ, so our own interest in Christ can very well be gauged by our interest in his church. We can well take up the lamentations of Jeremiah as we may take up the lamentations of another prophet: "Our holy and our beautiful house, where our fathers praised thee, is burned up with fire: and all our pleasant things are laid waste" (Isa 64:11). We cannot disassociate ourselves from the situation in which the church of Christ finds itself. There is a corporate responsibility, and we cannot possibly disassociate our own responsibility from that which afflicts the church of Christ in our particular day and generation. We cannot shrug our shoulders and say that we have no responsibility for the plight in which the church of Christ finds itself when our gold has become dim and our wine mixed with water (Lam 4:1; Isa 1:22). There is the grave danger that people in a particular location or in a particular denomination will shrug their shoulders and say that we have no responsibility. My friends, there is a corporate responsibility that we cannot divest ourselves of.

Not only is there this corporate responsibility for the defection and the impurity that are so rampant in the professing church of Christ, but we are responsible for our own individual, personal iniquities. Another prophet said, "I will bear the indignation of the Lord, because I have sinned against him, until he plead my cause, and execute judgment for me" (Mic 7:9). You cannot read this chapter of the lamentations of Jeremiah without recognizing, on the part of Jeremiah himself, a profound sense of his own sin and the indignation of the Lord against him for his iniquity. "I am the man that hath seen affliction by the rod of his wrath. He hath led me, and brought me into darkness, but not into light" (Lam 3:1–2). There is, here, profound recognition of his own individual, personal iniquity, and frustration in self-humiliation before God.

Not only do we find the reflection in this chapter of the indignation of the Lord against the sin of Zion and even against Jeremiah himself because of *his* own personal, individual iniquity, but we also find a reflection of those mysterious dispensations of God's providence that are ever tending to bewilder even the people of God. God's providences to his people are not all dictated by his anger and indignation. There are indeed providences that are the expression of his indignation for his people's iniquity, and there are indeed dispensations of chastisement, which, of course, are always for sin and for its correction. But there are also those dispensations of God's providence that do not find their explanation in God's indignation against the particular recipients of these dispensations.

If you take, for example, the patriarch Job, God did not visit him with afflictions because of indignation for his iniquity. Not at all! There was something in the unseen spirit world that was the explanation of Job's affliction. And yet, notwithstanding the fact that the dispensations of God's providence to him were not dictated by God's indignation against him, Job could nevertheless say, "Behold, I go forward, but he is not there; and backward, but I cannot perceive him: On the left hand, where he doth work, but I cannot behold him: he hideth himself on the right hand, that I cannot see him" (Job 23:8–9). Job was encompassed with great darkness and bewilderment because he did not understand at that time the unseen purpose of God in the tribulation that overtook him.

So it is often the case with the people of God, as Jeremiah says in this very chapter, "He hath set me in dark places, as they that be dead of old. He hath hedged me about, that I cannot get out: he hath made my chain heavy. Also when I cry and shout, he shutteth out my prayer" (Lam 3:6–8). And again, "Thou hast covered thyself with a cloud, that our prayer should not pass through" (Lam 3:44). When the people of God have to walk in darkness and have no light in the mystery or the abyss of God's providential dealings towards them, and they cannot understand the reason, it causes the bewilderment and the distress of heart, mind, and soul reflected in Lamentations 3.

Now all of that is simply by way of introduction, in order to appreciate that pinnacle of praise, of thanksgiving, and of hope that we find in the words of our text. In the face of all this perplexity, darkness, dismay, even bewilderment, in the face of this profound sense of the indignation of the Lord against Zion and against the prophet himself individually, is there any outlet of confidence, joy, and hope for the prophet in this unspeakable situation of grief and sorrow and travail? Yes, there is! "This I recall to mind, therefore have I hope." And what is the secret of this hope? Jeremiah remembered certain things; there were certain considerations that he called to mind, that entered into his thought, notwithstanding the bewilderment, the darkness, and the dismay that possessed the inmost recesses of his heart and being. Very briefly I'm going to call your attention to these particular considerations that the prophet called to mind.

First of all, there is his own self-humiliation before God: "It is of the Lord's mercies that we are not consumed" (Lam 3:22). The prophet recognized that he had not received, that there had not been visibly dealt to him, that which was equal to the measure of his deserts. God had visited him with much less affliction than his iniquities deserved (Ezra 9:13). We find this expression of his own self-humiliation and his abasement before God so eloquently set forth in Lamentations 3:28–30:

> He sitteth alone [that is, the person who is in this particular situation of self-humiliation] and keepeth silence, because he hath borne it upon him. He putteth his mouth in the dust; if so be there may be hope. He giveth his cheek to him that smiteth him: he is filled full with reproach.

He giveth his very cheek to God himself, who smiteth him! Here is humble recognition of what the prophet says again in a later part of this chapter, "Why should a living man complain, a man for the punishment of his sins?" (Lam 3:39).

Self-humiliation is far too frequently overlooked in our relationship to God and is the very starting point for deliverance. Of course, it is the very starting point for deliverance even at the inception of the Christian life, but it is also the starting point for deliverance for the people of God themselves when they are under God's afflicting hand and when they are experiencing those bewildering dispensations of his providence. Self-humiliation before God recognizes that however bitterly God may be dealing with us, however severe may be the dispensations of his providence, however stinging may be the aloes of his holy displeasure and wrath, we have not received anything yet that is equal to the measure of our deserts. Why should a living man complain for the punishment of his sins, when he thinks that what he deserves is not the afflictions of this life—however severe they may be—but the blackness of darkness forever (Jude 13)?

I tell you, my friends, that a great deal of the superficiality that is in the church of God today, and a great deal of the impiety that even characterizes the people of God, is due to this failure to recognize that we are ourselves in the presence of God. We fail to measure ourselves by the criterion of God's holiness, his majesty, his justice, and his truth. When we apprehend the glory and the majesty of God, then the only reaction that is proper and that can be appropriate to our situation is that of the prophet Isaiah: "Woe is me! for I am undone; because I am a man of unclean lips, and I dwell in the midst of a people of unclean lips" (Isa 6:5).

That, my friends, is the starting point for any deliverance—deliverance at the inception of Christian profession and faith, and deliverance in the pilgrimage of the people of God as they experience the bitterness of God's dispensations toward them. We shall never properly assess God's dispensations to us—whatever their character and whatever their purpose in the divine mind—until we prostrate ourselves before God in the recognition of our own iniquity. "It is of the Lord's mercies that we are not consumed. . . . Why should a living man complain, a man for the punishment of his sins?" (Lam 3:22, 39).

The second element in this text that fills the mind of the prophet with hope, with confidence, and with expectation—and that likewise must fill our minds with hope and expectation—is the mercy and the compassion of the Lord. "This I recall to mind, therefore have I hope. It is of the Lord's mercies that we are not consumed, because his compassions fail not. They are new every morning: great is thy faithfulness" (Lam 3:21–23). I tell you again, my friends, that we cannot have any true appreciation of those provisions of God's grace for our deliverance at the very inception of the Christian life on into the pilgrimage of the people of God until we have an apprehension of the mercy of God in Christ Jesus.

The fact that God is merciful is the outlet from our misery—our outlet from our misery at the beginning and in every onward step of our pilgrimage until we come to the "city which hath the foundations, of which God is the builder and the maker" (Heb 11:10). The fact that the Lord is the Lord God, merciful and gracious, slow to wrath, abundant in loving kindness and truth, forgiving iniquity and transgression and sin (Exod 34:6–7)—that's the outlet. You can see this so conspicuously in the case of Jeremiah. It is that great truth so emblazoned on one of the psalms so familiar to us: "For the Lord is good; his mercy is everlasting; and his truth endureth to all generations" (Ps 100:5). Don't you see that what the prophet here lays hold upon is the mercy and the faithfulness of God, and these are the key notes of this great psalm of thanksgiving: the Lord is good, his mercy is everlasting, and his truth—his *faithfulness*—endureth to all generations.

May I plead very humbly, my friends, that as we prostrate ourselves before God's majesty in recognition of what our iniquity deserves, let us also have the apprehension of the mercy of

God in Christ Jesus. Let us reach out our hand to him in faith. Oh, let it be humble faith, faith as of a grain of mustard seed. Nevertheless, in the outreach of that faith, we have the guarantee of experiencing the exaltation that the prophet Jeremiah reflects in this particular chapter.

The third element that Jeremiah recalls to mind, and therefore has hope, is found in verse 24 of this chapter: "The Lord is my portion, saith my soul; therefore will I hope in him." The Lord is my *portion*. You don't ascend to a higher pinnacle of faith in the whole of Scripture than that which the prophet enunciates at this particular point: "The Lord is my portion." We read, of course, in the Scripture that "the Lord's portion is his people" and that "Jacob is the lot of his inheritance" (Deut 32:9). God has peculiar delight in his people, which is why he sent his Son into the world that he might redeem his people from all iniquity and present them "faultless before the presence of his glory with exceeding joy" (Jude 24). The Lord's portion is his people; Jacob is the lot of his inheritance. But you also have the complementary truth: the Lord is the portion of his people.

Perhaps there is nothing in the New Testament that enunciates what you might call the very apex of the Christian privilege, the very apex of God's provision of grace, than that expression of the apostle Paul that "we might be filled unto all the fullness of God" (Eph 3:19). Being filled unto all the fullness of God is the New Testament counterpart of this Old Testament concept of the Lord being the portion of his people. It means that we come into the very possession of God himself, that God is ours. If Christ is ours, then all things are ours, and God himself is ours. You find it in that very psalm that we were singing,

"Whom have I in heaven but thee? And there is none upon earth that I desire besides thee. My flesh and my heart faileth: but God is the strength of my heart, and my portion forever" (Ps 73:25–26).

I tell you, my friends, that eternity will not exhaust the meaning of that truth that God is our portion; we can only have a very dim glimmering of it even at the very best. But it is something that is *true*, and it is something that you are to appropriate. "The Lord is my portion, saith my soul." And if God himself is the portion of his people, surely everything in his dispensations to them is the unrolling of his own favor and his own mercy. If God is our possession, then no evil can befall us (Ps 91:9–10).

That's the third; now the fourth: and that is hope. "The Lord is good unto them that wait for him, to the soul that seeketh him. It is good that a man should both hope and quietly wait for the salvation of the Lord" (Lam 3:25–26). Oh, my friends, what endless misery we reap for ourselves, and what dishonor we do to the God who is the portion of his people, when we take illegitimate methods of getting away from the bitter dispensations of God's providence. We must wait. God doesn't dispense to his people all his favor in this life or at any one time in this life. We have to wait; we have to have hope.

You know how utterly hopeless is a situation in which there is no hope. If a person is caught in the toils of tribulation, of distress, and perhaps of pain and torment, what a difference it makes if there is just a glimmer of hope. If a person is overtaken by a very serious disease and is racked with pain, what a difference between whether the person has absolutely no hope of deliverance from it and whether that person has even a glimmer of hope. Hope gives him endurance; it gives him a measure of patience. He is willing to endure it or she is willing to endure it because there is going to be deliverance. That is what is true in a much more transcendent realm in reference to our relationship to God and our relationship to the dispensations of his providence. "It is good that a man should both hope and quietly wait for the salvation of the Lord." To quote again the word of another prophet, "I will bear the indignation of the Lord, because I have sinned against him, until he plead my cause, and execute judgment for me: he will bring me forth to the light, and I shall behold his righteousness" (Mic 7:9).

It is this hoping and waiting of which the prophet Isaiah speaks, "But they that wait upon the Lord shall renew their strength; they shall mount up with wings as eagles; they shall run, and not be weary; and they shall walk, and not faint" (Isa 40:31). The secret of endurance, patience, and waiting with expectation is submission to God's providences until he brings us forth to the light, and we shall then behold his righteousness. This hope is well-grounded for the reasons that have been already enunciated: that the Lord is full of compassion and of tender mercy and that the Lord is the portion of his people. Therefore, there cannot possibly be anything else but a glorious finale; it can't be otherwise! If the Lord is the portion of his people, and if that has its issue in our being filled unto all the fullness of God unto the plentitude of that grace and truth that reside in the mediator Jesus Christ and that have been communicated to his people, then there cannot possibly be but a grand and glorious finale.

Now fifth and finally, what the prophet here brings to mind and what fills him, therefore, with hope and expectation is the vindication of God himself, that there is no arbitrariness in God. You might think that that's a sort of anticlimax. You might think that it is not on the plane of these other great truths like the lovingkindness and tender mercy of God or that the Lord's portion is his people and that God is the portion of his people. You might not think that it is on the plane of the glorious hope set before the people of God of a grand finale, a finale that will fill their hearts with praise and thanksgiving throughout the endless ages of eternity. But the vindication of God himself is not an anticlimax; it is on the very summit of faith. You find it in verses 33 to 36: "For he doth not afflict willingly nor grieve the children of men. To crush under his feet all the prisoners of the earth. To turn aside the right of a man before the face of the most High, to subvert a man in his cause, the Lord approveth not." That was no anticlimax for Jeremiah.

And it should not be an anticlimax for us, either. What is the secret of the fact that there is no arbitrariness in God, that he doth not afflict willingly nor grieve the children of men? It is just this: that the Lord is just in all his ways and holy in all his works (Ps 145:17), that the judge of all the earth will do right (Gen 18:25). I tell you, my friends, that whatever may be our affliction, however much we may cringe under the chastening hand of God, and however much the arrows of the Almighty may enter into the innermost recesses of our being (Job 6:4)—when we have come to the point of vindicating God's ways by recognizing that he is holy, just, sovereign, and good, then we have the outlet, then we escape. "As a bird under the snare of the fowlers, our soul is escaped and our help is in the name of the Lord who made heaven and earth" (Ps 124:7–8). "The Lord," we can then say, "will light my candle so that it shall shine full bright; the Lord, my God, will also make my darkness to be light" (Ps 18:28).

My friends, I would appeal to you, as I would address my own heart and soul, that the very secret of escape in the midst of tribulation and darkness and anguish is that we are able to justify God. And we are able to justify God in all his works because we recognize that we always have less than our iniquities deserve. There is a very close connection between that which the prophet first brings to remembrance—self-humiliation before God because of his own iniquities—and that which has just been enunciated in verses 33 to 36—the vindication of the justice and holiness and goodness of God.

We must never forget that God does not afflict willingly nor grieve the children of men. God is never motivated by vindictive revenge. He is, indeed, motivated by vindicatory justice, but never by unholy, vindictive revenge. And that's what is enunciated here as elsewhere. The Lord does not afflict willingly (that is, arbitrarily); he doesn't afflict simply for the sake of afflicting. God is not *vindictively* executing his wrath; he is *vindicatorily* executing his wrath. It is the same great truth in another connection that the prophet Ezekiel sets forth in the words of God himself: "As I live," saith the Lord God, "I have no pleasure in the death of the wicked; but that the wicked turn from his way and live" (Ezek 33:11).

It is well for us, my friends, whatever may be the dispensations of providence to us, to recognize his sovereign holiness and bow before his sovereign majesty. When we are able to do that, we shall also be able, in the strength of God's grace and by the energizing of his Spirit, to rejoice with the prophet: "The Lord is my portion, saith my soul, therefore will I hope in him. My flesh and my heart faileth: but God is the strength of my heart, and my portion forever" (Lam 3:24; Ps 73:26). In these days, when we are encompassed about with so much that causes dismay, that causes us to walk in darkness and have no light, may we, by the grace of God and by the effectual application of the Holy Spirit, be able to reproduce in our own experience, faith, and hope, that blessed assurance described by the prophet: "This I have called to mind, therefore have I hope."

Oh God, we praise and magnify thy name that thou hast not dealt with us after our sins nor rewarded us according to our iniquities. And we praise thee that thou dost give us the precious privilege of receiving thy Word in all its fullness. May it be reflected in our hearts in faith and love and hope. Oh, grant that we may be more than conquerors through him that loved us, knowing that neither death nor life, nor angels nor principalities, nor powers, nor things present nor things to come, nor height nor depth, nor any other creature will be able to separate us from the love of God, which is in Christ Jesus our Lord. For his name's sake, amen.

14

Where Two or Three Are Gathered

For where two or three are gathered together in my name, there am I in the midst of them.
—Matthew 18:20

Oh God, thou who dwellest between the cherubim, do thou shine forth. Graciously grant us thy holy presence as we come into thy courts in accordance with thine own appointment. May we enter into thy gates with thanksgiving and into thy courts with praise. May we be thankful unto thee and bless thy name. Create, oh Lord, within us a clean heart and renew a right spirit, so that we may worship thee in spirit and in truth, in the beauty of holiness, recognizing how great is the mercy thou hast bestowed upon us, that thou hast not cast us off from thy presence nor given us our desert in everlasting destruction from the presence of the Lord and from the glory of his power.

Oh Lord, do thou awaken each one of us to a profound sense of our great need. Particularly, do thou arouse us to a sense of our sinfulness, of our sinnership—that against thee, and thee only, have we sinned and done evil in thy sight. Blessed forever be thy great and holy name, that there is forgiveness with thee, that thou mayest be feared, that there is a fountain open for the house of David and for the inhabitants of Jerusalem for sin and for uncleanness, and that the blood of Jesus Christ, thy Son, cleanseth us from all sin. And so when he will appear in his undimmed glory, we shall not be ashamed before him in his presence.

Oh, how marvelous are the provisions of thy grace! How marvelous is that salvation that has been wrought by thee wherein thou art just and the justifier of the ungodly, so that, when Christ will appear and be manifested in all his glory, we shall be able to stand in his presence without abashment and even without shame. Oh Lord, do thou grant unto us that we may have a profound understanding of the riches of the provisions of thy grace in Christ Jesus. And may we understand the meaning of the great truth that God was, in Christ, reconciling the world unto himself, not imputing their trespasses unto them, and that thou hast committed unto us the Word of reconciliation.

Oh Lord, be merciful unto each one of us, and grant that not only may we have hope towards thee but that we also may walk in all godliness and sincerity and truth before thee. May we have respect at all times unto thy honor, and may we be jealous that we may be found of thee without spot and blameless. Forbid, oh Lord, that we should at any time be overcome by the allurement and the deceit of this present evil world or by the deceit of riches by which the Word is choked so that it becomes unfruitful.

Oh Lord, enable us to gird up the loins of our minds to be sober and to day-by-day walk as in the presence of our Savior, confessing with thy servant that the life I now live in the flesh, I live by faith of the Son of God, who loved me and gave himself for me. And may we be jealous for the institutions of thy grace, not forsaking the assembling of ourselves together as is the manner of some, but that we may exhort one another daily, so much the more as we see the day approaching.

Oh Lord, may we never forget that day of judgment, that last day, when we shall be judged according to the things done in the body, whether they be good or evil. And, oh Lord, make each one of us a vessel unto honor, sanctified and meek for thy use and prepared unto every good work. Enable us to bear good testimony day-by-day that we may never be forgetful of the claims of Christ, of his kingship and of his lordship, and that we may be ever ready to give the reason of the hope that is in us with fear and trembling.

Oh Lord, we pray not only for ourselves; we would remember the whole company of thy people to the very ends of the earth. Do thou build them up in faith and purity and holiness. Glorify thy work in these days and cause that the church of Jesus Christ might again be arrayed in garments of glory and beauty, that she may appear clear as the sun and fair as the moon and terrible as an army with banners. Do thou grant unto thy people a profound appreciation for the deposit of truth that thou hast given and of the opportunities that thou hast presented to thy people to bear witness to the Lord of Glory.

Oh Lord, grant that the nations of the world may be curbed by thine almighty restraint from the designs of iniquity. Do thou graciously grant that peace might be given in our time, and above all would we pray for the establishment of righteousness in the earth. Do thou bring the designs of the great arch-enemy to naught. Do thou bring the designs of his unholy instruments to naught so that thy kingdom, which is righteousness and peace and joy in the Holy Spirit, may be advanced.

Do thou, oh Lord, grant unto all who are in any affliction that measure of thy grace that is necessary in order to sustain them. May they ever have the assurance that thy grace is sufficient for them and thy strength is made perfect in weakness. Do thou remember those who are grieved, who are bereft of their dearest in the world. Oh give unto them the consolation that Christ himself affords when he reminds us that he is the resurrection and the life, and may we put all our confidence in him as the one who was dead but who is alive again and has the keys of hell and of death.

And now, while we wait upon thee at this time, graciously grant unto us thy Spirit, that he may take of the things of Christ and show them unto us, so that we shall see his glory and may be transformed by the vision of his glory, so that we may prove what is that good and acceptable and perfect will of God, for his name's sake. Amen.

There are people who appear to think that they bestow a great favor upon the church of God when they grace us with their presence, and the assumption is that they bestow a great favor upon the Almighty as well. How reprehensible is that conception of the living God and of their own importance! And how God-dishonoring is the frame of mind that entertains such a conception of the mercy and the grace of God bestowed upon us in the institution of his church.

There are other people who are so obsessed with the idea of numbers that they will not patronize the services of God's worship unless great crowds of people congregate there. You can readily see what standard they apply to the presence of God. They have more respect for numbers than they have for the presence of God, more respect for the presence of people than for the presence of the Savior. And if numbers are the criteria of our esteem of the presence of God, then we miss entirely the comport of our Lord in this particular passage: "Where two or three are gathered together in my name, there am I in the midst of them."

Let us suppose that on a particular occasion, where a much larger number of people is accustomed to gather, only two happen to come to the service. When the minister came to the pulpit and found that there were only two there, he said to them, "Well, since there are so few of us here today, we better suspend the service." Of course, the minister then would be doing the *gravest* dishonor to the promise of Christ. He would be offering the gravest insult to the Lord of Glory himself.

But let us suppose on one occasion that only *one* came—that when the minister entered the pulpit, he found that there was only *one* in the congregation. It might be a little embarrassing for him, and it might be a little embarrassing for the particular person concerned, but if the minister on that occasion had said, "There is only yourself here; we better suspend the service," he would be doing the gravest insult to the Redeemer. For Christ's institution is, "Where two or three are gathered together in my name, there am I in the midst of them." We must always remember that where there are only three, there are also *four*—and the fourth is the Lord of Glory. And where there are only two, there are always *three*—and the third is the head of the church, Christ himself.

Now, in connection with these words, there are three things that I want to mention: first, the institution; second, the requirement; and third, the promise, which Christ offers us in Matthew 18:20.

First, then, the institution. All of us—at least all of us who have gone to school—know the difference between the plural and the singular. Where there are more than one, we speak of the plural number, and where there is only one, we speak of the singular number. When we have many, we speak of plurality, and when we have only one, we speak of unity. So, we can speak of plurality in unity. That is the particular institution of which our Lord is speaking in this text: the plurality of at least two in the unity of one—"Where two or three are gathered together in my name."

We need to appreciate the place that this institution of plurality in unity occupies in the constitution of the human race. The basic institution—or at least one of the basic institutions—in the constitution of the human race is the family. A family always has more than one; it has at least two, the man and the wife. And the institution of God is that the two shall be one flesh (Gen 2:24). There is plurality and there is unity: the *two* shall be *one* flesh. The same principle is illustrated on a much broader scale in the political sphere. A commonwealth is comprised of a great many individuals, but they are united under one government and sometimes under one head. So you have, on a much broader scale, the institution of plurality in unity.

The same is true in the church of Christ. There are a great

many individuals, but nevertheless they are comprised in one body. You don't have the church of Christ unless you have that plurality in unity. The plurality is the great multitude of those who are united to Christ, and the unity is the unity of one body. "There is one body, and one Spirit, even as ye are called in one hope of your calling" (Eph 4:4).

Now what is it that lies back of this institution? It is simply the fact that God himself is plurality in unity: the plurality of three in the unity of one—Trinity in unity. Of course, he is not one who *became* three nor is he three who *became* one, but he is one in three and three in one eternally and necessarily. It could not be otherwise because God could not be any other than that which he eternally and perfectly is. You may have been asked the question why God is three in one and one in three. The answer is just this: God *is* three in one and one in three. It is just as sensible to ask the question "why" about this as it is to ask why God is at all. God necessarily and eternally and perfectly *is*! And he is three in one and one in three.

Of course, God is unique, and there is nothing in his whole creation that is really comparable to him. Who among the sons of men or what in the whole world of creation can be compared unto the Almighty himself (Ps 89:6)? He is absolutely transcendent, he's absolutely unique, and he's beyond all comparison. He's not in a class. He's absolutely unique because he alone is God, and "there is none else besides him" (Deut 4:35). And yet God has made man in his own image, and he has constituted the race, to a certain extent, after the pattern of that which he himself uniquely and transcendently and incomparably is.

It is in connection with the church of Christ that this pattern appears particularly. In the church of Christ, you have the great example of that which God has done in the human race after the pattern of his own unity. The church, of course, is an institution of redemptive grace, preeminently *the* institution of redemptive grace. It is made up of a great multitude drawn from every nation and kindred and people and tongue (Rev 7:9), but it is one body in Christ Jesus (Rom 12:5). And the assemblies of God's people in this world, met in accordance with the institution of Christ and in accordance with his commandments, are the way in which this unity that exists in the body of Christ is expressed. It is the way by which God's purposes of grace and salvation are promoted and fulfilled in the world. That is how the church is preeminently the institution of redemptive grace in this world.

It is well for us to remember the words of Scripture in another connection. The writer of the Epistle to the Hebrews says, "Let us consider one another to provoke unto love and to good works: not forsaking the assembling of ourselves together, as the manner of some is; but exhorting one another daily: and so much the more, as ye see the day approaching" (Heb 10:24–25). When he says there, "as ye see the day approaching," he is talking of the perfect and *last* day, the day of judgment—nothing else. "As ye see the day—the perfect day, the last day, the judgment day—approaching."

We might think that the expectation of that last day, when all the elect of God will be perfectly united together in one body, would interfere with our taste for the imperfect in this world. It might seem that our preoccupation with the eternal would impair our interest in the temporal and that our expectation of the final bliss, when the whole body of Christ will be made perfect, would interfere with the imperfections and the limitations that attach to the assemblies of God's people in this world. Oh, how much imperfection there is in all the assemblies of God's people in this world. And as we cast our eyes to the perfect day, when there will be no longer any imperfection attaching to the body of Christ, it might seem that that would interfere with our interests in the assemblies of God's people in this world, where sometimes there are only very few gathered and where there is always imperfection and limitation.

But you notice that the line of thought suggested in Hebrews 10:24–25 is just in the very opposite direction: "not forsaking the assembling of ourselves together, as the manner of some is; but exhorting one another daily: *and so much the more,* as ye see the day approaching" (Heb 10:24–25). You see, the thought is that it is the very expectation of the *perfect* day that is the incentive to, and the reason for, the assembling of the people of God in this world. When we examine the direction of thought expressed in this passage a little further, then we can see very well the reason: the imperfect assemblies of God's people in this world are a foretaste of that perfect presence of the Lord that will be enjoyed at the perfect day, at the last day, when Christ will gather out of all these kindreds and peoples the whole body of the elect and present them spotless to the Father, "without spot or wrinkle or any such thing" (Eph 5:27). It is the expectation of the permanent enjoyment of Christ's presence that gives renewed force and incentive to the necessity of gathering ourselves together, because that gathering of ourselves together is the expression of the unity that there is in the body of Christ, and it is a foretaste of that which will ultimately be dispensed in its fullness and in its perfection.

See the great grace that the Savior, the Lord of the church and the head of the church, has bestowed in this particular institution: "Where two or three are gathered together in my name, there am I in the midst of them." Two or three! It is sometimes impossible to gather together more than two or three in his name, that is, in the unity of the Spirit and the bond of peace (Eph 4:3). Christ has made provision in his marvelous grace for the minimum, not the maximum. There may be only two who can gather together unto his name because there are only two in a particular situation or community who can gather together *in* Jesus's name. Oh, blessed be his name! It is not always true that we are reduced to the minimum, but recognize the fact that Christ has made provision for the very minimum of plurality in unity and unity in plurality. "Where two or three are gathered together in my name, there am I in the midst of them."

Now second, we have the requirement: "Where two or three are gathered together *in my name*." Everything hinges upon that little expression "in my name." What does it mean? It's very difficult to determine exactly what Jesus had in mind in this particular instance, but there are certain things that are very clearly implied. In any case, if we cover the implications of this particular expression, we will arrive, by one way or another, at the meaning.

There are four things implied by the requirement to gather together in Jesus's name that I shall mention. The first is that we meet together in accordance with Christ's authority and institution. It is very profitable indeed for the people of God to gather because they draw water with joy out of the wells of salvation (Isa 12:3). There are innumerable advantages from the observance of Christ's institution. We derive inestimable benefits from this communion that the people of God have with one another in the unity of the faith and in the bond of peace. But that is not the basic reason why we gather together. Of course, it is very pleasant and a great encouragement; we like to meet people who are of kindred spirit and of kindred faith. And it is intended to be of assistance to the people of God for them to meet together to encourage one another. That, of course, is implied in the Word that I quoted already: "Exhort one another daily, and so much the more as we see the day approaching" (Heb 10:25).

But that is not the fundamental reason why the people of God gather together. It isn't from the profit that they derive from it that they principally gather together. They gather together principally for this reason: it is Christ's institution, it is his command. And that, after all, is the basic reason for everything that is done in the church of Christ. We gather together because *Christ* has commanded and instituted it.

The second thing that is implied in this little expression "in my name" is that we gather together in union with Christ. "In Christ's name" is simply "in himself." The name stands for the person. So, if you say, "Where two or three are gathered together *in my name*," it is synonymous with saying, "Where two or three are gathered together *in me*, in union *with me*." Remember that on another occasion it is said, "As many as received him, to them he gave the authority to become sons of God, even to them that believed on his name" (John 1:12). You have the same expression in John 1 as you have in Matthew 18: "in his name." To believe on his name is not to believe in an empty vocable; it's to believe in himself. The name stands for the person. And so, to gather together in his name is to gather together in him, that is to say, in the union which he himself has effected.

We are united, first of all, to him, and then, because we are united to him, we are united to one another and can be united in the unity of the faith and in the bond of peace. Oh, what grave prejudice is done to the church of Christ when that great principle is neglected or overlooked! We must first of all be sure that we are united to Christ himself, for from him all nurture and all vitality springs. "As the branch cannot bear fruit of itself, except it abide in the vine; no more can ye, except ye abide in me. I am the vine, ye are the branches" (John 15:4–5). Just as the branches derive all their sustenance and their vitality from the vine, so the people of God derive all their sustenance and their vitality from Christ. Oh, let us make sure that we are united to Christ in the bonds of love and faith and obedience, united to him in the efficacy of his death and the power of his resurrection. And then, my friends, we shall have fulfilled the condition that Christ speaks of in Matthew 18:20.

The third thing that is implied here is that there must be unity of faith and unity of confession. You remember the great confession that Peter made at Caesarea Philippi. He said, "Thou art the Christ, the Son of the living God" (Matt 16:16), and that is the central confession. Unless there is that confession in our hearts and unless there is that confession in our assemblies, we're not fulfilling the condition that Christ has laid down for his church. "Everyone that confesseth that Jesus Christ is come in the flesh is of God" (1 John 4:2). Let us make sure that we have a unity of confession. That is what is meant by the unity of the faith: the unity of confession in Jesus Christ as the Son of the living God, which means nothing less than that he is God himself manifest in the flesh. God himself, on an equality with God the Father and nevertheless distinguished from the Father as the Son of the Father. And there you have the kernel of the Christian confession.

The fourth thing that is implied in this condition is that we come together to meet with Christ. Surely, the condition is the counterpart of the promise. The condition is, "Where two or three are gathered together *in my name*," and the promise is, "*There am I* in the midst of them." We surely cannot get away from it, that when Jesus said, "Gather together in my name," he means, "Gather together in order to *meet with me*." And he never fails to keep that appointment if we fulfill the conditions.

You remember that under the Old Testament there was what is translated in our version as "the tabernacle of the congregation," but it can be more literally, and perhaps a little more perspicuously, rendered "the tent of meeting." And why was it called the tent of meeting? It wasn't called the tent of meeting because the people met together there, though it's quite true that the people came to the tabernacle. It was called the tent of meeting because the Lord himself met with them there. And Christ is the grand fulfillment of the tabernacle under the Old Testament dispensation. Remember what John said: "The Word was made flesh, and dwelt among us" (John 1:14)—that is to say, the Word was made flesh and *tabernacled* among us. It is in Christ Jesus preeminently that the tabernacle of God is with men; he is the grand fulfillment of all that was symbolized and typified in the tent of meeting.

So, when we come together in obedience to Christ's commandment—honoring his institutions; united together first of all with Christ; and united together in the unity of that single confession that "there is one body and one Spirit, one Lord, one faith, one baptism, one God and Father of all who is above all and through all and in all" (Eph 4:4–6)—then we can be sure that Christ will be present. When we come together in the expectation of meeting with him, in the assurance that his promise will be fulfilled and that he will disclose to us something of his matchless glory, then we may be sure that he will not disappoint us. If we ever go away disappointed, my friends, it is not because Christ has failed in the fulfillment of his promise but because we have failed in the faith and in the hope and in the assurance of expectation. Christ is always true to his Word because he is himself the Truth. If he failed in the fulfillment of his promise, he wouldn't be the Truth.

Now, finally, we have the promise: "There am I in the midst of them." It's very simple, isn't it? Christ is present with the assemblies of his people even when they are reduced to the minimum of two or three. And you ask the question, "Well, how is Christ present?" It is no wonder, indeed, if that question would baffle you. If you don't have a sense of bafflement in trying to answer that question, you don't really have appreciation of the mystery of Christ's presence with his people. The apostle Paul speaks of the love of Christ that surpasses knowledge (Eph 3:19), and in another epistle he speaks of the peace of God that passes all understanding (Phil 4:7). Therefore, it is no wonder at all that Christ's presence with his people in this world should be a great mystery that baffles our comprehension.

Never forget that there is something here, notwithstanding its reality in experience, that surpasses understanding, that surpasses all explanation on our part. No wonder. Can we comprehend what Jesus meant when he said, "I in them, and thou in me, that they may be made perfect in one; and that the world may know that thou hast sent me" (John 17:23)? Can we understand what Jesus means when he says in another location, "If a man loves me, he will keep my words: and my Father will love him, and we will come unto him, and make our abode with him" (John 14:23)? Can we fully understand it? Of course not; this is one of the greatest mysteries of the Christian faith. The first great mystery of the Christian faith is the incarnation of the Son of God—that's the mystery of godliness (1 Tim 3:16), and we cannot unravel all its truth. But one of the greatest mysteries of our Christian faith is the presence of Christ in and with his church.

But although it surpasses our understanding, remember this: It is not something that is unintelligible. It is not something that is a complete blank in our understanding; it's not all darkness, there is light at the center. Of course, as you extend the circumference of light, you extend the circumference of mystery—but remember that there is always the focal point of light. There is something intelligible about the presence of Christ with his people, something that comes within the scope of our understanding. It even comes within the scope of our experience if we are united to Christ in the bond of faith. If we don't have any experience or any understanding of the presence of Christ with us, then it is just because we do not know what it is to be united to Christ. It's a reality, after all, that is understood, that is apprehended, and that is experienced.

So, what shall we say about our understanding of this great

mystery? Well, you remember that when Christ ascended upon high, he said, "Lo, I am with you always, even unto the end of the world," or "Lo, I am with you all the days, even unto the end of the world" (Matt 28:20). If Christ were not present with his people in this world—if he were not in them, if they were not in him, and if he were not present with them—then there would be no such reality as the church of God, and there would be no experience of salvation.

There are two ways in which we can speak of the presence of Christ with his people. He is, first of all, present with his people by his Word. Remember the two on the way to Emmaus on the day of the resurrection. We only know the name of one of them (and that is Cleopas). They were on the way to Emmaus and were very sad, and Jesus drew near and went with them. You remember, they did not know him because their eyes were holden, and yet Jesus was speaking to them incognito about himself. Then, beginning from Moses and all the prophets, he expounded unto them in all the Scriptures the things concerning himself. And afterwards, when they discovered that it had been Jesus who was with them, you remember what they said: "Did not our heart burn within us, while he talked with us by the way, and while he opened to us the Scriptures?" (Luke 24:32).

It's just as true, my friends, that Christ is present in the church of God *now*. He is present with his people in all generations *now* when the Word of God is read and when the Word of God is preached. And I protest, my friends—if you know Christ, I protest—your experience of that fact that oftentimes in hearing the Word of God read in the assemblies of God's people or hearing the Word of God preached in the assemblies of God's people, afterwards you are able to say (though you didn't fully realize it at the time), "Did not our hearts burn within us while he talked with us by the way and while he opened to us the Scriptures?" Christ is present with us by his Word as really, as truly, and as efficaciously now as he was in the flesh on the day of the resurrection with the two on the way to Emmaus, and your heart will burn within you even when you're scarcely aware of it. You will be taken up so much with the presentation of the glory of the Redeemer that at that particular moment you will scarcely be aware of the fact that your heart is burning. Christ is present in his Word in accordance with his promise, and he will surprise you beyond all your expectations.

Then, in the second place, Christ is present by his Spirit. Jesus said to his disciples,

> I will pray the Father, and he will give you another
> Comforter, that he may abide with you for ever; even
> the Spirit of truth; whom the world cannot receive,
> because it seeth him not, neither knoweth him: but ye
> know him; for he dwelleth with you, and shall be in you.
> (John 14:16–17)

Yes, it is the unique prerogative of the Holy Spirit in the economy of salvation to take of the things that are Christ's and show them unto us (John 16:14). Where we fulfill the conditions, the Holy Spirit is there glorifying Christ, and he is glorifying him in our apprehension, in our understanding, and in our reception. It is the Holy Spirit who glorifies Christ.

I tell you, my friends, that if you, in reality, come in accordance with Christ's institution and fulfill the condition of his promise (coming "in his name"), then the Holy Spirit will be working, silently perhaps, very secretly indeed, but nevertheless efficaciously to glorify Christ in your apprehension. And that is the presence of Christ himself. John said, "We beheld his glory, the glory as of the only begotten of the Father, full of grace and truth" (John 1:14). As you get renewed visions of the fullness of grace and truth that are in Christ Jesus, out of his fullness you will receive grace for grace (John 1:16).

Therefore, let us not despise the gathering together of even two or three. Do not despise the day of small things, for to do so is to despise the presence of the Father, of the Son, and of the Holy Spirit. My friends, if you were invited to an interview with royalty, with Queen Elizabeth of England, would you deign to patronize because there would only be two there besides yourself? Would you refrain from going because there would only be two present? Would fewness of number in any way interfere with the great privilege and honor bestowed upon you to be ushered into the presence of royalty? It isn't the criteria of number that's the important thing, is it? It's the presence of Her Majesty the Queen!

And oh, how much more true that is in the transcendent world of the King of kings and Lord of lords, of him who is given all authority in heaven and on earth (Matt 28:18), who is exalted "far above all principality, and power, and might, and dominion, and every name that is named, not only in this world, but also in that which is to come" (Eph 1:21). Christ did not despise to speak to the Samaritan woman, did he? He spoke to her alone. And do you know that heaven will eternally resound with the praises that emanated from that interview with the woman of Samaria? Christ did not despise to speak to Nicodemus, and the repercussions will be eternal! And are we to despise the presence of Christ because perhaps only two or three human persons are present on that particular occasion? Don't you see the awful insult that we offer to the Lord of Glory when we despise the assemblies of God's people, however much they may be despised by this present evil world? I tell you this, my friends, that when Christ is present with two or three, it is like, if I may use the figure, a stone dropped into a pond. Ripples in endless cycles proceed from that event, and these ripples break on the shores of eternity. Let us not despise the day of small things because the veracity of him who is the Truth is pledged to the fulfillment of his promise, "Where two or three are gathered together in my name, there am I in the midst of them."

Don't despise the presence of Christ, because it is the presence of him who is the faithful witness, the first begotten from the dead, and the prince of the kings of the earth (Rev 1:5), the King of kings and Lord of lords. Is there any glory comparable to his glory? Is there any tabernacle that is comparable to that which is graced by the majesty of the King eternal, immortal, and invisible? Where there are two, there are always three, and the third is the Lord of Glory. And we go a step further, where there are only two gathered in Christ's name, there are always five. There are never less than five, and the third, the fourth, and the fifth are the Father, the Son, and the Holy Ghost. Jesus said, "I will pray the Father, and he shall give you another Comforter, that he may abide with you for ever; even the Spirit of truth" (John 14:16–17). And Jesus said, respecting himself and the Father, "That they all may be one; as thou, Father, art in me, and I in thee, that they also may be one in us. . . . I in them, and thou in me, that they may be made perfect in one" (John 17:21, 23).

And so, as we meet in humble expectation of Christ's presence, as we wait upon his Word, and as we pray for his Spirit to glorify Christ in accordance with his prerogative, then our hearts will burn within us and the bells will begin to ring in the deepest recesses of our spirit. And they are bells that have their responses in heaven. Then we shall be able to sing, "There is a river, the streams whereof shall make glad the city of God, the holy place of the tabernacles of the most High. God is in the midst of her; she shall not be moved: God shall help her, and that right early" (Ps 46:4–5). "One thing have I desired of the Lord, that will I seek after; that I may dwell in the house of the Lord all the days of my life, to behold the beauty of the Lord, and to enquire in his temple" (Ps 27:4).

How shall we be prepared for the communion of the saints in glory or the inheritance of the saints in light if we have despised the presence of the King eternal, immortal, and invisible in the institutions of his grace in this world? Oh, let us plead his promise; let us expect his grace: "Where two or three are gathered together in my name, there am I in the midst of them."

15

Appointed Once to Die

> *And as it is appointed unto men once to die, but after this the judgment: So Christ was once offered to bear the sins of many; and unto them that look for him shall he appear the second time without sin unto salvation.*
> — HEBREWS 9:27–28

Oh God who dwellest on high, glorious in holiness, fearful in praises, doing wonders, before ever thou hast formed the earth and the world, even from everlasting to everlasting, thou art God, the same yesterday, today, and forever. We acknowledge unto thee, oh Lord, with thanksgiving, the great privilege thou dost bestow upon us that we may come into thy courts, that we may come into that place where thy name is made known and where the institutions of thy grace are observed. Make us, oh Lord, deeply aware of the inestimable grace that thou hast bestowed upon us, for many prophets and kings and righteous men have desired to see the things that we see and have not seen them, and to hear the things that we hear but have not heard them. Thou hast cast our lot in the consummation of the ages, and do thou grant that we may know that in this perspective thou hast given us the privilege of that revelation that has been hid from ages and from generations but that has now been revealed by the appearing of our Lord and Savior, Jesus Christ.

We confess our sin, oh Lord—our blindness, the hardness of our hearts, the unresponsiveness of our will, and how remiss are the conceptions that we entertain of thee, the living God. Do thou cleanse our minds from that corruption and deliver our hearts from the deception of the Evil One and from the imaginations of our own evil hearts, so that we may come into thy presence with a true realization of thy great majesty and bow before thee in the deepest recesses of our spirit, acknowledging thee, the only true God, and realizing that it is only through the mediation of thine own Son, our Lord Jesus Christ, that we may draw near unto thee. Do thou, oh Lord, deliver us from the sacrifice that is an abomination in thy sight. Create within us a clean heart, oh God, and renew a right spirit within us, so that each one of us may offer unto thee sacrifices acceptable, well-pleasing unto God through Jesus Christ.

Do thou, oh Lord, confront us this night with the reality of thy being, with the reality of thy judgment, and with the reality of the truth thou hast revealed to us in thy Word, so that we may stand in thy very presence and realize that we are *thy* creatures, that to thee we are responsible, and that upon thee we are dependent for every breath we draw. And enable us, oh Lord, in spirit and in truth, to worship thee in the beauty of holiness.

Blessed forever be thy great and holy name—that it is a faithful saying and worthy of all acceptation, that Christ Jesus came into the world to save sinners, and we in all our destitution would come to that inexhaustible fountain of grace and of truth. Out of his fullness, in whom are hid all of the treasures of wisdom and knowledge, we would draw and would receive grace for grace. And do thou satisfy us with thy message, that we may rejoice and be glad all our days.

Grant unto us, oh Lord, thy Holy Spirit. How marvelous it is that we should be able to plead the promise, which thou hast given, that if we, being evil, know how to give good gifts unto our children, how much more shall the heavenly Father give the Holy Spirit to them that ask him. And may we, oh Lord, know the presence and the communion of the Holy Spirit because he glorifies Christ in our understanding, in our hearts, and in our wills.

Oh grant that Christ may be precious to us in all the glory that is his as our wisdom, righteousness, sanctification, and redemption. Enable us, oh Lord, to live in this world as those who are the trophies of his redemption, that we may gird up the loins of our minds, that we may be sober and hope to the end for the grace that is to be brought unto us at the revelation of Jesus Christ. Constrain our hearts to that commitment and to Jesus Christ in all the length and breadth and depth and height of his love.

And do thou, oh Lord, grant, not only unto us but to all thy people to the ends of the earth, a rich measure of thy grace. We would remember that thou hast redeemed to thyself a people out of every nation and kindred and people and tongue. So, may we realize more and more the preciousness of communion with the saints, communion with thy people unto the ends of the earth, and our communion not only with those who are here on earth but with that great company who have gone to be with Christ.

May we realize our communion with the church triumphant. And enable us, in the fellowship of the body of Christ, to have strong consolation and that faith as the anchor of the soul, both sure and steadfast.

Bless, oh Lord, the preaching of the gospel unto the very ends of the earth. May the Word have free course and be glorified so that it may come in that irresistible power—that mysterious, transforming, and converting power—so that sinners may be translated from darkness to light and from the power of Satan unto God. Do thou, oh Lord, grant that with us this night there may be thy abundant blessing so that thy doctrine may drop as the rain and thy speech distill as the dew, as the small rain upon the tender herb, and as the showers upon the grass. Grant us, oh Lord, a realization that we are in thy presence and that it is thee and thee alone that we worship, for Jesus's sake. Amen.

It is quite obvious that there is a certain comparison drawn in Hebrews 9:27–28. On the one side is the fact that "it is appointed unto men once to die, but after this the judgment." And on the other side there are the facts that "Christ was once offered to bear the sins of many; and unto them that look for him shall he appear the second time without sin unto salvation." There is a comparison instituted between these two series of facts, and the truth expressed turns on that comparison. It is well for us to observe the likeness that there is between the appointment of men to death and the judgment on the one hand, and the offering of Christ and his appearing again the second time, without sin, unto salvation, on the other. So, there are just these two main considerations in this text: first, that which is appointed for men, and second, that which pertains to Christ.

First, there is that which is appointed for men. It is appointed for men to die. Now that is not without any exception. "Enoch was translated that he should not see death; and he was not found, because God had translated him" (Heb 11:5). Those who will be living at the second coming of Christ will not die; they will be changed (1 Cor 15:52). But these, of course, are exceptions, and the general rule for humanity, the general rule of God's providence throughout the whole history of the world, is that it is appointed for men once to die.

Why do men die? Of course, it is quite proper to say that men die by natural processes. Oftentimes their bodies are attacked by disease, and that disease is too powerful for their life, and, consequently, there is a biological necessity that they should die. For God has so constituted men that there are certain forces that are too strong for the life that he has given men in this world. And sometimes, of course, men are the victims of assault and so are killed. A force that is extraneous to themselves, and too powerful for them, wrests life from them.

But the real facts of providence do not explain the reason *why*. Why is it so arranged in the providence of God that men should die? Beyond the answer to that question is that death is the wages of sin. The only ultimate reason why men die is that men have sinned. And because *all* have sinned and come short of the glory of God (Rom 3:23), and since the wages of sin is death (Rom 6:23), therefore it is appointed for men to die (Heb 9:27).

The emphasis, however, in this particular text, falls upon the fact that it is appointed for men *once* to die. There is a certain finality attaching to death as death and to the issues that are bound up with death. It is to that particular fact that our attention is drawn in this text. There are certain respects in which we may quite profitably reflect upon that text, that it is appointed for men *once* to die.

The first respect in which we may think of the finality of death is that of warning, of unrestricted warning. When we die we are not brought back again to this earth to remedy the opportunities that we have neglected or the privileges that we have squandered in this life. We are not able to come back again to redeem the time that we have wasted. "There is no work, nor device, nor wisdom, nor knowledge in the grave, whither we are going" (Eccl 9:10). And you remember very well how in the Old Testament you have these eloquent words: "There is hope of a tree, if it be cut down, that it will sprout again, and that the tender branch thereof will not cease. . . . But man dieth, and wasteth away: yea, man giveth up the ghost, and where is he?" (Job 14:7, 10).

There is a finality to death as death. It is not for us to waste, as it were, the precious opportunities that are given to us. Remember the man who had received one talent and went and hid his lord's money in the earth? What is the indictment against that particular man? It is just that he did nothing. And you know, we don't need to do a great deal in order to squander our opportunity, we just need to do nothing. See how eloquent is the indictment that was brought against him by his lord when he returned: "Thou wicked and slothful servant" (Matt 25:26). Wickedness and slothfulness lie together, and slothfulness is wickedness. It's the great lesson of that particular parable, and it's a great lesson of this text in respect to its warning. We cannot redeem lost opportunities or squandered privileges. "Behold, now is the accepted time; behold, now is the day of salvation" (2 Cor 6:2).

The second respect in which we may properly think of the truth that it is appointed unto men once to die is one of *both* warning and consolation. There have been men even in our own time who have made the earth to tremble, and some of you remember very well how these men made the earth to tremble. Less than twenty years ago the voice of Hitler could be heard all over the world by radio, and it certainly made the earth to tremble. And there have been other men who, in their time, even in our generation, have made the earth to tremble, and where are they? "I have seen the wicked in great power, and spreading himself like a green bay tree. Yet he passed away, and, lo, he was not: yea, I sought him, but he could not be found" (Ps 37:35–36).

You don't need to be afraid that these boasters are going to return to earth again. It is appointed to men *once* to die, and they are, after all, only men. If we are jittery, if we are overcome by undue trepidations with respect to the boasts or the claims of any man, it's just because we forget the appointment of the living God. It is appointed to men once to die, and once they die, all their glory descends with them to the grave. "I have seen the wicked in great power . . . yet he passed away, and, lo, he was not." There is warning for the vain boasters, but there is consolation for the meek of the earth.

The third respect in which we may quite properly think of this text is one of unrestricted consolation, and it is unrestricted consolation for the people of God. When they depart this life, they go to be with Christ. Because they go to be with Christ, it is far better to not be wrenched from the bosom of the Savior. We would quite properly hold onto our dear, faithful, believing friends, and it is not right for us to desire otherwise. It is right for us to pray for the recovery of our friends; that's *our* duty. But when God takes them, we ought to have this as our comfort: because they're bound to be with Christ, it is far better for them. We cannot bring them back, and it would be wrong for us to ask that the Lord would bring them back. They'll never be brought back again to the tribulations and the perplexities of this present pilgrimage. They have gone to unalloyed bliss, bliss in the presence of the Savior himself, and that is the consolation that belongs to us as we are confronted with the death of our departed loved ones. If they are in Christ, they go to be with Christ. And if they are with Christ, they are in the presence of him who is the exalted, risen, and glorious Redeemer, "the great high priest who has passed into the heavens, Jesus the Son of God" (Heb 4:14). That is the unrestrained consolation for those who believe in the sovereignty of the appointments of God.

Yes, there is a certain finality to death, and there is a gravity, of course, that is bound up with this finality—a gravity and seriousness that ought to make each one of us ponder what will be our situation when the fulfillment of the divine appointment arrives. But, after all, death is not the end; it isn't the ultimate finality. It is just because it is *not* the end that there is a gravity connected with death. The very finality of death as death is bound up with something else, with another finality, and that is the finality of judgment: "After this, the judgment" (Heb 9:27).

Death and judgment are placed together in Hebrews 9:27.

Because they are placed together in this particular way, the great lesson is that these are the two determinative, decisive events in the matter of eternal destiny. There's no decisiveness in what will transpire between death and resurrection, but there is a finality to death as death and a finality to judgment as judgment.

We often overlook the fact that we are to be judged according to the things done in the body, whether they be good or whether they be evil (2 Cor 5:10). There is a solemnity attaching to that fact of judgment where "God will bring every work into judgment with every secret thing whether it be good or whether it be evil" (Eccl 12:14). There is a great deal that will pass muster before man, a great deal that will be considered virtuous and noble before men, and yet be simply an abomination in the sight of God. But God searches the heart and tries the reins of the children of men (Jer 17:10; Rev 2:23). "Man looks on the outward appearance; God looks on the heart" (1 Sam 16:7). And because he judges according to the secrets of men's hearts (Ps 44:21; Rom 2:16), his judgment is one of absolute equity. Everything will come into judgment. The whole panorama of human history—of individual history, of collective history, and of world history—will come before God for judgment, and everything will be adjudicated with perfect judgment and equity.

But there isn't simply a solemnity to the fact of judgment. Oh, there is a grandeur to that fact of God's ultimate and absolute judgment. God will ultimately put everything and everyone in its proper place; he is not going to leave anything at loose ends. When a person dies and leaves an estate but leaves no last will or testament, what trouble it is! Everything is at loose ends. Sometimes you find that the whole estate is consumed by litigation, and there's really nothing left, and the lawyers get all of it. Everything so sadly left at loose ends, everything topsy-turvy. It's very calamitous, even in the individual sphere or in the sphere of family relationships, when people leave things at loose ends. But that's not what God is going to do. There's going to be absolutely nothing left at loose ends. He is going to bring every work into judgment with every secret thing, whether it be good or whether it be evil, and there is a grandeur to that fact. Everything will be perfectly adjudicated with equity.

Do we live as if there is no final judgment? Do we live as if bygones are bygones, as if the past is gone and we have nothing more to do with it? What utter folly! God will bring *every* work into judgment. Something far worse than the folly of living as if death ended all, however, is the dishonor it does to God. Do you know, my friends, that if we live in this world as if death ended all, *it is just because we don't believe in the one living and true God*? Justice and judgment are the habitation of God's throne (Ps 97:2), and *for that reason*, "he will judge the world in righteousness and the people with his truth" (Ps 96:13). Our realization of that fact is bound up with our belief in the living and true God.

If we are imbued with the love of the living God, we shall really, after all, be imbued with the love of his final judgment, because it would be a *hopeless* and *dismal* outlook for eternity if there were to be no absolute adjudication of everything that transpires in the history of this world. But it is not that dismal outlook that is presented to us, because God is a God of judgment and with him actions are weighed (1 Sam 2:3). He guards the paths of justice (Prov 2:8), and he will judge the people with righteousness and with his truth (Ps 96:13).

Now in the second place, we have in this text that which pertains to Christ: "He was offered to bear sin" (Heb 9:28). And again we have to ask the question: Why? Why was he offered to bear sin? And because of the comparison in this text between death and judgment on the one hand and the offering of Christ on the other, we must discover that the same real reason underlies the offering of Christ as underlies the appointment of men to death and the establishment of the judgment. The answer to the questions, "Why do men die?" and, "Why is there to be a final judgment?" is the same as the answer to the question, "Why was Christ offered to bear sin?" That may seem very strange, but it is true.

Why are men appointed to death? It is simply because truth must be vindicated and justice must be executed. "The wages of sin is death" (Rom 6:23), "The sinner must die" (Ezek 18:20), "Dust thou art and to dust thou shalt return" (Gen 3:19), and because that is the case, men must die. It is really for that very same reason that Christ was offered. Christ would not have been offered if there had been no sin. If sin did not deserve its wages in death, he would not have died upon the accursed tree. Christ indeed was offered as a sacrifice unto death, the death of the cross, for the very same reason that the claims of justice must be satisfied and truth must be vindicated. God had determined the salvation of a countless multitude, and because God had determined the salvation of a countless multitude, justice *must* be vindicated. And it is just Christ's vicarious death that satisfies and vindicates that justice.

But the answer again falls upon the fact that Christ was *once* offered—that's the leading thought in this text. Just as the leading thought in the earlier part of the text is that it is appointed unto men *once* to die and then there will be the *once-for-all* judgment, so he was *once* offered to bear the sins of many. And just as there is that once-for-all finality to *death* as death, just as there is that once-for-all finality to *judgment* as judgment, so there is this once-for-all finality to the offering of *Christ* once-for-all upon the cross of Calvary.

What is the great truth? It is the truth that belongs to the very center, to the very essence, of our holy faith. And it is this: that he made an end of sin, that he finished transgression (Dan 9:24), that "when he had by himself purged our sins, he sat down on the right hand of the Majesty on high" (Heb 1:3). He made an end of sin on behalf of his own people, and because he made an end of sin, there's no need for any repetition. You see, there is a finality, there is a completeness, there is a perfection attaching to the once-for-all sacrifice of Christ. That is something that never attached to anything else in the sphere of God's judgment upon sin. He made an end of sin and exhausted the judgment of God against sin in *himself* with the result that "there is no condemnation to them who are in Christ Jesus" (Rom 8:1).

But again, the vicarious sin-bearing of Christ is not the end; it isn't the *final* end. There is something more ultimate in the appointment of God than the once-for-all offering of the sacrifice of Jesus Christ upon the accursed tree. It is just because there is this finality and completeness and perfection belonging to the sacrifice of Christ that it is not the ultimate end. What is this final finality of which this text speaks? It is that "he will be seen again the second time, without sin, for them that look for him, unto salvation" (Heb 9:28). It is just the finality, the once-for-all-ness, the completeness, the perfection of the sacrifice of

Christ that makes so precious and, indeed, *necessary* that final consummation that he would be manifested again the second time, without sin, unto salvation.

Now how does that bear upon us? What is the focal point of hope and expectation for the people of God? What, after all, is it that looms highest on the horizon of our hope? You might say it's the death of the righteous, that my last end might be like his. May God grant that for all of us our last end of existence in this world will be like that of the righteous. But if that is what is central in our hope and expectation, we are completely off the track of the Christian revelation, completely off the track of the Christian hope! Remember what the apostle Paul says: "*Not* for that we would be *unclothed*, but *clothed* upon, that mortality might be swallowed up of life" (2 Cor 5:4). Paul, indeed, did say that to depart and to be with Christ was far better (Phil 1:23) and that to be absent from the body is to be present with the Lord (2 Cor 5:8), but *not* that we would be unclothed, but clothed upon, that mortality might be swallowed up of life. "For we know that if our earthly house of this tabernacle were dissolved, we have a building of God, an house not made with hands, eternal in the heavens" (2 Cor 5:1). And if it is the death of the righteous that is central and focal in your expectation, my friend, you're off the track of the Christian revelation and you have imbibed a *pagan* conception. You are still, as it were, chained in the forms of pagan thought. Let us deliver ourselves from it.

What *is* central and focal in the Christian hope is the appearing of the glory of the great God and our Savior, Jesus Christ (Titus 2:13). What is it, my friends, that looms highest on *our* horizon as we have respect to death, to judgment, and to the once-for-all offering of the body of Jesus Christ? It is in that way that we shall test the reality of our Christian faith as well as the reality of our Christian hope. What is central in the expectation of the people of God is that Christ will be seen *again* the second time, without sin, unto salvation.

Now, with reference to that central hope and expectation, there are three things that need to be stressed. The first is that Christ will be seen. Our version perhaps just slightly obscures that when it says that "unto them that look for him shall he appear" (Heb 9:28). But it isn't the fault of the English at all, but the fault of our reflection. "He will be *seen*" is a more literal rendering, and it draws our attention to the fact that *physical sense* is given its proper place and weight in the Christian expectation. The finality for the people of God is one that gives full satisfaction to the demands of physical sense experience. The Scripture doesn't place any disdain upon the human body. God created men at the beginning body and spirit, body and soul, and death is an abnormality. A normal state will not again be realized until the body will be resurrected from the dead. And physical sense experience will be given its full satisfaction and realization in the beholding of Christ himself, come again in his glorious body.

I'm just trying to emphasize, my friends, that the Christian hope is not that pagan hope of etherealized immortality. There's something very concrete, very material *itself*, in the Christian hope. He will be seen with our physical senses. Don't underestimate that. If we underestimate that, it is just because again we are caught in the coils of pagan thought. The body has its proper place, and redemption will not be consummated until the body of our humiliation will be transformed into the likeness of the body of Christ's glory (Phil 3:21). And we shall see him; we shall see him as he is; we shall see him in the glory of his glorified humanity. There will be something marvelous about that just as there was for Thomas when Jesus said to him after the resurrection, "Thrust thy hand and put it into my side, and thus put thy finger into the print of the nails, and be not faithless but believing" (John 20:27). My friends, it's an essential ingredient of the Christian hope that we shall see Jesus *in that body* that was crucified upon Calvary's accursed tree, that body in which he bore our sins and made an end of transgressions.

The second fact that is brought to our attention in this particular text is that he will be without sin. It is not bearing sin that Christ will come again the second time. He will not come enveloped in the clouds of humiliation but will come in undimmed glory. There will be no shadow to obscure that matchless glory that is his as the exalted Lord, as the one who is given authority in heaven and in earth, who is given the name that is above every name, and at whose name every knee will bow and every tongue confess that he is Lord, to the glory of God the Father (Phil 2:9–11).

Not only will he not come bearing sin, but he will not come again the second time to load his people with their sin. Don't you see, my friends, that that is the preciousness of the finality and the completeness and the perfection of the once-for-all offering upon Calvary's accursed tree: that he made an *end* of sin! And although he will come to judge, he will *not* come to load his people with their transgressions. "There is no condemnation to them who are in Christ Jesus" (Rom 8:1). There is no damnation for them. Although their sins will be judged, he does not come to lay upon them the guilt of their transgressions nor to burden them again with the grief that is entailed in that sin and guilt. There will be *unalloyed joy* for the people of God even in the final judgment, for Jesus will say to them on his right hand, "Come, ye blessed of my Father, inherit the kingdom prepared for you from the foundation of the world" (Matt 25:34).

The third point to be noted in connection with this central hope of Jesus's appearing is that it is unto salvation that Jesus will come. "He will be seen again the second time without sin, for them that look for him, *unto salvation*" (Heb 9:28). You must note that quite often in the Scripture that word *salvation* is used of the perfection or consummation of salvation, when salvation will be complete and the body of our humiliation transformed into the likeness of the body of Christ's glory (Phil 3:21). The people of God all long for that salvation in its completeness, in its thoroughness, in its all-inclusiveness, when the whole redemptive purpose of God will reach its final realization in the completion of the salvation that was once-for-all purchased by Christ when he "offered himself without spot to God" (Heb 9:14), when he purged our sins and sat down at the right hand of the Majesty in heaven (Heb 1:3). But I tell you this, my friends, that although it is a salvation that we long for, it's a salvation that will surpass all our expectations. The half has not been told.

In the passage I was reading to you earlier—that most graphic passage in describing the final judgment—Christ will come and sit upon the throne of his glory, and before him will be gathered all the nations. He shall separate them one from another, as the shepherd separates the sheep from the goats. He will set the sheep on his right hand and the goats on his left and mark it. Then shall the King say unto them on his right hand, "Come, ye blessed of my Father, inherit the kingdom prepared for you from the foundation of the world" (Matt 25:34). And what a surprise they will then get. He will say,

> "For I was an hungred, and ye gave me meat: I was thirsty, and ye gave me drink: I was a stranger, and ye took me in: naked, and ye clothed me: I was sick, and ye visited me: I was in prison, and ye came unto me." Then shall the righteous answer him, saying, "Lord, when saw we thee an hungred, and fed thee? Or thirsty, and gave thee drink? When saw we thee a stranger, and took thee in? Or naked, and clothed thee? Or when saw we thee sick, or in prison, and came unto thee?" And *the King* [remember, the King], shall answer and say unto them, "Verily I say unto you, inasmuch as ye have done it unto one of the least of these my brethren, ye have done it unto me." (Matt 25:35–40)

Less than two months ago, it was my sad duty to come to these parts of the country to bury our very highly esteemed and beloved friend and your highly esteemed and beloved pastor. It was a painful journey, but I considered it one of the greatest privileges that was accorded to me in this life that it should have been possible for me to come to pay these last respects of honor and esteem to my dearly beloved friend. I consider it one of the greatest honors that God, in his mercy and providence, has bestowed upon me in connection with that type of thing. And as I went back to Philadelphia on the next Sabbath afternoon, I was reflecting and was studying this particular passage. I never realized in my life before as I realized then how precious these words were and how appropriate to that person whom we had committed to his last earthly resting place just a few days before. I never saw them with such appropriateness in my life before.

Let me read them to you again, and just think:

> Then shall the King say unto them on his right hand, "Come, ye blessed of my Father, inherit the kingdom prepared for you from the foundation of the world: For I was an hungred, and ye gave me meat: I was thirsty, and ye gave me drink: I was a stranger, and ye took me in: Naked, and ye clothed me: I was sick, and ye visited me: I was in prison, and ye came unto me." Then shall the righteous answer him, saying, "Lord, when saw we thee an hungred, and fed thee? Or thirsty, and gave thee drink? When saw we thee a stranger, and took thee in? Or naked, and clothed thee? Or when saw we thee sick, or in prison, and came unto thee?" And *the King* shall answer [mark it, it is the King!], and say unto them, "Verily I say unto you, inasmuch as ye have done it unto one of the least of these my brethren, ye have done it unto me." (Matt 25:34–40)

Oh, let us emulate that example that had been so magnificently illustrated in our departed friend, that he loved the humblest of the poorest and the most obscure, whom he recognized to be the blood-purchased possession of Jesus Christ. It was not upon the great ones of the earth that he, as it were, poured out his affections; he did it unto one of the least of these his brethren.

Now let us come back to our theme: when Christ will come in his undimmed glory and when he will dispense to all those who look for his appearing that final salvation, it will surpass all their conceptions and expectations. How glorious, my friends, is the prospect and how grand is the assurance that is ministered unto us, that "Christ will descend from heaven with a shout, with the voice of the archangel, and with the trumpet of God, and the dead in Christ shall rise first" (1 Thess 4:16).

Do you like to go to cemeteries? I love to go to cemeteries where I know the people of God are. I just love to wander among these graves because I get a peculiar sensation, a peculiar delight, in recognizing that one day, when the trumpet will sound, the dead will be raised incorruptible, and those who are living will be changed, and this corruptible will put on incorruption, and this mortal will put on immortality:

> *Then* shall be brought to pass the saying that is written, Death is swallowed up in victory. O death, where is thy sting? O grave, where is thy victory? The sting of death is sin; and the strength of sin is the law. But thanks be unto God, who giveth us the victory through our Lord Jesus Christ. (1 Cor 15:54–57)

My friends, don't live as if this world ended all; don't live as if death ended all. That's folly, but it's worse than folly; it's blind unbelief, an assault upon the very foundation of God's government, and dishonor to him. My friends, in the perspective of Christ's glorious appearing, view death itself in this finality, view judgment itself in the finality that belongs to it, and view the once-for-all offering of Christ in the finality and the perfection and the completeness that belongs to it. For the issue of God's judgment for the people of God is nothing less than this: "Come, ye blessed of my Father, inherit the kingdom prepared for you from the foundation of the world" (Matt 25:34). Oh, judgment is a solemn event, but it has a grandeur too. And yet everything would be out of proportion, everything would be out of joint as far as *hope* would be concerned, if it were not for the appearing of the glory of the great God and our Savior, Jesus Christ.

Oh may I, as Christ's messenger, plead with each one of you to be joined to him in the bonds of a faith and a love and a hope that can never be dissolved. Then, when he will come again, he will usher you into the possession of that salvation, which you looked for, which you waited for, and which you longed for. And it will surpass all your expectations, because it is a salvation that is bound up with the glory of the presence of him who was given the name that is above every name. "The dead in Christ shall rise first: Then we who are alive and remain shall be caught up together with them in the clouds, to meet the Lord in the air: and so shall we ever be with the Lord" (1 Thess 4:16–17).

Oh God, the God and Father of our Lord Jesus Christ, the Lord Jesus Christ in all his glory, and the Holy Spirit as the Comforter, do thou graciously grant unto us thy blessing. May thy Word take hold of our hearts and bring forth abundant fruit in our lives, so that when Christ shall appear, we may be manifested with him also in glory, for his name's sake. Amen.

Appendix

Charge to Edmund Clowney

My dear friend and colleague, my esteem for your person and my high estimate of the qualifications you bring to the discharge of the Chair in which you have now been installed, make it very difficult for me to perform this assignment of giving you the charge. I am also aware that you are more sensitive than I could be to the demands of your office and to your complete dependence upon the grace of God for the fulfilment of these demands. To give you a charge then would seem superfluous and even presumptuous. But since I have been asked to do this I deeply appreciate the privilege, and in giving you the charge perhaps the chief result will be the recognition on our part of the harmony that exists between us respecting the aims to be realized in the conduct of the department now more fully committed to your charge.

1. First I would remind you that the responsibilities devolving upon you, arduous though they be, are at the same time unspeakable privileges. To the extent to which the responsibilities are arduous, to the same extent the privileges are magnified.

The proclamation of the gospel is the greatest vocation upon earth. The heralds of the gospel are the ambassadors of Christ, the King of kings and Lord of lords. Your task is preeminently to train men for this ministry. The task is overwhelming. But you are called to it, and grace is always according to need. And you are but Christ's chosen vessel into which, at each step of your responsible undertaking, he will pour from the plenitude of his wisdom, knowledge, grace, and power for the supply of all that is necessary for the fulfilment of your vocation.

2. Second, I would charge you to humility, humility for several reasons. You, like all of us, are still sinful. May you always be imbued with the broken spirit and the contrite heart, and before the vision of God's majesty say with the prophet, "Woe is me for I am undone. I am a man of unclean lips, and I dwell among a people of unclean lips, for mine eyes have seen the King, the Lord of hosts" (Isa 6:5). You, like all of us, are not sufficient for any of these things. Be increasingly aware of your dependence upon God's grace. Particularly would I now stress your dependence upon the Holy Spirit. For though your task is very largely concerned with the communication of the gospel, communication is never effective to the accomplishment of the gospel's purpose without the demonstration and power of the Holy Spirit.

3. Your department is that of practical theology. The bane of much that goes under this title is the divorce of practics from theology. You are well aware of this evil and you have determined to counteract it. But it may not be out of place to put you in remembrance. Practical theology is principally systematic theology brought to practical expression and application. And this means the whole counsel of God brought to bear upon every sphere of life, and particularly upon every phase of the life and witness of the church. He would be a poor theologian indeed who would be unaware of, or indifferent to, the practical application of God's revealed counsel. But likewise, and perhaps more tragically, he would be a poor exponent of practical theology who did not know the theology of which practics is the application. I charge you to make it your concern to be the instrument of inflaming men with zeal for the proclamation of the whole counsel of God and of doing so with that passion and power without

which preaching fails to do honour to the magnitude of its task and the glory of its message.

4. Your work is concerned with homiletics, the exposition and effective presentation of the Word of God. I charge you to continue to press home, as you have done in the past, the necessity of discovering, unfolding, and applying the particularities of each text or portion of God's Word. Few things are more distressing to the discerning, and more impoverishing to the church, than for a preacher to say much that is scriptural, indeed altogether scriptural, and yet miss the specific message of the text with which he deals. It is by the richness and multiformity of God's revealed counsel that the church will grow up into the measure of the stature of the fulness of Christ, and the witness of the church will be to all the spheres of life and to all the obligations of men.

5. I charge you to concentrate upon the discipline of the professorship of which you have been inaugurated. There are temptations to dissipate time and energy in devotion to other worthy tasks. But the only way of retaining and increasing the proficiency your installation expects is by concentrating on the tasks of the particular discipline which is your field of labor and by making all other activities contribute to your greater effectiveness in the field of practical theology.

May you long be spared to fulfill this high vocation in Westminster Theological Seminary, a seminary devoted, as few are, to the maintenance and proclamation of the whole counsel of God!

Indices

Scripture Index

Genesis		Job		51:10	219, 240
2:7	93	6:4	215	51:17	55*
2:24	224	14:7	244	57:5	89*
3:5	198	14:10	244	57:11	89*
3:19	94, 249	23:8–9	208	73:25–26	213
15:6	19	42:5–6	69, 176	73:26	217
17	20			80:1	219
18:25	215	Psalms		89:6	225
		4:8	117	90:2	239
Exodus		18:28	215*	90:14	241
15:11	239	19:7	107	91:9–10	213
28:2	57*, 221	19:14	1*, 171	96:9	219, 240
34:6–7	211	22:1	138	96:13	248
		22:3	35*	97:2	8, 248
Deuteronomy		22:12–13	80	100:4	219
4:35	225	22:16	80	100:5	211
32:2	242	25:7	28	103:3	55*
32:9	205, 212	27:4	238	103:10	217
		29:2	219, 240	103:16	42
1 Samuel		32:1–2	27	103:17–18	24
2:3	248	33:6	5	108:5	89*
2:8	11	33:9	5	113:7	3
16:7	247	36:6	90*	116:15	122
		37:35–36	42, 245	124:7–8	215
1 Chronicles		40:2–3	3	130:4	220
16:29	219	44:21	247	145:7	90*
		46:4–5	238	145:10	90*
Ezra		51:1–2	28	145:17	8, 215
9:13	209	51:4	219	148:13	89*

* Asterisks denote Scripture references cited in Professor Murray's prayers.

Scripture Index

Proverbs
1:10	102
2:8	248
6:6	118
15:8	240
20:13	118
21:27	240
23:21	118

Ecclesiastes
9:10	244
12:14	56*, 247

Song of Solomon
5:10	186*
6:10	221*

Isaiah
1:22	206
6:3	69
6:5	70, 210*, 262
8:19	200
8:20	199, 201
12:3	228
28:16	55*
30:33	78
40:31	37*, 214
42:1	137
44:22	27, 29, 85
52:13	137
53:6	76, 82, 152
53:10	76, 152
53:11	137
56:1	12
57:15	1*, 171*
61:11	92*
63:3	179
64:11	206

Jeremiah
17:10	247

Lamentations
1:1–3	203–4
2:1–3	204
3:1–2	207
3:6–8	208
3:1	205
3:21–24	203–17
3:21–23	211
3:22	209–10
3:25–26	213
3:28–30	209
3:33–36	215–6
3:39	209–10
3:44	208
4:1	206
4:1–2	204

Ezekiel
18:20	249
33:11	216

Daniel
9:24	51, 250

Micah
7:9	206, 214
7:19	27

Zechariah
13:1	220*
13:7	152

Matthew
5:29	174
6:25	180
8:11	192
8:19–20	172
8:21–22	172
8:26	148
10:25	142
13:17	239*
16:16	147, 230
16:17	147
16:18	33
16:24	171–86
16:25	180
16:27	183
17:5	4
18	229
18:20	1*, 171*, 219–38
20:28	136
24:12	168
24:30	126
24:38–39	126
25:26	244
25:34	254–5, 258
25:34–40	256
25:35–40	255
27:46	79, 138
28:18	38*, 236
28:20	234

Scripture Index

Mark
4:41	148
8:38	184
13:32	125
15:34	79, 138

Luke
8:14	220*
9:26	129
9:57–58	172
9:59–60	172
11:13	241*
16	200
16:19–31	187, 199
16:22	189–90
16:23	191
16:25	195
16:26	195–6
16:29	198
16:31	187–201
18:13	90*
19:14	150
20:18	55*
21:28	120
22:27	136
22:53	79
24:13–32	234

John
1:3	146
1:12	229
1:14	36*, 53*, 75, 200, 231, 236, 240*
1:16	36, 236*, 241*
1:18	75
3:19	15
3:35	75
4:23	219*
4:24	240*
4:34	77
5:18	74
5:20	75
6:38	136
6:39	87
10:15	73
10:17	75
11:12	117
11:25	222*
12:31	86
13:23	192
14:6	200
14:16–17	235, 237
14:23	233
14:27	167
14:30	167
14:31	75
15:4–5	230
15:19	86
16:14	222, 235
17:1	152
17:4–5	140, 152
17:5	166
17:14	86
17:21	237
17:23	233, 237
20:27	253

Acts
2:24	151
2:31	145
2:34	145
2:36	145–56, 160
3:13–15	149
4:27–28	150
5:30–31	149–50
26:18	242*

Romans
1:15	3
1:16	2–3, 119, 199
1:16–17	1–17
1:17	9, 30
1:18	6
1:24–32	2
1:25	175
2:1	95, 97
2:16	247
3:12–18	90*
3:21–22	8–9, 30
3:23	55*, 82, 243
3:25–26	8
3:26	39, 220*
4	33
4:3	29
4:6–8	27
4:7	29
4:9–11	19–34
5:19	11
5:20	40
5:21	32
6	35–53, 57–58, 65–67
6:1	39
6:2	41–43
6:4	51–52, 58, 151

6:5	35–53	8:1	83, 162, 250, 253	14:9	91*
6:6	43–46, 97			14:17	222*
6:7	46	8:3	135		
6:10	35–53	8:7	63–64	**1 Corinthians**	
6:11	51	8:23	120, 123	1:30	241*
6:12	47	8:28	81	2:2	186*
6:12–13	51, 97	8:29	70, 74, 81, 87, 169*	2:8	101
6:14	35–53			3:8	139
6:22	93*	8:31	81	3:10	33
6:23	243, 249	8:32	xxx, xxxiii, 73–88	3:12	56*
7	43, 57–58, 65–66, 70			6:19–20	98
		8:33	81	6:20	34*
7:4	58–59	8:37–39	37*, 217	10:11	205
7:4–6	59–60	10:3	31	12:14–21	111
7:5	66	10:10	119	12:26	111–2
7:6	55–72	11:25–26	92	15:25–26	94
7:7–13	60–62	12:1	95, 97, 108, 110	15:26	45
7:9	61–62			15:52	94, 125, 243
7:10–13	61	12:1–2	101		
7:12	59, 107	12:1–3	89–116	15:53–54	124
7:14	59, 65	12:2	91*, 100, 103, 107–8, 222	15:54	94
7:14–25	62–63, 65			15:54–57	257
7:15	62	12:3	108–10, 113–4	15:55	45
7:15–18	65–66			15:55–57	86
7:15–25	xxxiv, 62	12:4–8	108–9	15:56	58
7:17	67	12:5	111, 226		
7:18	67	12:6–9	115	**2 Corinthians**	
7:21	67	13	125	1:20	36*, 88*
7:22	63, 65	13:8–10	127–8	2:14	2
7:23	16	13:8–14	128	3:18	104, 142*, 169*
7:24	15–16, 63, 66, 69	13:11	117–30		
		13:12	129–30	4:4	4, 101
7:24–25	71	13:12–14	128	5:1	251
7:25	64–65, 67	13:14	45, 88*	5:1–3	123
8	70, 81	14:7–8	91*	5:4	123–4, 251

5:8	122, 251	4:10	162, 165	2:3	36*, 241*
5:10	221, 247	4:13	116	2:8	91*
5:14	143*	5:12	2	2:9	36*
5:14–15	80	5:25	73	2:15	80
5:16–17	13	5:25–27	206		
5:19	220*	5:27	227	**1 Thessalonians**	
5:21	9, 11–12, 31, 78, 152	**Philippians**		1:5	4
				1:9	173
6:2	245	1:21	186*	4:16	257
10:5	91*	1:23	122, 251	4:16–17	258
11:3	91*	2:4	136	5:5	130
12:9	36*, 222*	2:4–5	142	5:9	121
13:4	148	2:4–7	xxxvi–xxxvii		
		2:5	136	**2 Thessalonians**	
Galatians		2:5–9	131–43	3:1	242*
1:4	101	2:6	133, 135, 138		
2:20	83, 221*	2:6–7	137	**1 Timothy**	
3:13	77	2:8	135	1:15	71, 240*
5:17	68	2:9	56*, 139–40, 160	2:2	38*
6:14	2, 10, 143*			3:16	132, 233
		2:9–11	153, 253	4:1–3	174
Ephesians		2:12–13	120	6:6	117
1:17	151	3:5–6	10–11	6:16	35*, 89*
1:19–20	37*	3:8	185*		
1:19–21	151	3:9	9, 31	**2 Timothy**	
1:20–21	154	3:20–21	124	2:21	221*
1:21	141, 160, 165, 186, 236	3:21	253–4	3:16–17	201, 205
		4:7	232		
1:22	160	4:8	92*	**Titus**	
1:23	92*			2:13	124, 251
3:8	109	**Colossians**			
3:19	81, 212, 232	1:13	43	**Hebrews**	
4:3	116, 228	1:16–17	146	1:3	146, 154, 250, 254
4:4	225	1:17	154		
4:4–6	232	1:26	240*	1:14	121, 191

2:14	86	10:25	221, 229	**1 John**	
2:14–15	37*	10:26–31	158–9	1:5	89*
2:17	161	11:5	243	1:7	34*, 220*
2:18	166	11:10	15, 211	1:9	27, 36*, 90*
3:1	159	11:37	201*	2:1	163, 168
4:1	158	12:28	56*	2:2	162
4:12	4			2:16–17	103
4:14	143*, 159–60, 164–5, 168, 246	**James**		2:28	220*
		4:6	55*	3:2	69
				3:13	86
4:14–15	157–69	**1 Peter**		4:2	230
4:15	163–7	1:3–4	57*	5:4	37*
4:16	56*, 90*	1:4	201*		
6:4–6	158	1:5	121	**3 John**	
6:18	36*	1:8–9	56*	9	111
6:19	242*	1:12	141		
7:25	163	1:13	220*, 241*	**Jude**	
7:26	77, 135, 138, 143*, 162, 167	1:20	xxxiii	13	33, 210
		2:5	100, 240*	24	87, 212
		3:15	221*		
9:14	254	5:5	55*	**Revelation**	
9:27	127, 243, 246			1:5	56*, 185, 237
9:27–28	239–58	**2 Peter**		1:18	196, 222*
9:28	121, 249, 250, 252, 254	1:11	186*	2:23	247
		1:17	4	4:8	89*
		3:10	126	5:9	241*
10:22	36*, 56*	3:14	220*	7:9	226
10:24–25	226–7	3:17	91*		

Subject and Name Index

Abraham, 19–21, 25, 29, 149, 190–193, 195–6, 198–9
acceptance with God, 21, 24–26, 29–33, 39, 55, 60
adoption, 74, 84, 120, 123
angels, 37, 94, 121, 125, 129, 141, 183–5, 190–192, 217
apostasy, 37, 157–9, 163, 168
application, 50, 93, 155, 217, 262
appointed time, 119, 127, 128
assembling of people of God, 221, 226–7
assurance, 3, 4, 36, 49, 72, 84, 85, 87, 217, 222, 232, 257
atonement, 161, 163–4

baptism, 23–24, 232
belief, 159, 248
believers, differences among, 108, 110
bless, 19, 25–33, 35–36, 38, 50, 57, 90, 92, 116–8, 122, 124, 147, 169, 186, 201, 217, 219, 228, 240, 242, 254–6, 258
body
    of Christ, 58–59, 92, 108, 111–5, 160, 226–7, 242, 252–4
    of death, 16, 63–64, 69, 71
    as evil, 93–95
    holiness of, 97, 98
    as living sacrifice, 95
    Scripture does not disdain, 252
    of sin, 44–47, 50, 52, 65–66, 97
    as temple of Holy Spirit, 98
    transformed into likeness of Christ's glory, 252–3
    as well-pleasing to God, 98–99

calling, 36, 84, 159, 225
cemeteries, 257
Christian life, 68, 95, 142, 177, 209, 211
church, 10, 23–24, 37–38, 49, 57, 73, 92–93, 109–15, 122, 129–30, 132, 160, 172, 174, 179, 205–6, 210, 221–2, 224–6, 228–230, 233–4, 242, 262–3
circumcision, 19–21, 25
citizenship in heaven, 124
Clowney, Edmund, 261–3
commandments, 24, 102, 107, 182, 226
communion, 229, 238, 241–2

confession, 36, 90, 119, 147, 157, 159, 163, 168–9, 176, 230–232
conscience, 27, 29, 33, 36, 56, 102, 181–2, 185
corporate responsibility, 206
creation, 7, 44, 94, 123, 146–7, 155, 255
cross, 2, 10–11, 28, 75, 79–80, 93, 131, 137–9, 143, 147, 171–85
crucifixion, 2, 10–11, 43–47, 50, 52, 65, 95, 101, 143, 145, 148–50, 153, 160, 179–80, 185–6

darkness, 3, 15, 33, 35, 43, 79–80, 86, 89, 128–30, 200, 207–8, 210, 216–7, 233, 242
day of judgment, 39, 221, 226
day of the Lord, 126
deacon, office of, 114
death, 42
    as consolation, 245–6
    destruction of, 94
    as everlasting, 200
    finality of, 244–6, 250, 257
    as irreversible state, 188, 195–6, 199–200
    as last enemy, 45, 86, 94, 122
    reversal at, 189–95
    as separation of human body and spirit, 94
    sting of, 86, 257
    as wages of sin, 94, 197, 200, 243, 249
    as warning, 42, 244–5
definitive sanctification, 35–53
deliverance, 64, 209–14
discipleship, 171–85
disembodied state, 42, 191, 193–4
dogs, 80, 188–9
dominion of sin, 47–48, 52, 63–64, 66

earthly life, 188
economy of salvation, 153–6, 235
elder, office of, 114
Emmaus, 234–5
encouragement, 87, 159, 163–4, 167–8, 229
endurance, 177, 213–4
enmity against God, 63–64, 175
eternal life, 32–33, 180, 197

faith, 1, 5, 8–11, 13–17, 19–22, 27, 29–34, 36–39, 42, 49, 56–57, 60–61, 64, 71, 84, 88–90, 102, 108–9, 113–6, 119–24, 129, 155, 157, 159–61, 163, 168, 169, 178, 181–3, 185, 192, 199, 201, 205, 210–212, 215, 217, 220–221, 229–33, 237, 240, 242, 246, 250, 252–3, 258

family, 74, 84, 224, 248
Father, 1, 4, 19, 34, 51–52,
    58, 72–87, 103, 125, 129,
    136–40, 146–7, 149, 151–6,
    163, 166, 168, 171–2, 183–5,
    192, 201, 206, 227, 231–3,
    235–7, 241, 253–8
fear, 24, 35, 37, 45, 56, 79, 86,
    90, 92, 1134, 120, 158–60,
    220–221, 239
fellowship, 32, 50, 84, 167, 192,
    195, 242
Free Presbyterian Church, xx

gifts in the church, 109–10, 114
glorification, 84–85, 152
glory of God, 4, 55, 82, 153, 176,
    243, 253
God
    as creator, 135, 140, 146–8,
        153–5, 175
    goodness of, 197, 216
    holiness of, 6, 16, 30,
        35–36, 69, 83, 90, 138,
        210, 216
    incomprehensibility, 84,
        154
    as just, 8, 16, 30–31, 36,
        39, 83, 90, 197, 210,
        215–6, 220, 248
    no arbitrariness in, 214–5
    omnipotence of, 5, 9, 147
    as our portion, 212–3
godly ancestry, 24–25

gospel, 1–17, 22, 25, 36, 91, 119,
    123, 152, 172, 201, 242, 261–2
grace, 1, 5, 7, 17, 22, 24–25, 27,
    29, 32, 35–41, 47–49, 53,
    55–57, 72, 74, 84–85, 88–91,
    108–10, 113, 115, 121, 130,
    139, 158, 171, 185, 197, 199,
    211–2, 214, 216–7, 220–2,
    226, 228, 236–41, 261–2
guilt, 5, 27, 36, 55, 82–83, 85,
    162, 174, 181, 183, 254

heaven, 5–7, 38, 40, 72, 77, 106,
    123–6, 136–8, 141, 145–7,
    151, 153, 156–63, 165–6,
    168, 173, 191–2, 194, 196,
    199–201, 204, 213, 215, 236,
    238, 241, 246, 251, 253–4, 257
heirs, 57, 74, 121, 191
hell, 191–6, 199
Hilter, Adolf, 245
history, 125–6, 129, 247–8
holiness, 15, 51, 68–70, 97–98,
    122
Holy Spirit, 4, 91, 100, 235, 262
honesty, 70, 183–5
honoring Christ, 182
hope, 33, 36, 64, 71, 87, 122–4,
    129, 178, 201, 208, 210–217,
    221, 251–3
human laws, 106–7
human unrighteousness, 6,
    10–11, 16, 36
humility, 110–112, 142

image
- of Christ, 68, 72, 74
- of God, 39, 69

immortality, 123–4, 257
incarnation, 131–2, 140–141, 146–7, 154, 233
individuality, 81–82
indwelling sin, 67–68
intermediate state, 187, 200
Israel, 149–52, 160, 203–5

Jehovah's Witnesses, 133
Jeremiah, 203–12
- hope of, 208–12
- self-humiliation of, 207–9, 216

Jesus Christ. *See also* Son
- ascension of, 145–8, 234
- bore his cross, 137–9, 177–9
- compassion of, 164–9
- as Creator, 146–8, 153–5
- death of, 50–52, 58, 73, 137, 249
- deity of, 132–3, 147–8, 153–4
- dignity of being, 132–3, 136, 138
- dignity of station, 132–4, 136–8
- efficacy of heavenly ministry, 72
- equality with God, 132–4, 137–8, 231
- exaltation of, 139–41, 148, 153–5, 160, 162–4
- faithfulness of, 211
- forsakenness of, 79, 138
- as God-man, 146–8, 154–5, 165
- as High Priest, 159–69, 246
- as holy, harmless, undefiled, and separate from sinners, 135, 138, 142, 167–8
- humiliation of, 134–42, 148, 152–4
- intercession of, 163–4, 169
- kingly office, 160–161
- lordship of, 48, 145–56
- as Lord's servant, 134–41
- love of, 73, 80, 83, 206
- made himself of no reputation, 133–4, 137
- merited reward, 139–40
- obedience of, 11, 32, 76, 137–40, 91, 139
- as pattern of our vocation, 141–2
- presence by his Spirit, 235–6
- presence by his Word, 234–5
- presence with his people, 231–4, 236–8
- resurrection of, 50–52, 57–58, 68, 91, 145–8, 152, 178, 230

Subject and Name Index

sacrifice of, 76–77, 249–50
second coming of, 120–121, 123, 130, 156, 186, 250–253, 258, 243
sovereignty of, 155–6, 160–161, 163
temptation of, 164–9
two-fold dominion of, 155
unique sonship of, 74
was made sin, 77–78
works of mercy, 147

Jesus's name, 228–9

Job
abhorred himself, 69, 176
afflictions of, 207–8

joy, 7, 56, 87, 186, 208, 212, 222, 228, 254

judgment, 8, 23, 28, 33, 39, 47, 56, 76–78, 80, 83, 86, 89, 106, 127, 130, 138–9, 150, 152, 158, 184–5, 206, 214, 221, 226, 239–40, 242, 246–51, 254, 257–8

justice, 8, 16, 30–31, 36, 70, 81, 83, 91–92, 138, 181–2, 197, 210, 216, 248, 249

justification, 8, 12, 14, 16, 19–33, 38–39, 41, 47, 49, 60, 84, 137, 216, 220

keeping faith, 159
kingdom of God, 43, 102, 128, 192
kingdom of sin, 43

last day, 129, 221, 226–7
Last Supper, 192
law, 58–59
laziness, 114
life, 13, 23, 28, 30, 32–33, 37–38, 42, 44–45, 49, 51–52, 56–61, 63, 67–69, 73, 75, 90–93, 95–96, 98–99, 101, 103–7, 124, 126, 136, 138, 142, 149, 156, 173, 177–82, 184–6, 188–9, 191–2, 194–7, 199–201, 209–11, 213, 217, 220, 222, 238, 243–5, 251, 255–6, 262–3

living in sin, 43, 66–67
living sacrifice, 95–101, 108, 110
Lloyd-Jones, D. Martyn, xxi
Lord's Supper, 24
love, 15, 34, 37, 42, 44–45, 73–88, 91, 111, 115–6, 118, 127–8, 137, 141, 143, 153–4, 165, 168, 178, 183–6, 191–2, 197, 201, 203, 206, 217, 220, 226, 230, 232–3, 241, 246, 248, 255–8

man
as new, 44–46, 68
as old, 44–46, 52, 65–66
martyrdom, 180
means of grace, 24
ministry of the church, 110
Moses, 198–200

Murray, John, xix–xxviii
    character of, xx
    mannerisms of, xx
    preaching of, xx–xxi, xxiii–xxvi
modesty, false 113–4
mystery of godliness, 131–2, 137–8, 140–141, 233

nations, 2
nature, 63
newness of life, 51–52, 58, 67, 178

obedience, 107, 137–40, 199, 201, 230–231
Old Princeton, xx
overbearingness, 111, 112

patience, 214
Paul, crucified unto self-righteousness, 10–11
peace with God, 68
permanent, desire for, 103
persecution, 180
practical, 95–98, 100–102, 128, 176, 262–3

realm of sin, 43, 53
reasonable service, 96–97, 99–101, 108
reconciliation, 161–3
redemption, 120, 123, 178
Reformed theology, xxxi, xxxiv

repentance, 173, 176
resurrection, 50–52, 58, 68, 94, 145–8
reward, 139–40
righteousness, 5–20, 24, 26, 30–32, 41
    demands justification, 12, 32
    mediated through Jesus Christ, 8–12, 16
Roman Catholic Church, 93, 112–3

sabbath, 107
sacrifices, under the Old Testament, 95–96
salvation
    consummation of, 119–23, 128–9, 251–4,
    logic of, 39–41
    nearer than when we believed, 117–9, 122, 124–9
    as our great hope, 122, 124
    from ourselves, 175–6
    ready to be revealed, 121–2
    from sin and to righteousness, 41
    working out of, 120–121
sanctification, 39, 49–52, 69, 83–85
    and bitterness of sin, 69, 83
    not a second blessing, 49–50
    as progressive, 49
    and use of the body, 46

Satan
- as god of this age, 101
- temptation of Adam and Eve, 198

Scripture, sufficiency of, 198–9
self-assertiveness, 111–2
self-complacency, 61–62, 70, 72
self-denial, 174–9
self-detestation, 69–71
self-humiliation, 139–42, 207, 209–10, 216
selfishness, 6
self-renunciation, 175–6
self-righteousness, 11, 13, 16, 61–62, 72, 174
servanthood, 134–43
service, 99–101, 108, 136
sin
- of blessed man, 26–7
- brought to remembrance, 27–8
- condemnation of, 62–3, 78–9, 83,
- as contradiction of God, 6, 175–6,
- as contradiction of holiness, 6–7, 68
- conviction of, 14, 48, 60–62, 71
- dominion of, 47–52, 63–66
- end of, 51, 163, 250, 253
- enormity of, 28, 82–85
- hatred of, 64
- living in us, 43, 66–67
- particularity of, 82, 173
- presence of, 64
- slavery to, 47
- squalor of, 5–6

sleep, 117–9, 127, 129
sloth, 117–8, 129, 244
sober thinking, 108, 113–4
Son. *See also* Jesus Christ
- bore the stroke of the Father's wrath, 76–80
- glorification of, 84–85, 140, 149, 152, 155
- love for the Father, 75
- suffering of, 76–80, 166–7

sonship
- of the adopted, 74
- of the only begotten, 74–75

specific sins, renunciation of, 173–6
spiritual devotion, 100
spiritual indifference, 118
spiritual sloth, 117–8, 129
state of innocence, 59,
state of sin, 59–60
systematic theology, as exegetical, xxxiv–xxxv

temptation, 85
- particularity of 164–5, 168

tent of meeting, 231
this age and age to come, 101–3
time, 101, 118–9, 124–30
tongue, use of, 97–99

transformation, by renewing of the mind, 101, 103–5, 108
trial and temptation, 164–8
tribulation, 165, 213,
Trinity, 131, 133–4, 225,
triumph over sin, 70–72
truth, 3, 6, 8, 14, 16, 36–37, 39, 41, 43, 45, 47–48, 50, 53, 56, 65, 68–69, 71, 78, 83, 85, 91–92, 128, 131, 138, 140, 150, 155, 158–9, 162, 165, 174–5, 177, 181–5, 194–200, 210–216, 219–21, 232–3, 235–7, 240–242, 245, 248–50

unbelief, 150
ungodliness, sense of, 27–8
union with Christ, 12–14, 50–53, 58, 68, 229–38
unity in plurality, 224–6, 228
unity of confession, 230–232
unity of faith, 229–30
unregenerate, body of, 46, 97
unworthiness, 27

validation, 159–63
Van Til, Cornelius, xix
vestibule of faith, 61
vindicatory justice vs. vindictive revenge, 216
vine and branches, 230
vocation, 99, 113–4, 141–2
Vos, Geerhardus, xx–xxi

waiting upon the Lord, 120–123, 213–4
weak faith, 14, 17
well-pleasing to God, 98–9, 104–6, 240
Westminster Shorter Catechism
   on justification, 38–9
   on sanctification, 49
whole counsel of God, 57, 262–3
wickedness, 15, 26–27, 102–3, 199, 244
will of God, 99–108, 136–9, 201
Winslow, Octavius, 79
wisdom of God, 7, 17, 153–4, 197, 199, 261
women, responsibilities and functions in the church, 114
Word of God
   and faith and repentance, 13–14, 199
   in saving action, 3–5, 12–13, 199
   never void of power, 4
   tabernacled among us, 231
works of darkness, 128–30
works-righteousness, 31
worship, 24, 36, 90, 95–96, 100, 118, 175–6, 219, 223, 240, 242
wrath of God, 6–7, 10–13, 17, 78–83, 161–2, 204–7, 210–211, 216